101 Superheroes of the Silver Screen

A Compendium of Cinema's Costumed Crimefighters

John L. Flynn, Ph.D.

Galactic Books

Owings Mills, Maryland

Galactic Books
Post Office Box 1442
Owings Mills, Maryland 21117-9998

101 Superheroes of the Silver Screen
By John L. Flynn, Ph.D.

PRINTING HISTORY
Second Printing / September 2019

Illustrations: Many of the photographs and illustrations used in this book were issued by 20th Century-Fox, Warner Brothers, Columbia Pictures, M-G-M, New Line Cinema, Paramount Pictures, Cannon Films, New Horizons, Republic Pictures, and other companies for publicity purposes, and we make no claim to ownership or copyright. We are simply reproducing them here for the purpose that they were originally intended, and in much the same way they are used in newspaper and magazine articles and on websites throughout the World Wide Web. We are grateful for their use in this academic study. We also acknowledge that the use of these photographs does not suggest official endorsement. The figure of Captain Nice on the title page was drawn by Jack Kirby to illustrate the NBC series. We also wish to thank DC Comics, Marvel Comics, Image Comics, Warren Publishing, King Features, and numerous other publishers. The lyrics to "Holding Out for a Hero" are copyrighted by Bonnie Tyler (1986).

Editor: Edmund Dantes
Design & Layout: John L. Flynn
Book Cover Design: John L. Flynn

Library of Congress Cataloging in Publication Data
Flynn, John L.
101 Superheroes of the Silver Screen
1. Superhero Films. I. Motion Picture History.
II. John L. Flynn--Plots, themes, etc. III. Title.

ISBN: 978-0-9769400-1-2

PRINTED IN THE UNITED STATES OF AMERICA

Introduction

> I need a hero.
> I'm holding out for a hero 'til the end of the night.
> He's gotta be strong
> And he's gotta be fast
> And he's gotta be fresh from the fight.
> – *Bonnie Tyler, "Holding Out for a Hero"*

At the recent San Diego Comic-Con, while we were discussing the impact of comic books on popular culture at a well-attended panel, I blurted out, "Everything I know about life I learned from comic book superheroes." My sudden, ill-timed statement brought the panel to a screeching halt, and induced more than its fair share of laughs and chuckles, snickers and groans from the audience. But after a moment's consideration, each of my fellow panelists agreed with me, echoing my sentiments in their own particular way. Most of the fans who had gathered in that room also knew that I was right. Everything that we know about good and evil, compassion and justice, right and wrong, friendship and sacrifice, righteousness, integrity, honesty and atonement, and life in general we learned while reading comic books or watching superhero movies. In fact, I wondered where we would be without our comic books.

Since the debut of Superman in 1938, superheroes have been a ubiquitous part of our popular culture. They have dominated American comic books for nearly seventy years, and their stories have crossed over into other media. They have been featured in daily comic strips, filled the pages of pulp magazines, figured in radio dramatizations, appeared on television shows, and headlined cinema marquees around the world. In many ways, their legendary tales of courage and derring-do form a modern mythology that has deep roots in our culture, our moral and spiritual beliefs, and our whole way of life. Myths are, after all, nothing more than narratives about heroic beings that are intended to explain some broader truth about the universe and our place in it. Superheroes represent our innermost desires and ideals; they reflect our bravery and the noblest part of our human nature as we strive to rise above our own weaknesses and frailties. They show us how we wish to see ourselves…as individuals with a strong moral code and a responsibility to the safety of others that goes well beyond personal risk and reward.

For most of us "fanboys" who collect and trade comic books and attend comic book conventions, we've always known how important superheroes were to our world. In the 1940s, they fought a secret war against the fascist forces of Germany and Japan, while collecting for war bonds and keeping the home-front safe. In the 1960s, they struggled to hold the fabric of our world together when equally valid but divergent points of view threatened to tear us all apart. In the 1980s, they exposed corporate greed and scandal. And they were among the first responders to the events of 9/11 when America truly needed its heroes. They have always existed in a world or collection of worlds that was parallel to our Earth Prime, only we didn't need a cosmic treadmill or some divergent point in history to slide between worlds. We just needed a dime or a quarter (or some other denomination of currency) to purchase a comic book that featured their latest exploits, and the time to sit down and read about them.

Their superhuman feats have become the subject of more and more of our popular media. In fact, whether we're Baby-Boomers who grew up watching Flash Gordon or Congo Bill on the Saturday Matinee serials or Gen-Xers who played video games while listening to MTV, we all look forward to a good movie featuring our favorite superheroes. The X-Men trilogy, the Spider-Man movies, "Batman Begins" (2005) and "Superman Returns" (2006) have been among the highest-grossing films in motion picture history. And more comic book adaptations, featuring Iron Man, The Spirit, Wonder Woman, and many, many others, are on the way! Ironically, superhero films began as matinee serials aimed at children, but their entertainment value declined as audiences demanded greater sophistication. Those of you over thirty-five may remember a time when we considered ourselves lucky if Hollywood produced one science fiction or fantasy film a year, let alone one that featured a comic book character. The success of Richard Donner's "Superman" in 1978 changed all of that. Movies featuring costumed crimefighters spawned sequels and then whole franchises. Now, our summer blockbuster season, which starts early in May, has one superhero film scheduled right after another. Thanks in large part to improvements in special effects technology and a genuine respect for the material, comic books now drive our entertainment industry. Who would have guessed how important this medium would become?

Comic books have always been a major part of my life. I read my first comic book, which was an issue of "Batman" written by Gardner

Introduction

Fox, when I was five years old. The dozens of illustrations that were presented in panels like a movie's storyboard fascinated me. I also loved the fact that, once I had finished reading the story, I could go back and re-read my favorite parts again and again. As a child spoon-fed heavy doses of "Howdy-Doody" and "Buffalo Bob," "Tom Corbett" and "Buzz Corry," "The Lone Ranger" and "Tonto," and other pop culture icons of the 1950s, comic books were a welcome literary diversion because they were more than simple words on a page. Let's face it: Television will always be my first love, but without the modern conveniences of Tivo or digital video recorders, when that televised episode ended in 1955, my favorite characters went back into the "box" until the following week. Comic books gave me the opportunity to call upon my favorite characters whenever I wanted, and allowed me to relive my favorite adventures when I was sick at home with measles or chicken pox. They were my constant companions on long drives in the family car and on weekend outings in the country, and I didn't need batteries or an electrical outlet to plug them in.

When I turned eight years old, comic books figured in my first economic crisis! Up until that point, my aunt and godmother Shirley Konin had purchased all of the comic books that I read. She usually provided me with a nice assortment of superhero and science fiction titles, while my younger brother received Archie comics. Together, we secretly believed that our benefactor really enjoyed reading the comic books before she passed them onto us, and to this day, I've not abandoned that belief. My stay-at-home aunt had a keen intellect that had been developed and nurtured by something… Towards the end of the year 1961, however, she stopped giving us comics, and began passing along those trashy dime novels that featured a certain secret agent instead. My mother told me that I was old enough to purchase my own comic books, and insisted that I use my pop-bottle money for something other than sweets. So, with less than a dollar in my pocket, I went to Kroger's grocery store in Mt. Greenwood, Illinois, and purchased my first comic books, including "Fantastic Four #1." I must confess that it was a major financial undertaking to keep up with my favorites every month, but I certainly learned the value of a dollar each time I cut a neighbor's grass or shoveled a neighbor's driveway free of snow. Each difficult task I accomplished simply meant that was one more comic book that I could purchase to read.

Less than ten years later, I put away all of my comic books in a trunk, and went off to college to study writing. I thought that I had outgrown them, but they had not outgrown me, for comic books are what inspired me to become a writer. I worked hard at my studies, eventually earning a teacher's certificate and my much-coveted Ph.D. Thankfully, when I came home from school, my comics were still there! My parents had not thrown them away, but had merely put them aside for safe keeping. So, when I did start writing, they were there to inspire me all over again.

In the summer of 1980, I opened one of the first comic book shops in the Baltimore area, more specifically the southeastern suburb of Glen Burnie, Maryland. I had been a customer of Steve Geppi when he had his first shop in the basement of a home on Edmonson Avenue in Catonsville, and I envied his lifestyle as a shopkeeper without realizing how much work was actually involved. He had traded his job as a hard-working postal carrier to sell comic books! I wanted that lifestyle as well, and I traded my job as a high school English teacher to open Galactic Enterprises. I offered my customers a subscription service where I reserved their favorite titles for them each month, and I had a well-stocked section of back-issues, comprised mainly of the comics that I had collected as a kid. In addition to comic books, I sold science fiction books, toys and novelties. I also treated my loyal customers to the first showings of big screen extravaganzas like "Superman 2" and "Sheena" with movie passes I had managed to wrangle from local theater managers. Superhero movies are also what brought new customers into the shop.

I'll admit that the first year was the hardest; I slept in the back of the store in a dingy little room without hot-running water to save on rent, and ate around the corner at the local diner, but I felt that I was living my dream as an entrepreneur. Gradually, as news rippled through the fanboy community that I was an honest dealer, business picked up, and I hired college kids from the local university to help me keep up with all of my customers. I paid them in comics, naturally. When Geppi started what would eventually become Diamond Comic Distributors, I was one of his first wholesale customers, and kept my orders up every month. And I remained a loyal customer for the five years that I ran my shop.

During my slow periods, on rainy days or days bleached white with snow, I read every comic book that I could get my hands on. I re-read the ones that I had read as a child, and I read all of the new titles that came out. I also read the ones that I bought or traded with customers. I read the Phoenix saga in "The Uncanny X-Men" on the plane to my grandmother's funeral. I labored through Tony Stark's battle with alcoholism in "Iron Man" the same year my father died, loosing his own private battle with the same disease. I cried over Electra's tragic death in "Daredevil," while reflecting back over the broken promises and lost relationships in my own life. Every comic book I read seemed to have something personal to say to me. Batman, Thor, the Teen Titans, Green Lantern, the Amazing Spider-Man, Flash, Fantastic Four, Superman, the Incredible Hulk, Wonder Woman – I read them all! Hundreds of thousands of words and thousands of images over a five-year period! I had just finished reading my last comic book when the "Crisis on Infinite Earths" maxi-series debuted. At the time, I could honestly say that my encyclopedic knowledge of every single character was put to the test and passed with flying colors; in fact, I felt that I could have written the twelve-part saga myself without ever breaking a sweat. That's when I realized I had spent the last five years of my life working as a shopkeeper in a comic book store instead of pursuing my dream of becoming a writer. I guess I had always imagined that I'd write the great American novel in between waiting on my customers, but the reality was that I never did find the right time.

I had little difficulty selling my shop; like me, most of my customers had dreamed of running a comic book store themselves, and all I had to do was mention it to one or two of them before I had found the new owner. In September of 1985, I packed up a couple of boxes filled with my favorite comics, and turned the lights out for the last time. Galactic Enterprises is still there; the store has changed owners several times, and it has a new name, but the business I created in 1980 still caters to those fanboys and fangirls who read comic books.

Eventually, I took a job teaching English at a local university to pay the bills, while I devoted my spare time to writing short stories, articles, reviews, columns, novels, and nonfiction books; I wrote whatever a publisher was willing to write me a check for. Seventeen years later, in 2002, I was nominated for a Hugo award for my science fiction writing. I didn't win the coveted statue of a rocketship on a wooden base, but I was nominated again in 2003 and 2004. I didn't win the Hugo award in those years either, and yet I still felt like a winner because my peers had thought enough of my writing to nominate me along with four other writers for the top prize in the field of science fiction. Had I actually won the Hugo, I probably would have thanked everyone from my mother to my college writing teacher in my "thank you" speech, but most of all, I would have acknowledged my Aunt Shirley for introducing me to the imaginary worlds of comic books where everything was possible.

Last year, at the 2006 San Diego Comic-Con, I was invited to participate in the four-day conference as an attending professional on several panels. At one panel, I sat between two of the giants in the industry, Forrest J. Ackerman and Basil Gogos, and while I have no pretenses of being in the same league with them, the fact that I was paired with them told me that I had somehow arrived at a certain point in my career. Mind you, I have been on panels at conventions for the last twenty years, but this was different. As I looked out on the standing-room-only crowd of five or six thousand fans, answered their questions, and traded stories with the other panelists as an equal, I realized that I had achieved my goal of becoming a successful writer.

My love of comic books and my determination to become a writer had brought me full circle. From that wide-eyed, five-year-old boy in Chicago, I now found myself right in the middle of the world's largest gathering of comic book artisans, science fiction writers, and media members in San Diego. Comic books were all around me, and I was there with 114,000 other fans for the same reason: To celebrate an art-form that had penetrated all aspects of our popular culture, from literature and music to television and movies. Right then and there, like a thunderbolt from Thor that struck me right in the middle of my forehead, I decided to write this book. I wanted to write something truly special that was a celebration of comic books and popular culture. I also intended the book to be for that little five-year-old inside of each of us that still looks with bright eyes on the wondrous things of imagination. I do hope that you will enjoy reading it as much as I have had writing it.

–John L. Flynn, Ph.D.
January 18, 2007

Note to the Reader: Each entry is arranged alphabetically by the name of the superhero; in certain cases, team names, like the Fantastic Four or the X-Men, take precedence over an individual, like Mr. Fantastic or Wolverine. A complete index of superheroes is included at the end of the book. For each entry, I have endeavored to include the character's first comic book appearance (if any), his or her origins, media appearances, a short plot synopsis and commentary of the film version, some trivia, and the "fanboy" rating. The rating is based on an informal, highly unscientific poll that I've taken at the San Diego Comic-Con and other conventions. Fans rated each movie version based on Babes, Special Effects, Action and Brainwaves. I admit that my rating system is far from perfect, but it is more fun that a handful of stars or a thumbs-up-or-down. Enjoy!

Introduction

Aeon Flux

Aeon Flux (2005). Paramount Pictures, 93min. **Director:** Karyn Kusama. **Producers:** David Gale, Greg Goodman, Martha Griffin, Gale Ann Hurd, and Gary Lucchesi **Screenwriters:** Phil Hay and Matt Manfredi. Based upon characters created by Peter Chung. **Cinematographer:** Stuart Dryburgh. **Film Editor:** Jeff Gullo, Peter Honess, and Plummy Tucker. **Cast:** Charlize Theron, Marton Csokas, Jonny Lee Miller, Sophie Okonedo, Frances McDormand.

First Appearance: MTV's "Liquid Television" (October 10, 1991)
First Comic Book Appearance: "Aeon Flux: The Herodotus File" (1995)
Origins: Korean-American animator Peter Chung created the avant garde science fiction series which first appeared on MTV's "Liquid Television" in 1991 to reflect the great cultural and societal divides that he saw in the United States. Chung's unique artistic style borrowed from "Rugrats," which he had worked on, Moebius and Japanese anime. In his bizarre, dystopian world of the future, two separate countries, adjacent to each other but separated by a wall, have evolved into two distinct worlds, Bregna and Monica. The totalitarian Bregna is ruled by Trevor Goodchild and other technocrats devoted to science and a centralized, scientifically-planned state. They rely on cloning, mutant creatures and robots to advance their technologically superior world. On the other hand, Monica, a free society, has dispatched Aeon Flux, a tall, beautiful, often scantily-clad secret agent, to infiltrate Bregna. She is a highly effective assassin who is so fast that she can catch a fly in her eyelashes. Even though the two countries were once a single nation called Berognica, the Breen citizens have had their memories erased (according to "The Herodotus File" graphic novel), and the Monicans seek to re-acquaint the Breens with their past by launching the Relical, an airship containing artifacts that prove the existence of Berognica. In each of the early shorts that were produced by Chung, Aeon Flux died a violent death, and was replaced by an identical clone; in the later half-hour series, which followed in 1995, she dies only once. Another distinc-

tive mark of the six-part serial of shorts (often no more than five minutes in length) no intelligible dialogue is ever heard (other than the words "no" and "plop"); the rest of the soundtrack consists of sound effects and non-human utterances. As the series evolved, viewers learned that Aeon Flux and Trevor Goodchild were linked romantically. In 1995, while the MTV series was at the height of its popularity, a graphic novel, titled "Aeon Flux: The Herodotus File," appeared. Unlike a comic-strip story, the graphic novel was actually a collection of documents and an assortment of story-boards (apparently taken from security cameras). It helped to fill in much of the backstory, and also expanded on Aeon Flux's character, making her a part-time model who posed for fetish magazines. In 2005, Dark Horse Comics published a four-issue miniseries that was based on the film. Even though the story represented a major departure from the series, the animation style reflected Chung's artistry.

First Media Appearance: Peter Chung directed a live-action Pepsi commercial, titled "Something Wrong," for Super Bowl 30, but the spot which featured Cindy Crawford as Aeon Flux and Malcolm McDowell as Trevor Goodchild was pulled by the network and later aired on MTV.

The 2005 Film Version: For years, fans of the original series had clamored for a live-action version, but when "Aeon Flux" finally debuted in 2005, the film bore little resemblance to its source material. 400 years in the future, a virus has exterminated most of the world's population. The last remnants of humanity live in the totalitarian city-state of Bregna, ruled by Trevor Goodchild (Marton Csokas). The resistance, known as the Monicans, have assigned Aeon Flux (Charlize Theron) to kill Trevor and overthrow the government. But Aeon Flux disobeys the Handler (Frances McDormand) to protect Trevor from his brother's plot to overthrow him.

Trivial Matters: Even though the film was decidedly different from the series, it did borrow a number of character names (Una and Clavius) and plot devices (cloning, a weaponized no man's land, and secrets passed by French kisses) from the series. Michelle Rodriguez was initially cast as Aeon Flux when the film was set to shoot in 2003.

Fanboy Rating: Babes-9 Effects-7 Action-5 Brainwaves-1 Total=22

Aeon Flux

Ant-Man

Ant-Man (2008). Paramount Pictures in association with Marvel Enterprises. 120min. **Director:** Edgar Wright. **Producers:** Avi Arad, Nira Park, and Edgar Wright. **Screenwriters:** Joe Cornish and Edgar Wright. Based upon characters created by Stan Lee and Jack Kirby. **Cinematographer:** TBA. **Editor:** TBA. **Production Designer:** TBA. **Cast:** TBA. This motion picture is still under pre-production, and will not be released until 2008.

First Comic Book Appearance: "Tales to Astonish #27" (January 1962)
Origins: Created by Stan Lee and Jack Kirby, the Ant-Man (also known as Henry Pym) debuted at a time when costumed superheroes were back in vogue and Marvel Comics were churning out superheroes by the dozen. Ant-Man was Marvel's second modern superhero after the Fantastic Four. Thor, Iron Man, the Hulk, Spider-Man, and the Daredevil, to name a few, were among his contemporaries. But he still managed to distinguish himself as the World's Smallest Superhero, the Atom (at DC Comics) notwithstanding. Dr. Pym was Marvel's most brilliant scientist. He was a chemist, biologist and inventor of artificial intelligence. His "Pym particles" allowed him to shrink just about anything, including himself, to the size of an ant, and employed his shrinking device in his personal war against crime. His first adventure finds him reduced down to size in an anthill, facing impending doom at the pinchers of an army of ants. By the time of his second adventure, he had created a "cybernetic helmet" with which to communicate with ants. He also discovered, that even though he was ant-sized, he still retained his normal human strength, and this made him incredibly powerful. As Ant-Man, he fought villains as diverse as Egghead, the Scarlet Beetle, and the Man with the Voice of Doom. Later, in June 1963, he was teamed with the Wasp, a female superhero capable of changing into a wasp, and the pair fought some of Marvel's marvelous stable of villains. They also paired up with Thor, Iron Man, and the Hulk, and were founding members of the Avengers. He also worked as a member along-

side the Fantastic Four when Mr. Fantastic went missing and was presumed dead. By Issue #49 of "Tales to Astonish," Pym reversed the polarity of his invention, and turned himself into Giant Man. He married the Wasp in 1969, and loaned his Ant-Man costume to Scott Lang for a personal emergency. Lang later became the new Ant-Man, but like his predecessor, his tenure was short-lived. Pym also had several different costumed identities as Goliath and Yellowjacket.

First Media Appearance: Henry Pym (as Ant-Man) made his first official media appearance as a regular on the short-lived "The Avenger: United They Stand" (1999) animated cartoon series. He was voiced by Rod Wilson on the Saturday morning cartoon.

Other Media Appearances: He aided the Fantastic Four in "Fantastic Four: World's Greatest Heroes" in 2006 when one of Reed's microverse experiments failed and caused them to be shrunk to the "World's Tiniest Superheroes." Ant-Man was voiced by John Payne. He also played a major character in the two direct-to-video animated films, "The Ultimate Avengers" (2005) and "Ultimate Avengers 2" (2006).

The 2008 Film Version: For several years, Edgar Wright, the director most famous for "Shaun of the Dead" (2004), has been trying to get a live-action version of "Ant-Man" made for the Silver Screen. Sharing scripting chores with Joe Cornish, Wright promises the live action version with feature both the original Ant-Man, Henry Pym, and his successor, Scott Lang. The very rough outline of the script, which is still in development, finds Biochemist Dr. Hank Pym using his latest discovery to create a size-altering formula. Though his first self-test goes awry, Pym develops an instrument that helps him communicate with and control insects. As this book goes to press, we are anxiously awaiting any new information as this film's pre-production moves forward.

Fanboy Rating: Babes-? Effects-?
Action-? Brainwaves-? Total=??

Ant-Man

Barbarella

Barbarella (1968). United Artists, 98min. **Director:** Roger Vadim. **Producer:** Dino De Laurentiis. **Screenwriters:** Terry Southern, Roger Vadim, Tudor Gates, Brian Degas et. al. Based on characters by Jean-Claude Forest. **Cinematographer:** Claude Renoir. **Film Editor:** Victoria Mercanton. **Cast:** Jane Fonda, John Phillip Law, Anita Pallenberg, Milo O'Shea, Marcel Marceau, Claude Dauphin.

First Appearance: "Barbarella" in *V-Magazine* (1962)
First Comic Book Appearance: "Barbarella" Graphic Novel (1968)
Origins: Jean-Claude Forest, one of France's most talented comic book artists, created the character of Barbarella in 1962, and published her first adventures in serial form in *V-Magazine*, one of France's leading publications. Each of the panels were drawn in black and white, then shaded by one sepia-like color for each adventure. The comic book panels were gathered together into a graphic novel and published by Grove Press in 1968 as a tie-in to the movie. In this first adventure, Barbarella acts as a mediator for two warring races that threaten to break the planet Lythion apart; rebel factions within each group seek peace, and Barbarella is their only hope. However, when her Astroship crashlands in an enormous greenhouse on Lythion and Barbarella emerges to look at the damage, her clothes are shredded by sentient rose bushes. She is then forced to complete most of her mission topless. Barbarella later meets Captain Dildano while traveling on a ocean-going ship, and sleeps with him to pass the time. Their ship is captured by an enormous sea creature, and they are taken to Medusa, an alien woman who steals the faces of the women she captures. Naturally, she is no match for our space-faring heroine who easily dispatches the monster. In her third adventure, Barbarella discovers a lost world beneath the surface of Lythion, and helps the inhabitants defeat a sadistic hunter named Trident. She then gets swept away to another part of the planet by a mad scientist who wants to make love to her. She escapes and meets an old man named Durand and a blind angel named

Pygar. The plots for most of her adventures were pretty absurd, and functioned mostly as an excuse to render her naked and at the mercy of some madman. Barbarella, who was modeled after French model and actress Brigitte Bardot, is often portrayed as being very naïve and helpless; she is unaware of her sexuality, and seduces nearly everyone, including men, women, aliens, and robots, with her naviete about sex. At other times in the comic strip, Barbarella is quite fearless and determined, and uses her sexuality as a distraction. Barbarella was the forerunner of Vampirella, Lady Death, and other bad girls in comic books.

First Media Appearance: Jane Fonda played the character of Barbarella in the 1968 Roger Vadim film, titled "Barbarella."

Other Media Appearances: A big budget musical version of "Barbarella," featuring the songs and lyrics of British composer Dave Stewart, premiered in Vienna, Austria, on March 11, 2004, with Nina Proll in the title role. Recently, Warner Brothers and 20th Century-Fox agreed to co-finance and co-produce a new "Barbarella" movie, with Drew Barrymore in the lead role. The film has tentative release plans for 2008 or 2009.

The 1968 Film Version: Jean-Claude Forest's innocent and sexy, comic book heroine came to life in Roger Vadim's psychedelic adaptation "Barbarella" (1968). In the far flung future, an oversexed, intergalactic secret agent named Barbarella (Jane Fonda) is ordered to stop an evil scientist, Durand-Durand (Milo O'Shea), from upsetting the balance of universal peace. During her mission, Barbarella encounters a tyrannical queen (Anita Pallenberg), a blind angel (John Phillip Law), and flesh-eating children that start gnawing at a person's ankles. She never finds herself in a situation where it isn't possible to lose at least part of her already minimal clothing. Fonda captures the innocence and naivete of the character perfectly. The film is now considered a cult favorite among sci-fi fans.

Trivial Matters: The rock group Duran-Duran took its name from the evil scientist. Virna Lisi was ordered to play the part of Barbarella by United Artists, but tore up her contract instead.

Fanboy Rating:
Babes-9 Effects-6 Action-5 Brainwaves-1
Total=21

Barbarella

Barb Wire

Barb Wire (1996). Columbia Pictures in association with Dark Horse Entertainment. 98min. **Director:** David Hogan. **Producer:** Mike Richardson. **Screenwriters:** Ilene Chaiken and Chuck Pfarrer. Based upon characters created by Chris Warner. **Cinematographer:** Rick Bota. **Film Editor:** Peter Schink. **Production Designer:** Jean-Philippe Carp. **Cast:** Pamela Anderson, Temuera Morrison, Victoria Rowell, Jack Noseworthy, Xander Berkeley, Udo Kier, Clint Howard.

First Comic Book Appearance: "Comics Greatest World: Steel Harbor, Week 1" (1993)

Origins: Barbara Kopetski, also known as Barb Wire, was the creation of Chris Warner and Paul Gulacy, and debuted as a superhero in "Steel Harbor, Week 1," published by Comics Greatest World, an imprint of Dark Horse Comics, in 1993. Razor sharp, tough as nails, Barb Wire refused to take "shit" from anybody and hated being called "babe" ("Don't call me Babe!") by men who want to possess her. In the not-too-distant future (2017 A.D.), America has been devastated by a civil war between a fascist dictatorship, known as the "Congressional Directorate," and a ragtag group of freedom fighters. Barb runs a bar (called the Hammerhead) in the last bastion of freedom, Steel Harbor, during the day, and at night, works as a bounty-hunter, enforcer, somewhat reluctantly. Parallels between her character and that of Humphrey Bogart's Rick Blaine in "Casablanca" (1943) are purposely contrived by creator Chris Warner. She's a woman with really high standards as she tries to remain neutral in a world where everyone is trying to force her to take sides. No man can have her, and she refuses to waste her time with a man unless he has a really big one (a brain, that is) and knows how to use it. Her town of Steel Harbor is a fascinating cross between World War 2 Lisbon (and Casablanca) and Frank Miller's Sin City, with its odd collection of characters. Barb Wire herself is often portrayed in the comics with a form-fitting leather bustier, an arsenal of heavy firepower, and a motorcycle with all manner of lethal accessories. She was supported in her quest to destroy the Prime Moviers by Charlie Kopetski, her blind, mechanical genius brother. Other allies included Yo Mama, Ghost, The Machine, Motorhead and Wolf Pack. Dark Horse Comics spun-off several limited series comics based on Warner's characters as Barb Wire became of the most popular heroes to appear in the try-out series, "Comics Greatest World." Unfortunately, the failure of the movie spelled certain doom for the character, which has since disappeared.

First Media Appearance: Barb Wire's one and only media appearance outside the world of the Dark Horse Comics was in the persona of Pamela Anderson-Lee, the Playboy centerfold-turned-actress.

The 1996 Film Version: Three years after her debut in the Dark Horse Comic series, Barb Wire made the transition to the Silver Screen, with Pamela Anderson-Lee in the lead role. Most fans of the comic book were titillated by the Playboy bunny's appearance, in particular her buxom assets, but could not make much sense of the film version. Sometime in the 21st century, a second civil war has divided the United States between a fascistic Congress that now rules with an iron fist and a group of freedom fighters struggling to restore order. Steel Harbor, headquarters for the resistance, is the last free city in the whole country. Barb Wire (Pamela Anderson-Lee) owns a night club named "Hammerhead" where parties from both sides meet to have a drink. She lives by the motto not to take sides, and serves both parties equally. Of course, by night, she is a bounty hunter and enforcer who lives only to survive with her brother (Jack Noseworthy). When her former lover Alex Hood (Temuera Morrison) arrives in town, seeking her help, she must walk a careful tightrope between the two political forces. The film was a huge bomb when it debuted in 1996, and went on to be nominated for a Razzie Award for the Worst Picture of the Year.

Trivial Matters: The entire "Don't call me, Babe" motif comes from the original advertising for the Barb Wire Dark Horse comic book, in which she said those words to differentiate herself from other buxom comic book heroines. Barb's motorcycle is a 900cc Triumph Thunderbird; it was made as a water-cooled three cylinder model by the new Triumph factory at Hinckley in Leicestershire.

Fanboy Rating: Babes-9 Effects-2 Action-6 Brainwaves-2 Total=19

Barb Wire

Bash Brannigan

How to Murder Your Wife (1965). M-G-M/United Artists, 118 min. **Director:** Richard Quine. **Producer:** George Alexrod. **Screenwriter:** George Alexrod. The character of Bash Brannigan illustrated by Mel Keefer. **Cinematographer:** Harry Stradling. **Film Editor:** David Wages. **Cast:** Jack Lemmon, Virna Lisi, Eddie Mayehoff, Claire Trevor, Terry-Thomas, Sidney Blackmer, Jack Albertson, Mary Wickes.

First Comic Strip Appearance: "Bash Brannigan" (January 26, 1965)
Origins: Bash Brannigan is a fictional comic strip character that was drawn by cartoonist Mel Keefer for the Jack Lemmon comedy "How to Murder Your Wife" (1965). The comic strip by Alex Toth ran in the *Hollywood Reporter* and several newspapers for 10 days in January 1965 as part of the publicity for the film. In the strip, Bash Brannigan is a secret agent who works for an unknown American intelligence agency. He is just about to solve the mystery of a missing diamond (with micro-film in it) when the film begins. Bash tracks gunmen and Chinese assassins down to the docks in New Jersey, and rescues a naked belly-dancer with a diamond in her navel. Case closed. In the Skyscraper Gaper Caper, a man is murdered while looking at the top of the Empire State Building, and Bash is summoned to investigate. Not long after his last case, Bash Brannigan finds himself married to an Italian woman who emerges from a cake at a friend's bachelor party. Initially, Bash finds the sexy woman desirable, and plays along as the dutiful husband who is unable to do anything right. Soon, he tires of that role, and seeks to return to his life as a secret agent. There's just one problem: He's married to a woman who refuses to give him a divorce. The only solution is murder, and of course Bash Brannigan plots the perfect murder by drugging her with "goof balls" and dumping her body (Brrrp! Blasp!) into a cement mixer. "A tomb of gloop from a gloppida-gloppida machine," he schemes dreamily. Bash succeeds with his plan, and returns to his life as a secret agent, fighting to save the world.

First Media Appearance: Bash Brannigan made his one and only media appearance in the guise of Jack Lemmon in the romantic comedy "How to Murder Your Wife" (1965), and has not resurfaced in nearly forty years.

The 1965 Film Version: Bash Brannigan plays second fiddle to alter ego Stanley Ford (Jack Lemmon). In the 1965 film "How to Murder Your Wife," Ford is a rich, unmarried playboy who writes and illustrates the newspaper comic strip "Bash Brannigan, Secret Agent" for a powerful syndicate. Since Stanley Ford refuses to make Brannigan do anything that he himself hasn't done, he runs a series of exciting crime capers across New York City with faithful valet Charles (Terry-Thomas) in tow, photographing everything that he does. Ford then commits all of his adventures to pen and paper. At 47 years old, he is living a life that most men dream about but rarely have. However, after one night at a drunken bachelor's party, he finds himself married to a beautiful woman (Virna Lisi) who popped out of a cake, nearly naked. Charles leaves him to care for another bachelor, and despite all of Ford's attempts to get a divorce, he is trapped by this Italian beauty who doesn't speak one word of English. Stanley Ford becomes the laughing stock of the city as he recounts his marital misadventures in the "Brannigans" comic strip, which has replaced his action-adventure strip. His humiliation becomes complete when his wife invades his private men's club. Unable to take any more, Ford develops a plan for Bash Brannigan to murder his wife. Of course, since Stanley refuses to make Brannigan do anything that he himself hasn't done, he follows through with his plan in real life, or so we are meant to think. When his wife disappears, he is charged with her murder, and now Bash and Stanley face the most difficult adventure of their lives. Jack Lemmon is at his best in the dual role opposite the gorgeous talents of Virna Lisi who all makes us wish we spoke Italian. George Axelrod's comedy is rife with satire and comic exaggeration that shoots Cupid's arrows at many of the institutions that we hold so sacred. So clever, the script works on many levels…as a battle of the sexes as well as a lampoon and tribute to the James Bond movies.

Trivial Matters: In the Italian version, Virna Lisi's character is Greek. The cartoonist Mel Keefer who brought Johnny Quest, Scooby-Doo, Spider-Woman and other great comics to life also drew the movie strip. Virna Lisi's husband made her promise not to do a nude scene in the movie, and then showed up unexpectedly on the day when they were shooting her first bedroom scene, nude, but tastefully covered. He was so enraged that he chased Jack Lemmon around the M-G-M lot.

Fanboy Rating: Babes-8 Effects-2 Action-5 Brainwaves-5 Total=20

Bash Brannigan

Batman

The Batman (1943). Columbia Pictures, B&W, 260min. **Director:** Lambert Hillyer. **Producer:** Rudolph C. Flothow. **Screenwriters:** Victor McLeod, Leslie Swabacker, and Harry Frazer. Based upon characters created by Bob Kane. **Cinematographer:** James S. Brown. **Film Editors:** Dwight Caldwell and Earl Turner. **Cast:** Lewis Wilson, Douglas Croft, J. Carrol Naish, Shirley Patterson, William Austin.

First Comic Book Appearance: "Detective Comics #27" (May 1939)
Origins: In 1939, cartoonist Bob Kane with the help of writer Bill Finger created a masked hero who was equal parts of Zorro and the Scarlet Pimpernel, and unleashed the Bat-Man (now known simply as Batman) to rid the city of Gotham of its criminal element. Unlike Superman and most of the other superheroes of his day, Batman did not have any superhuman powers or abilities. He did possess a keen intellect and an extraordinary physical prowess, both of which he had honed since witnessing the murder of his parents as a child. His secret identity as Bruce Wayne, a billionaire industrialist, gave him access to cutting-edge technology and the wealth to employ that technology in his war on crime. Wayne also provided him with a foppish alter ego, which allowed him to move through Gotham as a philanthropist and playboy. At night, he donned a cowl and cape inspired by a chance encounter with a bat – feared by criminals – and moved through the seedy underworld of the city as a bat-shaped avenger. Batman added a utility belt in "Detective Comics #29" and a batarang and the Batmobile in "Detective Comics #31." Early on, his character was written in the pulp style of the Shadow and the Spirit, with the Bat-Man possessing little humor or humanity. With "Detective Comics #38," he was given a sidekick named Robin (alter ego Dick Grayson), the best-known and longest-running of all of the comic book sidekicks. The Dynamic Duo were inseparable, and battled criminals as a team. Soon, Batman also had a butler named Alfred Beagle (later changed to Pennyworth), a friend and

ally in Commissioner Gordon, and a whole host of supervillains, starting with the Joker and the Catwoman in "Batman #1" (April 25, 1940). Other supervillains like the Penguin, False Face, Mr. Feeze, and the Riddler soon followed. In the 1950s, Batman teamed up with Superman for the first time, in "Superman #76" (1952), experienced more science-fiction themes in his stories, and ultimately joined the Justice League of America (in 1960). Unfortunately, as sales of the Batman titles fell off in the early sixties, DC considered killing the character off altogether. Editor Julius Schwartz stepped in, and gave Batman a complete overhaul which saved his character from oblivion. The popularity of the campy, zany television series in the 1960s, the addition of Barbara Gordon as Batgirl, and the artistry of Neal Adams in the 1970s resurrected Batman as one of DC's most popular titles. In 1986, Frank Miller's "The Dark Knight Returns," which featured an aged Batman coming out of retirement, became one of the most successful and seminal works in comic book history. The limited series sparked a major revival in the character. When Dick Grayson left Batman's shadow to become Nightwing, Batman took on Jason Todd (who was subsequently killed off), then Tim Drake, and finally, Stephanie Brown, as Robin. "Crisis on Infinite Earths" (1985) 12-issue series helped to resolve a number of continuity errors, including Bruce Wayne's marriage to the Catwoman and their subsequent daughter, Huntress, and allowed Batman to be relaunched, starting with "Batman: Year One," in 1986. The popularity of the Tim Burton Batman movies and "Batman Begins" (2005) guaranteed that Batman was here to stay. Today, the Batman series of comic book titles are among the most popular in the line of DC Comics, and easily rival those of Superman.

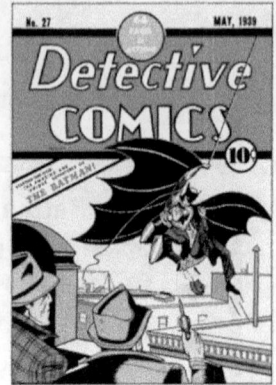

First Media Appearance: Batman's first media appearance outside the pages of DC comics and a weekly comic strip produced by the McClure Syndicate was in the 15-chapter serial, featuring Lewis Wilson as Batman and Douglas Croft as Robin. (See below.) Several attempts were made in 1943 and 1950 to launch a radio drama featuring the Caped Crusader, but none of those ever became a reality. The closest Batman came to radio was alongside Robin in a few guest appearances opposite Superman on "The Adventures of Superman" radio drama for the Mutual Broadcasting System.

Batman

The 1943 Film Serial: In his first Silver Screen appearance, the Caped Crusader (Lewis Wilson) of Gotham City and his faithful sidekick, the Boy Wonder (Douglas Croft), battled the sinister Dr. Daka (J. Carrol Naish), the Japanese mastermind behind several wartime plots to sabotage the infrastructure of the United States. First, Daka unleashes a radium-powered death ray that pulverizes walls; then he creates a classic alligator pit in which to dispose of the Dynamic Duo; and finally, after trying to kill Batman in a plane crash, he constructs a video ray that turns men into electronic zombies and sends them out to destroy Batman and Robin. Lambert Hillyer's 15-part serial for Columbia captures the innocent imagery of the comic book in a way that none of the other Batman movies have managed. And while there is no Batmobile and Bruce Wayne actually brandishes a revolver at one point in the serial, it's great to see our favorite superheroes aiding the war effort by dealing with Japanese spies and enemy saboteurs. The site of the Batman silhouetted against the night sky made white by a deep red filter is a wonderful image that remains a favorite one from the serial. In 1966, when the "Batman" television series was at the height of its popularity, Columbia struck new prints of the serial and released them under the title "An Evening with Batman and Robin." Loyal fans of the Dynamic Duo made the serial's revival a successful one, as they patiently sat through all fifteen episodes (shown one right after the other) in one sitting.

Trivial Matters: The serial first introduced Batman's underground headquarters, now known as the Batcave, to the Caped Crusader's mythol-

ogy. Bob Kane liked the idea so much that the Batcave was later incorporated into the comics. Batman and Robin were portrayed as FBI agents, not vigilantes, due to restrictions with Hollywood's ratings board. The serial's low budget forced Batman and Robin to rely on the same black Cadillac that Bruce Wayne had used; alas, the budget also prevented the serial from producing a Batmobile.

Fanboy Rating: Babes-1 Effects-3 Action-7 Brainwaves-5 Total=16

Batman and Robin (1949). Columbia Pictures, B&W, 263min. **Director:** Spencer Gordon Bennet. **Producer:** Sam Katzman. **Screenwriters:** George Plympton, Joseph Poland, and Royal Cole. Based upon characters created by Bob Kane. **Cinematographer:** Ira Morgan. **Film Editors:** Dwight Caldwell and Earl Turner. **Cast:** Robert Lowery, Johnny Duncan, Jane Adams, Lyle Talbot, Ralph Graves, Don C. Harvey, William Fawcett, Leonard Penn.

The 1949 Film Serial: Director Spencer Gordon Bennet took the multi-part serial to greater heights in this superior sequel to 1943's "The Batman." Without the racist overtones of the first serial, Bennet introduces audiences to a post-war Batman and Robin who are working to rid Gotham City of its criminal element. Enter the Wizard (Leonard Penn), a black-hooded mastermind, and his gang of cutthroats. He steals Professor Hammil's remote control device, and takes control of every motor vehicle within a fifty-mile radius. The Dynamic Duo (Robert Lowery and Johnny Duncan) are powerless to stop him when he commandeers their standard-model convertible. (This would have never happened to the Batmobile!) The Wizard needs diamonds to power his device, and sets his gang on obtaining them. When magazine photographer Vicki Vale (Jane Adams) learns of the Wizard's plan to bring the world to a stand still, she sets out to get the story, but constantly needs rescuing from a series of perils created for Batman and Robin. In the end, they use a remote controlled submarine to find the Wizard's hidden base, and unmask the Wizard to reveal his true identity. He was Professor Hammil's valet. This second serial was far better than the first, and even though fans were cheated out of the Batmobile, they got the first ever Bat signal and met Commissioner Gordon for the first time. Vicki Vale was actually a creation of the serial that was later incorporated into the comic book series.

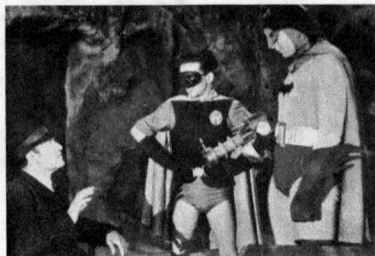

Trivial Matters: During the film's reception banquet, Bob Kane met Marilyn Monroe, and was so im-

Batman

pressed with the budding actress that he decided to incorporate the character of Vicki Vale into the comic book with Monroe's likeness. Robert Lowery re-appeared as Batman (albeit an animated Batman) in the opening credits of "The Pink Panther Strikes Again" (1976).

Fanboy Rating: Babes-1 Effects-3 Action-7 Brainwaves-5 Total=16

Batman: The Movie (1966). 20th Century-Fox,105min. **Director:** Leslie Martinson. **Producer:** William Dozier. **Screenwriter:** Lorenzo Semple. Based upon characters created by Bob Kane. **Cinematographer:** Howard Schwartz. **Film Editor:** Harry Gerstad. **Cast:** Adam West, Burt Ward, Lee Meriwether, Cesar Romero, Burgess Meredith, Frank Gorshin, Alan Napier, Neil Hamilton.

The 1966 Film Version: The huge success of the campy television series from creator William Dozier spawned a big-screen epic that featured a team-up of four supervillains that had threatened the lives of the Dynamic Duo (Adam West and Burt Ward) twice a week for the previous six months. The action-adventure series, which had two weekly installments (Wednesday night and Thursday night), debuted on ABC on January 12, 1966, replacing the long-running "Adventures of Ozzie and Harriet," and within a couple of weeks, fans and critics alike had deemed the series a major hit. Despite the comic book's dark origins, the television series embraced a lighter tone that often bordered on silly, high camp humor. Adam West and Burt Ward played their roles as Batman and Robin respectively, with very little humor, but the addition of outrageous villains, a pompous-sounding narrator (Dozier), psychedelic sets, and comic book style sound effects delivered as "WHAM!" or "POW!" on screen made the series funny. The character of Batgirl (Yvonne Craig) was added in the third season. Dozier and 20th Century-Fox were anxious to cash in on the series' popularity, and launched a movie version

which was little more than an extension of the series with bigger sets and props. (Originally, the movie version had been planned to launch the series, but when ABC pushed up the debut date to January 1966 instead of September 1966, the movie was placed on hold.) In addition to the Batmobile, which was a staple of the series, Batman and Robin were given a Batboat and other gadgets. Three of the supervillains were played by series regulars, including Cesar Romero as the Joker, Burgess Meredith as the Penguin, and Frank Gorshin as the Riddler. Lee Meriwether essayed the role of the Catwoman when Julie Newmar was unavailable. In the fantastic plot, these supervillains hijack a yacht containing a superdehydrator and use the device to reduce nine members of the United Nation's Security Council to dust. Batman and Robin to the rescue! The film and its live-action television show were popular among kids and intellectuals, but after less than 3 seasons, the show's popularity declined, and the series was canceled.

Trivial Matters: The "Batman" movie was originally planned to be the pilot film for the television series, but was delayed when ABC moved the released date for the series up six months. Julie Newmar was busy filming "McKenna's Gold" (1968) when the movie was shot, and thus, was not able to reprise her role as the Catwoman; Lee Meriwether played the role instead; later, in the series, Newmar was replaced by Eartha Kitt.

Fanboy Rating: Babes-5 Effects-5 Action-5 Brainwaves-2 Total=17

Batman

Batman (1989). Warner Brothers, 126min. **Director:** Tim Burton. **Producers:** Peter Guber and Jon Peters. **Screenwriters:** Sam Hamm and Warren Skaaren. Based upon characters created by Bob Kane. **Cinematographer:** Roger Pratt. **Film Editor:** Ray Lovejoy. **Production Designer:** Alan Furst. **Cast:** Michael Keaton, Jack Nicholson, Kim Basinger, Michael Gough, Robert Wuhl, Pat Hingle, Billy Dee Williams, Jack Palance.

The 1989 Film Version: Michael Keaton stepped into the role of Batman, opposite Jack Nicholson's Joker and Kim Basinger's Vicki Vale, in Tim Burton's big budget version of "Batman" (1989). Sam Hamm's wonderful screen story wisely jettisons the Boy Wonder and the campiness of the 1966 series to create a Gotham City that is a dark and dangerous place to live. Enter the Dark Knight, a mysterious figure whose parents were murdered on the streets of Gotham City many years earlier. Since all criminals are a superstitious, cowardly lot, billionaire Bruce Wayne disguises himself as a bat to strike terror into their hearts and sets about cleaning up the city of its criminal element. Reporter Alexander Knox (Robert Wuhl) teams with prize-winning photographer Vicki Vale to get the exclusive on the "bat-man." At the same time, one-time mob enforcer Jack Napier (Nicholson) emerges horribly disfigured from a firefight at a chemical factory, kills Boss Grissom (Jack Palance), and seizes control of Gotham's underworld as the psychotic Clown Prince of Crime, the Joker. Batman relies on his scientific gadgets –
"toys" as they are called by the Joker
– to keep the Joker at bay. But when
the Joker abducts Vicki Vale from a
dinner date with Bruce Wayne, the
Batman jumps into his Batmobile and
speeds to the rescue. While
Nicholson's over-the-top portrayal
of the Joker may steal the show from
Keaton's understated Batman, the film is all about production design. Alan Furst's designs for Gotham are simply stunning, translating Frank Miller's images for the Dark Knight comic book series into a reality. The film was a huge blockbuster, and inspired three other films in the franchise.

Trivial Matters: Adam West initially sought the role of Batman, but lost out to Michael Keaton who was Bob Kane's choice; other potential Batmans were Alec Baldwin, Charlie Sheen, Bill Murray, Pierce Brosnan and Tom Seleck. Tim Curry, Ray Liotta, Robin Williams, Willem Dafoe, David Bowie, John Lithgow and James Woods were all considered for the role of the Joker. Tom Mankiewicz, who had contributed to the 1978 version of "Superman," wrote a draft of "Batman" in 1980 in which he told the origins of Batman and Robin and pitted the Dynamic Duo against the Joker and the Penguin. In 1985, after Tim Burton had been assigned the role of director, he and his then girlfriend Julie Hickson wrote a 30-page treatment of their own, which ultimately became the basis of Sam

Hamm's screenplay. The Batmobile was built on the chassis of a Chevy Impala, and the Bat suit weighed over 70 pounds.

Fanboy Rating: Babes-8 Effects-7 Action-7 Brainwaves-7 Total=29

Batman Returns (1992). Warner Brothers, 126min. **Director:** Tim Burton. **Producers:** Tim Burton, Peter Guber and Jon Peters. **Screenwriters:** Daniel Waters and Sam Hamm. Based upon characters created by Bob Kane. **Cinematographer:** Stefan Czapsky. **Film Editor:** Bob Badami and Chris Lebenzon. **Production Designer:** Bo Welch. **Cast:** Michael Keaton, Danny DeVito, Michelle Pfeiffer, Christopher Walken, Michael Murphy, Pat Hingle.

The 1992 Film Sequel: As the title indicates, Batman (Michael Keaton) returns for yet another battle with the criminal forces that rule Gotham City. Having defeated the Joker (in the previous film), the Caped Crusader now faces the Penguin (Danny DeVito), a deformed and deranged criminal mastermind whose respectable parents abandoned him to a bunch of penguins at the zoo. Mysteriously, the penguins raised Oswald Cobblepot to adulthood, and gave him a purpose to survive. Now, as an adult, he wants to become Mayor of Gotham City. He coerces megalomaniacal businessman Maxwell Schrek (Christopher Walken) to help him with his political ambitions, while they both work together to frame Batman for a series of crimes. The plot is further complicated when secretary Selina Kyle (Michelle Pfeiffer) discovers her boss's criminal enterprise, and Schrek throws her from the top of a building. She dies from the impact, but is resurrected as the Catwoman by a group of alley cats. The Catwoman seeks revenge against Max Schrek, and ultimately crosses paths with Batman. He understands her more than she knows, but does not know what to do with her. He must also work to clear his name. In many ways, "Batman Returns" is better than the 1989 "Batman." The characters are much more alive in this movie, and all of the material dealing with Batman's origin has already been covered in the previous film. Keaton does an acceptable job as a dark and brooding Batman, but the real stars of the Batman movies are the villains. DeVito is outstanding as the Penguin, and the Catwoman in the guise of Michelle Pfeiffer never looked so good.

Batman

Trivial Matters: Annette Bening was originally cast as the Catwoman, but had to step down from the role when she became pregnant. Sean Young wanted the role so badly that she arrived at the studio in a Catwoman costume and demanded to see Tim Burton. Burton refused to see her. Lena Olin and Madonna were briefly considered as replacements for Bening. In the end, Burton's original choice for Vicki Vale, Michelle Pfeiffer, became the Catwoman. The name "Max Schreck" was borrowed from the actor who had played Dracula in the 1922 version "Nosferatu." Marlon Wayans was hired to play Robin in two movies, but when his character was dropped from "Batman Returns," Joel Schumacher selected Chris O'Donnell for "Batman Forever."

Fanboy Rating: Babes-8 Effects-7 Action-7 Brainwaves-5 Total=27

Batman Forever (1995). Warner Brothers, 122min. **Director:** Joel Schumacher. **Producer:** Tim Burton. **Screenwriters:** Lee Batchler, Janet Scott Bachler, and Akiva Goldsman. Based upon characters created by Bob Kane. **Cinematographer:** Stephen Goldblatt. **Film Editors:** Mark Stevens and Dennis Virkler. **Production Designer:** Barbara Ling. **Cast:** Val Kilmer, Tommy Lee Jones, Jim Carrey, Nicole Kidman, Chris O'Donnell, Michael Gough, Pat Hingle.

The 1995 Film Sequel: Director Joel Schumacher took the "Batman" franchise in a completely different direction from Tim Burton, discarding many of the darker elements in favor of a far more commercial approach. "Batman Forever" is crafted like a Hollywood blockbuster with big budget stars Jim Carrey, Nicole Kidman and Tommy Lee Jones and a special effects budget that cost twice as much as the first film. In the end, it is less artistically rendered. The Dark Knight of Gotham City (Val Kilmer) discovers that the former district attorney, Harvey Dent (Jones), is responsible for the wave of crime attributed to the supervillain Two-Face. Two-Face blames Batman for his disfigurement. At the same time, Edward Nygma (Carrey), a computer genius and former employee of the Wayne Foundation, has found a way to drain information from the brains of Gotham City's elite, and sets his sights as the Riddler on Bruce Wayne. To further complicate matters, Dr. Chase Meridan (Kidman) has fallen in love with Wayne, but sees a higher calling as Bruce's personal psychiatrist; she knows that he is troubled by some deep dark secret. When his family is killed by Two-Face, former circus acrobat Dick Grayson (Chris O'Donnell) becomes Wayne's ward, and Batman is forced to accept his new partner, Robin the Boy Wonder, to protect his own identity. WHAM! POW! Schumacher's Caped Crusader is suddenly thundering along in his Batmobile, Batwing, Batboat, Batsub…well, I think you get the idea. This third film comes the closest to emulating the 1966 television series.

Trivial Matters: Before Jim Carrey won the role of the Riddler, Brad Dourif, Damon Wayans, and Mark Hamill were all briefly considered. At one moment in the film, Robin exclaims, "Holey rusted metal, Batman!" This was a tribute to Robin's trademark expression from the 1966 television series. In the 1989 "Batman," Billy Dee Williams played District Attorney Harvey Dent, and was contracted to play Two-Face when the character was eventually used. Warner Brothers had to honor the contract and pay him off when they cast Tommy Lee Jones. Christian Bale, Corey Feldman, Corey Haim, and Matt Damon all auditioned for the role

Batman

of Dick Grayson/Robin; of course, Bale later went on to play the role of Batman in "Batman Begins" (2005).

Fanboy Rating: Babes-6 Effects-5 Action-5 Brainwaves-3 Total=19

> **Batman and Robin** (1997). Warner Brothers, 125min. **Director:** Joel Schumacher. **Producer:** Tim Burton. **Screenwriter:** Akiva Goldsman. Based upon characters created by Bob Kane. **Cinematographer:** Steven Goldblatt. **Film Editors:** Mark Stevens and Dennis Virkler. **Production Designer:** Barbara Ling. **Cast:** George Clooney, Chris O'Donnell, Uma Thurman, Arnold Schwarzenegger, Alicia Silverston, Michael Gough, Pat Hingle, John Glover.

The 1997 Film Sequel: Warner Brothers continued to mine the Batman comic book series for all that it was worth, and produced what many critics and fans alike consider the worst film in the Batman franchise. "Batman and Robin" (1997) was again directed by Joel Schumacher, and featured a third actor in as many films in the role as the Caped Crusader. George Clooney may well be the best actor who has donned the famous cape and cowl, but his portrayal of Batman raised more than its share of eyebrows. In a 1997 interview with Barbara Walters, Clooney admitted that he played the role as gay. "I was in a rubber suit and I had rubber nipples. I could have played Batman straight, but I made him gay." That portrayal reflected a decades-old assertion by Psychologist Fredric Wertham in his 1954 book *Seduction of the Innocent* that Batman and Robin are gay, and had been promoting homosexual values for years in the guise of innocent children's entertainment. "They live in sumptuous quarters, with beautiful flowers in large vases, and have a butler," Wertham wrote. "It is like a wish dream of two homosexuals living together." Whether Clooney's Batman was gay or not, O'Donnell's Robin was clearly heterosexual in his pursuit of beautiful Uma Thurman as Poison Ivy. Throw in Alicia Silverstone as Batgirl and Elle Macpherson as Bruce Wayne's love interest, Julie Madison, and the film fulfills nearly every heterosexual fanboy's wet-dreams. Who really cares about the plot? The plot is a jumbled mishmash in which Mr. Freeze (Arnold Schwarzengger) plans to turn Gotham City into an icebox because his dead wife is doomed to live her life in a

cryogenic tube. Meanwhile, Poison Ivy (Thurman) seeks revenge on Jason Woodrue (John Glover) for stealing her new invention, and comes between the Dynamic Duo when Robin decides it's time to sew his wild oats. Come to think of it, the background subtext provided by Clooney is far more interesting than the actual story. The motion picture bombed at the box office, and the Batman franchise seemed all but dead. Screenwriter Akiva Goldsman had managed to do what most supervillains for decades had threatened to do, and he was not even a major player in the action. Goldsman had succeeded in killing off the Batman franchise. The fifth and final installment, "Batman Triumphant," was canceled by Warner Brothers when the box office receipts failed to match the high cost of the film.

Trivial Matters: Anthony Hopkins, Patrick Stewart, Sylvester Stallone and Hulk Hogan were all considered for the role of Mr. Freeze that Arnold Schwarzenegger eventually played. Director Otto Preminger had initially played Mr. Freeze on the television series. Julia Roberts, Sharon Stone and Demi Moore were all in the running for the part of Poison Ivy. Dr. Jason Woodrue and Bane were recurring characters in the comic book series from DC Comics.

Fanboy Rating: Babes-7 Effects-3 Action-3 Brainwaves-1 Total=14

The 2005 Film Version: For several years, after the huge box office failure of "Batman and Robin" (1997), Warner Brothers attempted to revive the Batman franchise. At first, executives considered making Frank Miller's "Batman: Year One" into a motion picture with director Darren Aronofsky. They went as far as hiring a screenwriter to write an extended treatment, but when the screen story came back, Alfred was an African-American mechanic named "Big Al," the Batmobile was a souped-up Lincoln Towncar, and Bruce Wayne was a homeless man. Next, Larry and Andy Wachowski were approached to re-launch the franchise with Frank Miller's "Dark Knight Returns" graphic novel, but turned the offer down to make their "Matrix" sequels instead. The Warner executives then consulted Alan Moore and Brian Bolland, who had created one of DC's standalone titles, the exceptional "Batman: The Killing Joke," but Warner eventually decided the graphic novel was wrong for their Batman franchise. They even

Batman

went back to Tim Burton who was shepherding a Broadway show, titled "Batman: the Musical," for a 2005 run on the Great White Way. Finally, David S. Goyer wrote a screen treatment that borrowed elements from

Batman Begins (2005). Warner Brothers, 140min. **Director:** Christopher Nolan. **Producer:** Larry Franco, Charles Roven, and Emma Thomas. **Screenwriters:** Christopher Nolan and David S. Goyer. Based upon characters created by Bob Kane. **Cinematographer:** Wally Pfister. **Film Editor:** Lee Smith. **Production Designer:** Nathan Crowley. **Cast:** Christian Bale, Michael Caine, Liam Neeson, Katie Holmes, Gary Oldman, Cillian Murphy, Rutger Hauer.

two graphic novels by Jeph Loeb, "The Long Halloween" and "Dark Victory," and the production was green-lighted with director Christopher Nolan. Goyer left to direct "Blade Trinity" (2004), and Nolan took over the writing chores as well. "Batman Begins" is more an origin story than anything else. The film tells the story of how young Bruce Wayne watched in horror as his millionaire parents were slain right in front of his eyes, and how that trauma led him to become obsessed with revenge. As a disillusioned young man (Christian Bale), he travels to Asia to seek the training of a great Ninja master named Ra's Al Ghul (Ken Watanabe). He trains hard, and becomes the top Ninja assassin in Al Ghul's service. One day, he awakens to the reality of what he is doing, and flees home to Gotham City to act as its lord and guardian. He becomes the Bat-Man. In his new guise, and with the help of a rising cop on the police force, Jim Gordon (Gary Oldman), Batman battles a Mafia don named Falcone (Tom Wilkinson) and supervillain Scarecrow (Cillian Murphy). He is aided by Alfred (Michael Caine) and a weapons inventor named Lucius Fox (Morgan Freeman). Eventually, his past catches up to him, and he must kill an old mentor (Liam Neeson). The motion picture does a wonderful job in re-launching the Batman franchise with youthful Christian Bale under the cape and cowl of Batman. Katie Holmes is all wrong as Batman's love interest Rachel Dawes as she appears little more than a teenager herself, but that seems like the only mistake this near flawless production takes. A big budget follow-up, titled "The Dark Knight," is scheduled for 2008 with Christopher Nolan returning as director. No details about the plot were available at the time this book went to press.

Trivial Matters: Christian Bale was cast as Batman after many other actors, including Ashton Kutcher, David Boreanaz, Cillian Murphy, Billy Crudup, Henry Cavill, Jake Gyllenhaal, Eion Bailey, Joshua Jackson and Hugh Dancy, auditioned for the part. Marilyn Manson was considered for the role of the Scarecrow, but after Nolan saw Cillian Murphy's screentest for Batman, he was cast in the role. Parts of the Chicago skyline were used to represent the city of Gotham. The film was originally titled "Batman: The Frightening."

Fanboy Rating: Babes-3 Effects-6 Action-7 Brainwaves-6 Total=22

Other Media Appearances: In addition to the various movies, the television show and the one radio appearance, Batman has been featured in several animated series. From 1969 to 1970, Filmation's "The Adventures of Batman and Robin" aired on CBS. "Batman: The Animated Series" ran for three years (1992 to 1995) as a syndicated cartoon series with Kevin Conroy as the voice of Batman. Mark Hamill played the Joker. In 1997, "The New Batman Adventures" played on the WB network, while "Batman Beyond" featured Will Friedle as the Caped Crusader. Several direct-to-video films were produced relying on the same artistic techniques Fleischer Studios had produced for the Superman cartoons from the 1940s. "Batman: Mask of the Phantasm" (1993) was the first of these releases, followed by "Batman and Mr. Freeze: SubZero" in 1998 and "Batman: Mystery of the Batwoman" in 2003. More recently, "Batman: The Animated Series" (1999) has drawn a great deal of attention for its Emmy-award winning scripts and outstanding animation. Batman will be forever with us!

Batman

Birds of Prey

Birds of Prey (2002). Warner Brothers Television, 60min, 13episodes. **Director:** Shawn Levy. **Producer:** David Carson. **Screenwriters:** Melissa Rosenberg, David M. Goodman, Laeta Kalogridis, Julie Hess. Based upon characters created by Bob Kane. **Cinematographer:** Christopher Faloona. **Film Editors:** Robert Ferretti and Michael Stern. **Cast:** Ashley Scott, Dina Meyer, Rachel Skarsten, Shemar Moore, Ian Abercrombie, Mia Sara, Mark Hamill, Maggie Baird.

First Comic Book Appearance: "Birds of Prey One Shot" (1996).
Origins: Created by Chuck Dixon and Gary Frank based upon a concept by Jordan Gorfinkle, "Birds of Prey" (1996) was a one-shot comic book that brought together Black Canary and the Oracle, two of the DC Universe's female superheroes, into one team. The standalone comic book was so successful that it became a regular series in 1999, featuring several other members. The roster includes: Barbara Gordon, formerly Batgirl, is now the wheelchair-bound leader of the team known as the Oracle. Black Canary (also known as Dinah Laurel Lance) assumed the role of the tough streetfighter when her mother stepped down as the superheroine. As the daughter of Batman and Catwoman, the Huntress relies on her skills as a trained assassin to affect a certain kind of justice. And Lady Blackhawk (Zinda Blake), time-displaced by events in "Zero Hour," the 1940s woman uses her skills as an aviator to pilot the Aerie One. Together, they use their kills to battle the dark criminal element that has crept back into Gotham City. Occasionally, they are aided by Nightwing (Dick Grayson), the Blue Beetle (Ted Kord), and Catwoman (Selina Kyle). The comic book series was imagined to take place at a future time when Batman has retired at the Dark Knight and guardian of Gotham, but like most DC Comics, the continuity is not always maintained. With issue #100, Big Barda, Judomaster and Manhunter were invited to be new team members.
First Media Appearance: "Birds of Prey" was launched as a live-action television series for the WB on October 9, 2002, and featured some of

the characters from the comic book series. Created and produced by David Carson, the sixty-minute television show was poorly received by critics and fans and was cancelled after only 13 episodes. *The 2002 Film Version:* In the European market and Far East, several of the television episodes were spliced together and released theatrically. In the future, long after the Dark Night has retired and gone into a self-imposed exile, his legacy lives on in the form of the Birds of Prey – three superhuman women dedicated to serving the public and ridding Gotham City of its criminal element. Batman's former protégé Batgirl was caught in the crossfire of the war between the Caped Crusader and the Joker, and now must fight crime from a wheelchair as the Oracle (Dina Meyer). The Huntress (Ashley Scott), daughter of Batman and the Catwoman, has taken up her father's cape and cowl, and fights criminals under the cover of knight, striking terror into their hearts. Together, they have taken in a young runaway, Dinah Lance (Rachel Skarsten) as Black Canary, who has secret powers, and have begun to train her to use these powers in the battle against evil. They are assisted by Alfred Pennyworth (Ian Abercrombie). The series was hot, stylish, and just right for the WB's youthful demographics; unfortunately, the show never caught on. Discussion of a big screen adaptation is still ongoing.

Trivial Matters: The character of Harley Quinn from the comic books was turned into Dr. Harleen Quinzel in the series, and played by Mia Sara. Maggie Baird made two appearances as the Catwoman, and Mark Hamill finally got his opportunity to play a live-action Joker in two episodes.

Fanboy Rating: Babes-10 Effects-4 Action-6 Brainwaves-3 Total=23

Birds of Prey

Blackhawk

Blackhawk (1952). Columbia Pictures, 242min. **Directors:** Spencer Gordon Bennet and Fred Sears. **Producer:** Sam Katzman. **Screenwriters:** Royal Cole, Sherman Lowe, and George Plympton. Based upon characters created by Will Eisner. **Cinematographer:** William Whitley. **Film Editor:** Earl Turner. **Production Designer:** Herbert Leonard. **Cast:** Kirk Alyn, Carol Forman, John Crawford, Michael Fox, Don Harvey, Rich Vallin, Larry Stewart.

First Comic Book Appearance: "Military Comics #1" (August 1941)
Origins: Blackhawk was the brainchild of Will Eisner, the creator of the Spirit. Along with Chuck Cuidera (as Charles Nicholas) and Bob Powell, he introduced the Blackhawks – Andre, Olaf, Chuck, Hendrikson, Stanislaus, Chop Chop, and their leader Blackhawk himself – as an elite band of fighter pilots during World War 2 who lived on a private island and battled the Nazis and other forces that threatened democracy and peace of the free world. The team first debuted in Quality Comics' "Military Comics #1," and then, after Quality Comics became part of the DC Universe, they appeared in a comic series, simply titled "Blackhawk." With "Blackhawk #230," the pilots became superheroes with individual names like the Leaper, the Golden Centurion, Dr. Hands, etc. But it was really during the war years and shortly thereafter that the Blackhawks made their mark. According to the original storyline, Janos Prohaska (Blackhawk) was a Polish pilot who flew a PZL P.50a Jastrzab against the German invasion of Poland in 1939. Shortly after his country was overrun by the Nazis, he formed a small team of ace pilots from various nationalities: Andre was French; Olaf, Swedish; Chuck was a Texas-born American; Hendrickson was Dutch; Stanislaus, Polish, and Chop-Chop, a stereotypical Chinese. They flew Grumman XF5F-1 Skyrockets, launched from a secret base known as Blackhawk Island. Zinda Blake, a Russian aviatrix, became the team's first and only Lady Blackhawk. (When Zinda Blake was displaced in time due to "Zero Hour" and became a member of

the Birds of Prey, Natalie Reed took her place.) The silliness of making the Blackhawks into superheroes eventually led to the title's cancellation in 1968. Several other short-runs and limited series have kept the Blackhawks active, but far from a bestselling series.

First Media Appearance: The Blackhawks made their first media appearance on a radio series that was broadcast on Wednesdays at 5:30 on ABC from September to December 1950. Blackhawk was played by Michael Fitzmaurice.

Other Media Appearances: Outside of the 1952 film series, the Blackhawks have made relatively few other media appearances. In 1982, William Rotsler wrote a Blackhawk novel in anticipation of a Blackhawk movie that never got off the ground. In 2001, the Blackhawks appeared on two episodes of the "Justice League" animated television series; the episodes were "The Savage Time" and "I Am Legion." A laudatory reference to the Blackhawk team is also made in "Sky Captain and the World of Tomorrow" (2003).

The 1952 Film Serial: At the end of the era of the Saturday matinee serial, Sam Katzman produced what many consider to be the last great action serial. Based on the comic book that featured seven flyers who banded together during World War 2 to fight the Nazis, the serial picks up shortly after the war, and follows the exploits of the Blackhawks as they battled spies and saboteurs in each cliffhanging episode. Kirk Alyn, who had played Superman in two previous serials, was cast as Blackhawk, and the lovely Carol Forman, a favorite serial villainess, was hired to play the femme fatale of an unnamed foreign power bent of stealing a secret fuel cylinder. The cylinder changes hands several times in the fast-paced action-adventure, but ultimately the Blackhawks emerge victorious. Columbia's last foray in the serial business is also one of its best.

Trivial Matters: Due to budgetary restraints, the 15-chapter serial only has one airplane at its disposal, and that airplane is shared by the Blackhawks. The various hideouts all look the same because the production team had to keep reusing sets that had already been built for a previous chapter.

Fanboy Rating: Babes-1 Effects-2 Action-5 Brainwaves-4 Total=12

Blackhawk

Black Scorpion

Black Scorpion (1995). Concorde Pictures, 92min. **Director:** Jonathan Winfrey. **Producers:** Roger Corman and Mike Elliott. **Screenwriter:** Craig J. Nevius. **Cinematographer:** Geoffrey George. **Film Editors:** Gwyneth Gibby and Thomas Peterson. **Production Designer:** Eric Khan. **Cast:** Joan Severance, Rick Rossovich, Michael Wiseman, Bradford Tatum, Casey Siemaszko, Kimberly Roberts, Kyle Fredericks, Terri Vaughn, Garrett Morris.

First Comic Book Appearance: None.

Origins: From the creative imagination of Craig J. Nevius, the Black Scorpion (also known as Darcy Walker) roared into our lives in her high-tech "Scorpionmobile" in 1995 in the low budget "Black Scorpion." The Black Scorpion was imagined as a female version of Batman. She has no superpowers, but thanks to her large assortment of gadgets, a background in computers, and martial arts training, she battles the criminal element in the City of Angels (not to be confused with Los Angeles). Her real name is Darcy Walker, and she is a police detective. When her father was shot by the city's crooked district attorney, the D.A. was arrested but never prosecuted. She donned her superhero costume and took to the streets as a vigilante in order to exact revenge against those who bend the law for their own purposes.

First Media Appearance: The Black Scorpion's first media appearance was in the 1995 film "Black Scorpion," produced by Roger Corman.

Other Media Appearances: In 1997, she returned for a second film, titled "Black Scorpion: Aftershock," and starred in a short-lived, live-action television series that aired on the Sci-Fi Channel in 2001. Joan Severance played her character in the two movies, and Michelle Lintel took over in the television series.

The 1995 Film Version: Police Detective Darcy Walker (Joan Severance) takes on the identity of "Black Scorpion" at night to catch evildoers. She strikes a deal with a petty thief named Argyle (Garrett Morris) to assist her. Argyle becomes her personal mechanic and helps to create her hi-tech equipment. Together they fight against Dr. Goddard (Casey Siemaszko), an asthmatic mad scientist who has developed an airborne toxin that he plans to release over the city. .Joan Severance is beautiful and seductive in her skin-tight Catwoman costume, but the film is definitely a low-rent version of "Batman," complete with a Batmobile.

Trivial Matters: In the 1995 movie, Darcy's boots (when dressed as Black Scorpion) change height; when she is fighting or running, they are flat; when she is merely standing or posing, they are high heels. In the 2001 television series, both Adam West and Frank Gorshin appeared in roles as supervillains.

Fanboy Rating: Babes-7 Effects-1 Action-3 Brainwaves-2 Total=13

Black Scorpion: Aftershock (1997). Concorde Pictures, 85min. **Director:** Jonathan Winfrey. **Producers:** Roger Corman and Mike Elliott. **Screenwriter:** Craig J. Nevius. **Cinematographer:** Geoffrey George. **Film Editors:** Gwyneth Gibby and Thomas Peterson. **Production Designer:** Eric Khan. **Cast:** Joan Severance, Garrett Morris, Whip Hubley, Sherrie Rose, Stoney Jackson, Matt Roe, Stephen Lee, Shane Powers, Terri Vaughn.

The 1997 Film Sequel: Professor Ursula Undershaft (Sherrie Rose) plots the destruction of Angel City in order to take advantage of the Mayor's federal earthquake relief money, and the Black Scorpion (Joan Severance) must stop her and find her stolen Scorpionmobile before it's too late. Meanwhile, a low-rent version of the Joker, named Gangster Prankster (Stoney Jackson) is stirring up trouble of his own. Again, Joan looks great in her dominatrix attire, but the film doesn't have much more than T&A going for it.

Fanboy Rating: Babes-7 Effects-1 Action-3 Brainwaves-2 Total=13

Black Scorpion

Blade

Blade (1998). New Line Cinema, 120min. **Director:** Stephen Norrington. **Producers:** Robert Engelman, Peter Frankford and Wesley Snipes. **Screenwriter:** David S. Goyer. Based upon characters created by Marv Woldman and Gene Colan. **Cinematographer:** Theo Van de Sande. **Film Editor:** Paul Rubell. **Production Designer:** Kirk Petruccelli. **Cast:** Wesley Snipes, Stephen Dorff, Kris Kristofferson, Donal Logue, Udo Kier, Traci Lords.

First Comic Book Appearance: "Tomb of Dracula #10" (July 1973)
Origins: The character of Blade, the Vampire Hunter, was brought to life by writer Marv Wolfman and artist Gene Colan, and appeared for the first time as an adversary of Dracula in "Tomb of Dracula #10" (July 1973). Born in a London whorehouse in the unsavory neighborhood of Soho on October 24, 1929 (Black Thursday), Eric Brooks was part human and part vampire. His mother, Tara Brooks, had been a prostitute at Madame Vanity's Brother when she experienced complications due to labor. Deacon Frost, a local doctor, was summoned to care for her, but he turned out to be a bloodthirsty vampire who instead feasted on her blood as the infant was born. Accidentally, Frost passed on certain of his vampiric enzymes to the baby, and this resulted in Blade's superhuman abilities; he inherited a longer-than-average lifespan, unusual strength, immunity to vampires, and the ability to "smell" supernatural creatures; the enzymes also caused him to have sensitivity to bright lights. Tara's fellow prostitutes drove Frost away before he could kill the infant as well. He was raised in the Brothel until age nine, and then trained by Jamal Afari, a vampire hunter, as a young man. When Afari was killed by Dracula, Blade joined a group of fellow vampire hunters who were dedicated to ridding the world of Dracula (believed to be the father and king of all vampires). The group was known as the "Drac Pack," and included Quincy Harker (son of Jonathan Harker), Rachel Van Helsing (granddaughter of Abraham Van Helsing), Taj Nital, and Frank Drake. For years, he pursued Dracula and

eventually learned of the existence of Frost, the vampire that had killed his mother. He left the Drac Pack and sought out and killed Frost with the help of Hannibal King, a private detective and vampire. Vampires were totally eliminated from the Marvel Universe in the 1980s, and Blade went to work as a private detective. When they were brought back, Morbius was the embodiment of a living vampire that Blade sought to destroy. The vampire hunter also worked alongside Doctor Strange, Spider-Man, Luke Cage, and S.H.I.E.L.D. At age 78, he still wages his lifelong battle against the forces of evil.

First Media Appearance: In 1996, two years before the first "Blade" movie, Blade made his first media appearance on an episode of the "Spider-Man" animated series. The episode "Neogenic Nightmare" finds Blade teaming with Spider-Man to track down the living vampire, Morbius. He also meets his friend and mentor Whistler, who had never appeared in any version of the Marvel Universe before.

The 1998 Film Version: "Blade" (1998), featuring Wesley Snipes in the title role, was an uncommonly good adaptation of the comic book series. While David Goyer's screenplay deviates slightly from the Marvel Universe, it remains faithful to the spirit of the character that was created by Wolfman and Colan. When Blade's mother dies during childbirth, the victim of a brutal vampire attack, she passes along to her infant son all the strengths of the vampire in combination with the best human skills. He is raised by Abraham Whistler (Kris Kristofferson), a life-long friend and vampire hunter, and trained to become the "day walker," a human-vampire hybrid that is unaffected by the sunlight. Apparently, vampires have managed to infiltrate nearly every major organization on the planet, and they plan to summon La Magra, the blood god, to establish dominion over the Earth's population like human cattle. But they need Blade's special blood! Deacon Frost (Stephen Dorff) and his minions are sent to capture Blade, but thanks to Dr. Jaren Kenson (N'Bushe Wright) the vampire hunter makes easy work of them. He also learns to control the last of his vampiric passions. The movie with its combination of vampires, martial arts, and techno music was a big hit among teenagers and young adults, and spawned two other films and a television show in the series.

Trivial Matters: Blade relies on a samurai sword to eliminate his vampire victims; apparently, an obscure reference in Bram Stoker's novel *Dracula* suggests that vampires can be killed by blades, in this case a Bowie knife. Udo Kier, one of the vampire elders, played Count Dracula in "Blood for Dracula" (1974). Though Denzel Washington and Laurence Fishburne were

Blade

considered, only Wesley Snipes was the living embodiment of the comic book character Blade.

Fanboy Rating: Babes-4 Effects-5 Action-7 Brainwaves-5 Total=21

Blade 2 (2002). New Line Cinema, 117min. **Director:** Guillermo del Toro. **Producers:** Patrick Palmer, Peter Frankford and Wesley Snipes. **Screenwriter:** David S. Goyer. Based upon characters created by Marv Woldman and Gene Colan. **Cinematographer:** Gabriel Beristain. **Film Editor:** Peter Amundson. **Production Designer:** Carol Spier. **Cast:** Wesley Snipes, Kris Kristofferson, Ron Perlman, Leonor Varela, Norman Reeus.

The 2002 Film Sequel: Guillermo del Toro took over the directing reigns for "Blade 2" (2002), and produced a sequel that may, in fact, be better than the original. In the story, also scripted by David Goyer, Blade (Wesley Snipes), Whistler (Kristofferson) and a weapons expert named Scud (Norman Reedus) join forces with the Bloodpack, an elite team of vampires trained in combat, to defeat the Reapers, a new breed of vampires that feed off humans and vampires. The Bloodpack is led by Reinhardt (Ron Perlman). They venture into the sewers below the city, presumably Chicago (as it was in the first), and hunt the Reapers down one by one. The alliance between Blade and the Bloodpack is a tenuous one that allows for incredibly snappy dialogue and intrigue all along the way. In the end, Blade discovers the Reapers are genetic experiments gone wrong. Damaskinos (Thomas Kretschmann) has betrayed not only Blade and his team but all vampires in attempting to concoct the ultimate vampire.

Trivial Matters: Scud wears a T-shirt featuring the logo of the Bureau of Paranormal Research and Defense, a reference to Mike Nignola's "Hellboy" comic book. Scud also

refers to Wesley Snipes' Blade as "the Dark Knight," a reference that is better suited for another kind of bat man. On the DVD version, an extended opening scene in Prague establishes the relationship between Blade and Whistler.

Fanboy Rating: Babes-4 Effects-6 Action-8 Brainwaves-5 Total=23

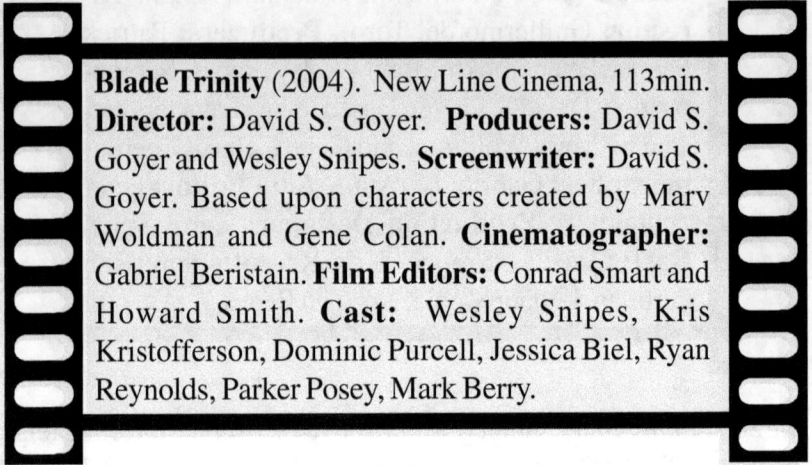

Blade Trinity (2004). New Line Cinema, 113min. **Director:** David S. Goyer. **Producers:** David S. Goyer and Wesley Snipes. **Screenwriter:** David S. Goyer. Based upon characters created by Marv Woldman and Gene Colan. **Cinematographer:** Gabriel Beristain. **Film Editors:** Conrad Smart and Howard Smith. **Cast:** Wesley Snipes, Kris Kristofferson, Dominic Purcell, Jessica Biel, Ryan Reynolds, Parker Posey, Mark Berry.

The 2004 Film Sequel: In the third and final film, "Blade: Trinity" (2004), the vampire hunter (Snipes) joins forces with Hannibal King (Ryan Reynolds) and Abigail Whistler (Jessica Biel), the Nightstalkers, to destroy the newly resurrected Dracula (Dominic Purcell), the first of all the vampires. Their only hope of destroying him is to unleash a virus that will kill every vampire on earth, but they have only one change to make it work. The third film was not as well received as the first two in the franchise, and plans for a fourth motion picture were dropped. Instead rapper Kirk Jones took over from Snipes, and played Blade on a short-lived television series that aired on Spike TV.

Trivial Matters: When Hannibal King is telling Blade about the return of Dracula, he shows Blade a copy of "Tomb of Dracula #55." Guillermo del Toro was set to direct the third installment, but passed when his dream project, "Hellboy" (2004), got the greenlight. Abigail Whistler was originally written by David S. Goyer as Rachel Van Helsing, but when he learned of the "Van Helsing" movie at Universal, he changed the character to be Whistler's daughter.

Fanboy Rating: Babes-5 Effects-2 Action-5 Brainwaves-3 Total=15

Blade

Buck Rogers

Buck Rogers (1939). Universal, B&W, 237min, 12 episodes. **Directors:** Ford Beebe and Sam Goodkind. **Producer:** Barney Sarecky. **Screenwriters:** Norman S. Hall and Ray Trampe. Based upon characters created by Philip Francis Nowlan. **Cinematographer:** Jerome Ash. **Film Editors:** Joseph Gluck, Louis Sackin, Alvin Todd. **Cast:** Buster Crabbe, Constance Moore, Jackie Moran, Jack Mulhall, Anthony Warde, C. Montague Shaw.

First Appearance: "Armageddon 2419 A.D." in *Amazing Stories* pulp magazine (August 1928)

First Comic Strip Appearance: "Buck Rogers" (January 7, 1929)

Origins: Philip Francis Nowlan adapted his novella, which had first appeared in the pulp magazine *Amazing Stories*, for the National Newspaper Service syndicate, and created the first science fiction comic strip with "Buck Rogers in the 25th Century A.D." First published on January 7, 1929, the same date when the first "Tarzan" daily comic also began, Nowlan's strip followed the adventures of Anthony "Buck" Rogers five hundred years in the future. The story began by recapitulating the plot of the novella "Armageddon 2419 A.D." in comic strip form. Buck Rogers, an American living in the 20th Century, is overcome by fumes while trapped in a mineshaft collapse. He falls into a coma, and awakens in the 25th Century. Apparently, the gas has a preservative effect because he does not age one day over the 500-year period. He is discovered by Wilma Deering and Dr. Huer who attempt to bring Buck up to date. The future America has been conquered by evil Asian warlords, and the two need an intrepid leader like Buck to help them fight the Mongols. Not long after the Mongols are overthrown, Earth is invaded by alien legions, and Buck has to fight them as well. The comic strip introduced readers to most of the familiar conventions of sci-fi, including rocket ships, robots, space voyages, ray guns, and the like. "Buck Rogers" became the number one comic strip, and spawned a host of imitators, including "Flash Gordon" at rival

King Features. The strip ran until 1967, less than two years before Americans landed on the moon. In 1969, Chelsea House published *The Collected Works of Buck Rogers in the 25th Century,* a coffee table book of reprints, with an introduction by Ray Bradbury.

First Media Appearance: Buck Rogers made his first media appearance outside the world of the pulp magazines and comic strips in 1932. The "Buck Rogers" radio show – the first science fiction program on radio – aired four times a week for fifteen years, from 1932 to 1947. Actors Matt Crowley, Curtis Arnall, Carl Frank, and John Larkin all had the opportunity to play Buck, while Wilma Deering was voiced by Adele Ronson and Dr. Huer was played by Edgar Stehli.

Other Media Appearances: At the 1933-34 World's Fair in Chicago, Buck Rogers appeared in the guise of John Dille in a 10-minute short, titled "Buck Rogers in the 25th Century: An Interplanetary Battle with the Tiger Men of Mars." Several years later, Buster Crabbe, the actor who had brought Flash Gordon to life in three Universal serials, played Buck Rogers in a 12-part serial. A short-lived television series aired on ABC in 1950, with Earl Hammond as Buck and Eva Marie Saint as Wilma Deering. A second television series, with Gil Gerard as Buck Rogers, aired for two years on NBC in 1979.

The 1939 Film Version: After scoring big numbers with its serial adaptations of "Flash Gordon," Universal struck gold with its "Buck Rogers" serial in 1939. In this version, Buck Rogers and his sidekick Buddy Wade (Jackie Moran) crash-land a dirigible on a mountaintop and are put into suspended animation by a strange gas. When they awaken 500 years later, the Earth is ruled by a tyrannical despot named Killer Kane (Anthony Warde). They join forces with Wilma Deering (Constance Moore), Professor Huer (C. Montague Shaw), and Prince Tallen (Philson Ahn) of the Saturn men to bring law and order back to their planet. All references to Asians and Mongols were dropped from the serial because the studio didn't want to offend potential audience members in Asia, and the villain Kane was imagined as a European. Rocketships, ray-guns, light bridges, matter transportation tubes, and all of the trappings of a bad sci-fi novel were added to make certain audiences bought tickets. The 12-part serial was not as well received as

BUCK ROGERS
25TH CENTURY A.D.
The Big Little Book

Buck Rogers

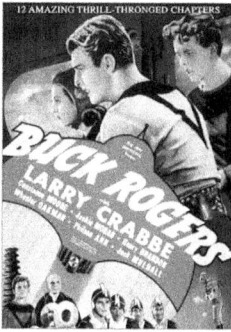

the "Flash Gordon" serials, but it still ranked in dollars at the box office.

Trivial Matters: The character of Killer Kane was changed from the comic strip; in the original, his real name was Oba Kane. Buck Rogers was also changed from a mine surveyor to a World War One pilot. The bullet cars used in the movie were the same ones used in "Flash Gordon's Trip To Mars" (1938). George Lucas borrowed huge parts of the futuristic technology in "Buck Rogers" and "Flash Gordon" serials for his "Star Wars" epic.

Fanboy Rating: Babes-4 Effects-4 Action-5 Brainwaves-5 Total=18

The 1953 Cartoon Satire: In 1953, Chuck Jones spoofed science fiction movies with the first of a series of cartoons featuring Daffy Duck as "Duck Dodgers in the 24th-1/2 Century." The animated short from Warner Brothers featured one of its most popular characters in a role not that dissimilar from Buck Rogers, intergalactic hero. Duck Dodgers and his sidekick Porky Pig in the role of "Eager Young Space Cadet" arrive on Planet X to claim the unknown world for Earth. Marvin the Martian lands on the same planet to claim it for Mars. The lines are subsequently drawn for a battle of wits between the two cartoon characters. The short has since become a cult favorite, and two other shorts were later produced featuring Daffy Duck as Duck Dodgers.

Buck Rogers in the 25th Century (1979). Universal, 89min. **Director:** Daniel Haller. **Producer:** Richard Caffey. **Screenwriters:** Glen Larson and Leslie Stevens. Based upon characters created by Philip Francis Nowlan. **Cinematographer:** Frank Beascoechea. **Film Editors:** John J. Dumas, David Howe, and Bill Martin. **Cast:** Gil Gerard, Erin Gray, Pamela Hensley, Henry Silva, Tim O'Connor, Joseph Wiseman, Felix Silla.

The 1979 Film Version: Glen Larson, who had created "Battlestar Galactica," and Leslie Stevens, who had created "The Outer Limits," collaborated on a remake of the famous comic strip with Gil Gerard in the lead. Initially, they created a pilot to launch a weekly series for NBC, but the network was so impressed with the final product that it was first shown in theaters in the Spring of 1979. Captain William "Buck" Rogers was a 20th Century astronaut whose Ranger 3 spacecraft develops a problem and puts him into suspended animation for 500 years. His dormant ship is captured by the Draconians, led by Princess Ardala (Pamela Hensley) and Kane (Henry Silva). They revive Buck and trick him into leading them through Earth's defenses. The Terran Space Force intercepts him, and Buck Rogers learns from Wilma Deering (Erin Gray) and Dr. Huer (Tim O'Connor) that Earth is engaged in a war with the Draconians. Buck proves himself, and eventually turns their suspicions about him into trust and admiration. The television series, which aired on NBC in September 1979 and ran for two seasons, followed Buck's further adventures as he attempted to adjust to life in the future. One episode paid tribute to Buster Crabbe, the original Buck Rogers, as a squadron of former pilots is called out of retirement to help in Earth's defense. The show started out strong, with many episodes devoted to the clash of cultures, but then dropped off with Buck being thrust into one weird situation after another. An attempt during the second season to launch Buck Rogers on a starship seeking lost and forgotten Earth colonies was the final nail in the proverbial coffin of this initially engaging series. "Buck Rogers in the 25th Century" was canceled in May 1981.

Trivial Matters: The robotic character Twiki (Felix Silla) was modeled after the robot C-3PO in "Star Wars," and first choice for the voice of Dr. Theopolis was Douglas Rain who had provided the voice of HAL-9000 in "2001: A Space Odyssey" (1968).

Fanboy Rating: Babes-8 Effects-5 Action-5 Brainwaves-5 Total=23

Buck Rogers

Bulletproof Monk

Bulletproof Monk (2003). M-G-M, 104min. **Director:** Paul Hunter. **Producers:** Terence Chang and John Woo. **Screenwriters:** Ethan Reiff and Cyrus Voris. **Cinematographer:** Stefan Czapsky and Anthony Nocera. **Film Editor:** Robert Lambert. **Production Designer:** Deborah Evans. **Cast:** Yun-Fat Chow, Sean William Scott, Jaime King, Karel Roden, Mako, Marcus Jean Pirae, Roger Yuan, Sean Bell.

First Comic Book Appearance: "Bulletproof Monk #1" (Flypaper Press and Image Comics, 1999)

Origins: In 1999, Michael Avon Oeming created a most unusual kind of superhero for Flypaper Press, and saw his Bulletproof Monk debut in a three-part miniseries that was released by Image Comics. Tim Sale drew the covers, and Dave Johnson provided some of the interior art. A flip-book, titled "Bulletproof Monk: Tales of the Bulletproof Monk," which included two prequel stories with the original material, was released to coincide with a film version in 2003. In the first of the two prequels, we learn that Bulletproof Monk was an ordinary man who sought the peace and solace of Tibetan monastery. He journeyed through the war-torn landscape of the Japanese-Chinese war and World War 2 to reach the Himalayas. Once there, he studies with a martial arts and spiritual Master, and learns to channel his inner "chi" for nearly superhuman powers. When Nazis invade the sacred monastery and gun-down the Master, Bulletproof Monk becomes the protector of the Tibetan monks. In the second of the two prequels, readers are taken all the way back to the beginning, before the modern-day Monk, to the Buddhist monasteries of 16th Century Tibet. Here, we learn of the first Bulletproof Monk and how he saved the Dalai Lama from the descendents of Genghis Khan. The lead story, from the original miniseries, told of how the Bulletproof Monk came to the United States in search of a replacement, and found a youthful pickpocket named Kar to take his place.

First Media Appearance: The Bulletproof Monk first appeared in media form outside the world of comic books in 2003 in the film "Bulletproof Monk" (see below).

The 2003 Film Version: For sixty years, a mysterious monk with no name (Chow Yun-Fat), a mighty martial arts warrior, has been entrusted with an ancient scroll – a scroll that holds the key to unlimited power. He protected the Scroll of the Ultimate from the Nazis when they invaded his monastery in Tibet in 1942, and has been its protector ever since that time. (Apparently, anyone who reads the scroll aloud in its entirety will be granted ultimate, unlimited power.) Now, the Monk wishes to retire; even though he appears to be a forty-year-old man, the scroll has extended his life so he is actually much older than he seems. But before he can step down as the scroll's protector, he must find a new scroll-keeper. An evil man named Strucker (Karel Roden) wants the scroll so that he can rule the world. He's been chasing the Monk ever since he obtained the right to protect the scroll. Now, in present day New York City, Strucker is still chasing the Monk. Monk finds an unlikely candidate in Kar (Sean William Scott), a pickpocket and street hustler. Kar has inadvertently saved Bulletproof Monk from capture, and keeps fulfilling prophecies that the next scroll-keeper must fulfill. With the help of a sexy and elusive young woman named Jade (Jaime King), the three come together as one to fight off Strucker and save the scroll. The film version of the underground comic book was not very well received by the critics and fans alike and virtually died at the box office. At the present time, there are no plans for a sequel.

Trivial Matters: Burt Ward's visual effects company, "Boy Wonder Visual Effects," handled the special effects in the movie. Heath Ledger was originally considered for the role of Kar, but turned it down to star in "Ned Kelly" (2003). Though the film takes place in New York City, it was actually filmed in Toronto, Canada.

Fanboy Rating: Babes-2 Effects-2 Action-2 Brainwaves-2 Total=8

Bulletproof Monk

Captain America

Captain America (1944). Republic Pictures, B&W, 244min, 15 episodes. **Directors:** Elmer Clifton and John English. **Producer:** William J. O'Sullivan. **Screenwriters**: Royal Cole, Harry Fraser, Joseph Poland, Ronald Davidson, et al. Based upon characters created by Jack Kirby and Joe Simon. **Cinematographer:** John MacBurnie. **Film Editors:** Wallace Grissell and Earl Turner. **Cast:** Dick Purcell, Lorna Gray, Lionel Atwill, Charles Trowbridge, Russell Hicks.

First Comic Book Appearance: "Captain America #1" (March 1941)
Origins: In 1941, during a period when most comic books had a patriotic flavor, Jack Kirby and Joe Simon created one of the most popular and iconic of all patriotic superheroes, Captain America, for Timely Comics. The first story in "Captain America Comics #1" told the familiar tale of how a man named Steve Rogers – born on the Fourth of July (1917) – attempts to enlist in the Army to fight the forces of fascism. Too weak and puny to fight in World War 2, he is rejected for service. But a U.S. Army officer offers him a chance to take part in a top-secret experiment (co-named "Operation: Rebirth") to create soldiers who are physically superior to other men. He is injected with a Super-Soldier Serum and develops an enhanced physique, thanks to a blast of "Vita-Rays" that activate and stabilize the chemicals in his system. Rogers is the second hero, and the first American character, to possess such an enhanced physique (the first hero being Ilya Morowez, the Russian King Arthur). Unfortunately, before Professor Erskine can create any other super-soldiers, he is killed by a Nazi spy. Steve Rogers kills the spy in retaliation and vows to fight enemies of America. He becomes Captain America, a counter-intelligence agent, with a costume modeled after the American flag, a bullet-proof shield, and handgun. Together with Bucky Barnes, a teenaged soldier and sidekick he met at Camp Hehigh in Virginia, he fights a never-ending battle against the forces of fascism around the globe. His main enemy was the Red Skull, head of terrorist operations for Nazi Germany.

During the closing days of World War 2, Bucky is presumably killed while trying to defuse a bomb aboard a plane that explodes in mid-air and Rogers' body is hurled into the freezing waters of the North Atlantic. Many years later, in "Avengers #4" (March 1964), Steve Rogers' body is discovered frozen, perfectly preserved in a block of ice in the North Atlantic. The Sub-Mariner subsequently unthaws him, and he becomes a loyal and trusted member of the Avengers. Captain America's adventures have continued to this day in the pages of Marvel Comics.

First Media Appearance: Captain America first appeared in the 1944 Saturday-morning matinee serial, "Captain America."

Other Media Appearances: In 1966, for the "Marvel Super-Heroes" animated television series, Captain America was given his own theme song, with the lyrics: "When Captain America throws his mighty shield/All those who choose to oppose his shield must yield!/If he's led to a fight and a duel is due/Then the red and the white and the blue will come through/When Captain America throws his mighty shield!. The series adapted and condensed many of Captain America's stories, but provided a wonderful premier for those who may not have known much about the superhero. In the 1970s, Captain America appeared on two live-action television movies that reduced the character to a hard-driving stunt motorcyclist. Reb Brown played Captain America. Captain America's other live-action appearance in 1991 was less than stellar. He faired much better as a superhero in several appearances on "Spider-Man" (1981), "Superman and His Amazing Friends" (1981), "Spider-Man: The Animated Series" (1994), "The Secret Wars" (1997), and "Avengers: United They Stand" (1999). He became a regular cast member on the two "Avengers" movies.

The 1944 Film Version: This 15-part Republic serial recast the familiar character of Super-Soldier Steve Rogers from the comic books as District Attorney Grant Gardner (Dick Purcell). Not only did the story jettison his official origins but also discarded his sidekick Bucky and his trademark shield. Instead what remains is a costumed character in name only who battles the evil forces of Archvillain Scarab (Lionel Atwill). Scarab has stolen a secret device capable of destroying buildings by sound vibrations, and Captain America, armed only with a .38 caliber revolver, must stop him before he does some serious damage to a big city. The serial is competent, but without the character's signature traits, fairly generic stuff.

Trivial Matters: Royal K. Cole and his team of writers started work on "Captain America" without ever having read the comic book series; by the time the production was already under way, Republic Pictures felt it would

Captain America

have required costly retakes to make the backstory as it had originally been intended, and decided to go forward with its different story.

Fanboy Rating: Babes-1 Effects-1 Action-2 Brainwaves-2 Total=6

Captain America (1979). Universal, 120min. **Director:** Rod Holcomb. **Producer:** Allan Balter. **Screenwriters:** Don Ingalls, Chester Krumholz, Patricia Payne, and Wilton Schiller. Based upon characters created by Joe Simon and Jack Kirby. **Cinematographers:** Ronald W. Browne and Vincent A. Martinelli. **Film Editor:** Michael Murphy. **Production Designer:** David Snyder. **Cast:** Reb Brown, Len Birman, Heather Menzies, Steve Forrest, Robin Mattson, Lance LeGault.

The 1979 Film Versions: In "Captain America" (1979), Steve Rogers (Reb Brown), a commercial artist, is nearly killed when spies from a foreign government come looking for his late father's Cold War secrets. He is saved by the FLAG formula which, when injected into his bloodstream, turns him into an invincible one-man army. An unknown U.S. government agency equips him with a special motorcycle and detachable shield, and sends him out to fight against the nation's enemies as Captain America. The production values are so shockingly poor that one wonders how they managed to keep gas in the motorcycle that keeps going and going like the energizer bunny. The story is so laughable that you'd be better off renting the 15-part serial from Republic than sitting through two hours of this dreck. "Captain America 2: Dead Too Soon" was released the same year with virtually the same cast and motorcycle footage. In this one, as directed by Ivan Nagy from a script by Patricia Payne and Wilton Schiller, Captain America (Brown) must prevent a mad doctor's plan from poisoning America with a chemical that speeds up the aging process. The great Christopher Lee does a nice turn as Miguel.

Trivial Matters: The skin-tight costume that Reb Brown sports in both movies looks nothing like the costume Captain America wore in the comic books. His shield, since it is also the shield on his motorcycle, is clear, not solid. The two films from Universal bear almost no resemblance to the original source material.

Fanboy Rating: Babes-1 Effects-1 Action-1 Brainwaves-1 Total=4

Captain America (1990). Columbia, 97min. **Director:** Albert Pyun. **Producer:** Menahem Golan. **Screenwriters:** Stephen Tolkin and Lawrence Block. Based upon characters created by Joe Simon and Jack Kirby. **Cinematographer:** Philip Alan Waters. **Film Editor:** Jon Poll. **Production Designer:** Douglas Leonard. **Cast:** Matt Salinger, Ronny Cox, Scott Paulin, Ned Beatty, Darren McGavin, Michael Nouri, Melinda Dillon, Bill Mumy, Fancesca Neri.

The 1991 Film Version: Panned by both fans and critics alike, the 1991 direct-to-video version of "Captain America" did nonetheless get a few things right. Matt Salinger played Steve Rogers as a brave, patriotic soldier who volunteers for some top-secret genetic experiments during the dog-days of World War 2. One of the experiments transforms him into a new super-soldier named Captain America. His first mission is to stop the Red Skull (Scott Paulin) from launching the V-1 and V-2 rockets on London and other cities throughout the United Kingdom. Racing to Germany to sabotage the rocket base, Captain America's plane is shot down, and he plummets into the freezing waters of the English Channel. Years later, he is unthawed, and battles the Red Skull who is now plotting to kidnap the President of the United States (Ronny Cox). The film was released to capitalize on the superhero craze of the early 1990s, and did not do very well. Rumors of a new Captain America movie have circulated since 2005, but have thus far not produced anything concrete.

Trivial Matters: Dolph Lungren and Arnold Schwarzenegger were considered for the part of Captain America before Matt Salinger was hired for the role. At a pre-screening, Stan Lee exclaimed, "Director Albert Pyun did it so well and so excitingly that everyone in the audience kept clamoring for more." The film did not get a theatrical release in the United States, but was released internationally.

Fanboy Rating: Babes-3 Effects-3 Action-3 Brainwaves-3 Total=12

Captain America

Captain Avenger

Hero At Large (1980). Metro-Goldwyn-Mayer, 115min. **Director:** Martin Davidson. **Producer:** Stephen J. Friedman. **Screenwriter:** A.J. Carothers. **Cinematographer:** David M. Walsh. **Film Editor:** David Garfield. **Production Designer:** Albert Brenner. **Cast:** John Ritter, Anne Archer, Bert Convy, Kevin McCarthy, Harry Bellaver, Anita Dangler, Allan Rich, Leonard Harris, Rick Podell, Kevin Bacon.

First Comic Book Appearance: None

Origins: Throughout the years, many fans and critics alike have debated the origin and history of Captain Avenger. Some have claimed that he was the superhero who received Captain America's shield as his successor in the original Captain's place in the Legion of Honor. Others have linked him to the character Rick Jones created by Scott Edelmann, Steve Leialoha and Al Gordon for the "Avengers" comic book series. According to a story set between "Avengers #s15-16," Rick Jones appeared in the Avenger's meeting room one day, and stumbled into their viewscreen, electrocuting himself. When he arose from his mishap, he was not a super-hero, clad in a colorful costume and possessing superhuman strength. He decided to call himself "Captain Avenger." And when Baron Zemo and his army of agents burst into Avengers' headquarters, and froze the members of the team, Captain Avenger was the only superhero not affected by the freezing ray. He attacked Zemo and destroyed his ray-gun. Zemo informed him that the gun was the only way to restore the Avengers. Just then, Rick woke up and discovered that he had dreamed the whole thing. And finally, still others have claimed that Captain Avenger was nothing more than a promotional gimmick for an upcoming movie that went array. Well, the truth of the matter is that Captain Avenger was just an ordinary man who was thrust into the spotlight for one brief moment in time and managed to accomplish some amazing things before retiring to anonymity. He played a fictional superhero that was created by A. J. Carothers for the movie "Hero

At Large." and taught us all a lesson about what it means to be a hero.

First Media Appearance: Actor Steve Nichols (actually John Ritter) appeared dressed in a Captain Avenger costume as a promotional gimmick for the fictional "Captain Avenger" movie in "Hero At Large" (1980). He made his one and only media appearance, and has not resurfaced in over twenty-five years.

The 1980 Film Version: Made at a time when there was a huge revival of interest in comic books and superheroes, "Hero At Large" tapped right into many deconstructionist theories about the genre and offered an interesting glimpse into what the real world of comic book heroes would be like. An idealistic but struggling actor, Steve Nichols (John Ritter), has taken the only job that he can get: Appearing dressed in pink spandex tights, a purple visor and cape as Captain Avenger to promote an upcoming film. His life becomes unexpectedly complicated when he stops at a convenience store on his way home from the gig, still dressed as Captain Avenger, and scares away a group of hoods robbing the owner. His selfless act gains news headlines, and soon, Nichols' Captain Avenger is a flesh-and-blood hero in New York City. Steve Nichols decides to dabble at being a superhero, and makes subsequent appearances to fight crime dressed as Captain Avenger. Of course, he also discovers that it's far more difficult and often deadlier to turn a comic book figure into reality. To further complicate his life, the film's PR manager Walter Reeves (Bert Convy) exploits Nichols' self-less acts as Captain Avenger to help Calvin Donnelly (Kevin McCarthy) with his flagging mayoral re-election campaign. Reeves arranges for Nichols to catch criminals who are nothing more than actors playing out a role. The people begin to see through the act and turn their backs on Captain Avenger. Even girlfriend J. Marsh (Anne Archer) thinks he is a fake. In the end, Steve rescues a child from a burning building, without the help of his Captain Avenger persona, and shows that heroes are just ordinary people, like you and me. Regrettably, the film's cool premise was not enough to save it from box office oblivion.

Trivial Matters: The fictitious actor playing Captain Avenger in the movie was actually Ryan McGraw. A very young Kevin Bacon puts in a minor appearance (one of his first film roles) as one of the teens that derides Ritter during his appearance in costume as Captain Avenger at the theater.

Fanboy Rating: Babes-5 Effects-2 Action-2 Brainwaves-5 Total=14

Captain Avenger

Captain Invincible

The Return of Captain Invincible (1983). Seven Keys Production, Australia. 90min. **Director:** Philippe Mora. **Producer:** Andrew Gaty. **Screenwriters:** Steven E. De Souza & Andrew Gaty. **Cinematographer:** Mike Molloy. **Film Editor:** John Scott. **Production Designer:** David Copping. **Cast**: Alan Arkin, Christopher Lee, Kate Fitzpartrick, Bill Hunter, Michael Pate, David Argue, John Bluthal, Chelsea Brown.

First Comic Book Appearance: None.

Origins: Captain Invincible is a fictional comic book character that was created by Steven E. De Souza and Andrew Gaty for the Alan Arkin comedy "The Return of Captain Invincible" (1983). He never actually appeared in book or comic strip form, but for the purposes of the film, he was a real-life superhero. Like Captain America, Captain Invincible used his superpowers to fight against the Nazis during World War 2. His exploits during the war become the subject of several mock newsreels that borrow details from the comic books that flourished during the war. He also fought spies, saboteurs, black marketeers and the like. His greatest nemesis was Mr. Midnight, a Nazi scientist and evil master criminal. Unlike a lot of those superheroes who wrapped themselves in the flag, Captain Invincible outlasted World War 2 and continued fighting all enemies of freedom until 1950. He was forced to retire during the 1950s when his integrity and patriotism were brought into question during Senator Joe McCarthy's witch-hunts. Some had even accused him of being a communist supporter and sympathizer because he wore a red cape and because he was often caught violating U.S. airspace without a proper license. Captain Invincible left the public stage and retired to Sydney, Australia. He took to drinking alcohol, and became a homeless man living on the streets. Thirty years later, when his nemesis Mr. Midnight resurfaced with a super secret weapon that had been stolen from the United States, Captain Invincible was asked to return. He was sobered up by FBI agents, and sent to save the world, one last time. He stopped Mr. Midnight from killing millions of innocent people in a land-fraud deal.

First Media Appearance: Captain Invincible made his one and only media appearance in the guise of Alan Arkin in the Seven Keys comedy "The Return of Captain Invincible" (1983), and has not resurfaced in nearly twenty-five years.

The 1983 Film Version: When the evil master criminal Mr. Midnight (Christopher Lee) re-emerges with an ingenious scheme to sell worthless property to people and use a top secret super weapon, known as the Hypno-Ray, to convince them the land is prime real estate (rather than a testing ground for nuclear missiles), the President (Michael Pate) sends out his best agents to find Captain Invincible (Alan Arkin). Captain Invincible was once a popular hero who fought the Nazis in World War 2, but fell out of favor during the McCarthy witch-hunts in the 1950s. He has been living as

a drunk in Sydney, Australia, ever since. The FBI helps sober Captain Invincible up, and with his new found confidence, the aged superhero takes to the skies once again to stop the criminal mastermind from killing millions of innocents. Philippe Mora's "The Return of Captain Invincible" came out during a period when the public had a renewed interest in comic book superheroes. The lavish big-budget adaptation of "Superman" (1978) led to a number of superhero spoofs, including "Hero At Large" (1980), "Condorman" (1981), and "The Greatest American Hero" (1980-82). "The Return of Captain Invincible" was considered to be the most and most underrated of all those efforts.

Trivial Matters: Alan Arkin played another comic book character as "Peevy" Peabody in Disney's 1992 "The Rocketeer." Christopher Lee has had a long career playing bad guys, including Dracula in the long-running Hammer Horror films, Lord Saruman in "The Lord of the Rings" films, and Count Dooku in "Star Wars 2: Attack of the Clones" (2002).

Fanboy Rating: Babes-1 Effects-2 Action-2 Brainwaves-2 Total=7

Captain Invincible

Captain Marvel

The Adventures of Captain Marvel (1941). Republic Pictures, B&W, 12-Episode Serial, 216min. Directors: John English and William Whitney. Producer: Hiram S. Brown Jr. Screenwriters: Ronald Davidson, Norman Hall, Arch Heath, Joseph Poland, Sol Shor. Cast: Tom Tyler, Frank Coghlan Jr., William Benedict, Louise Currie, Robert Strange, Harry Worth, John Davidson, Bryant Washburn, George Pembroke.

First Comic Book Appearance: "Whiz Comics #2" (February 1940). *Origins:* Created in 1939 by artist Charles "C.C." Beck and writer Bill Parker, Captain Marvel first came to life as "Captain Thunder" in "Flash Comics #1" from Fawcett Publishing. Shortly after its first printing, however, Fawcett discovered that "Captain Thunder" and "Flash Comics" were trademarks of another company. Thus, the superhero was renamed "Captain Marvelous," shortened to "Captain Marvel," and published in "Whiz Comics #2" (February 1940). The character was distinctly different from Superman and Batman, two other popular comic book superheroes of the period, in that he was the alter ego of a young orphan named Billy Batson. One day, the newspaper boy meets the ancient wizard Shazam, and is endowed with the superhuman abilities of six legendary figures: Solomon's wisdom, Hercules' strength, Atlas' stamina, Zeus' power, Achilles' courage, and Mercury's speed. All he has to do is say the magic word "Shazam," which is an acronym for the six heroes, and he transforms into "the strongest and mightiest man in the world – Captain Marvel!" Talk about wish-fulfillment for every adolescent who read the comic book! Captain Marvel was an overnight success, quickly outselling the similar books being offered by National Comics. By 1941, he debuted in his own series, known as "Captain Marvel Adventures." Throughout the series of comic book adventures, he battled Nazis, renegade robots, ancient evils, and other nefarious villains of the world. Each month, Captain Marvel's comic books outsold those of rival Superman at National Comics. Eventually, National Comics Publications (under the banner of DC Comics) sued Fawcett Comics for copyright infringement. The litigation stretched out for seven long years, and in 1951, the court found in favor of Fawcett. DC appealed the decision in 1952, and a second round of litigation was stopped when Fawcett agreed to settle out of court. The character of Captain Marvel became part of the DC universe, and was revived in the mid-1960s.

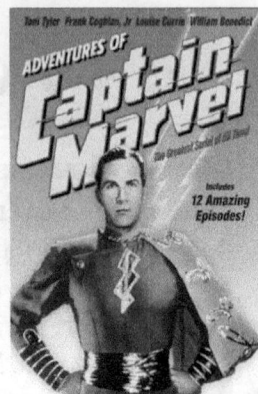

First Media Appearance: Captain Marvel was the first superhero to be depicted on film, and the twelve-part film serial from Republic Pictures in 1941 is often cited as the finest example of the serial form. Young Billy Batson (Frank Coghlan, Jr.) discovers the ability to transform into the super-powered Captain Marvel (Tom Tyler) while on a scientific expedition to Siam. The wizard Shazam (Nigel De Brulier) has endowed Billy with these powers to protect the magic talisman of the Golden Scorpion idol. Scientists believe it is the most powerful weapon in the world, and attempt to safeguard it by removing the idol's powerful lenses. Once back in the US, Captain Marvel wages a battle with the Scorpion (Gerald Mohr), who hopes to gather all five lenses, thereby gaining control of the super-powerful weapon.

Other Media Appearances: In 1974, more than thirty years later, Filmation produced a live-action television show that ran on CBS. Titled "Shazam!," the series featured Michael Gray as Billy Batson and both Jackson Bostwick and John Davey as Captain Marvel. When ratings began to flag in 1975, the show was team with a live-action show about "Isis," and became "The Shazam/Isis Hour." The show ran until 1977. Hanna-Barbera Productions resurrected Captain Marvel, now played by Garrett Craig, for two low-budget specials, titled "Legends of the Superheroes" in 1978. Three years later, Filmation tried again with an animated series, titled "Shazam!" The series ran for two years on NBC. More recently, New Line Cinema has begun pre-production of a live-action film with director Peter Segal and producer Michael Uslan. No release date has been set for this big-budget Hollywood production.

Fanboy Rating: Babes-2 Effects-2 Action-7 Brainwaves-5 Total=16

Captain Marvel

Captain Nice

Captain Nice (1967). National Broadcasting Company, 30min., 15 Episodes. **Director:** Richard Kinon et al. **Producer:** Jay Sandrich. **Screenwriter:** Jay Sandrich. Series and characters created by Buck Henry. **Cast:** William Daniels, Alice Ghostley, John Dehner, Ann Prentiss, Liam Dunn, Bill Zuckert, Byron Foulger.

First Comic Book Appearance: "Captain Nice #1" (Gold Key, 1967)
Origins: Created by Buck Henry, who was a co-creator of the spy spoof "Get Smart" (1965), "Captain Nice" was a half-hour comedy series featuring a police chemist-turned-superhero that ran from January through May 1967 on NBC. At the time when the series ran on television, all of the major networks were trying to compete with ABC and the overwhelmingly popular "Batman" (1966). Each of them was looking to capitalize on the superhero craze of the 1960s. So, NBC created a forensics scientist who drank a special portion that made him into a superhero, and CBS sketched up similar plans for its own superhero. Both shows debuted on the same Thursday night, January 9, 1967, a half hour apart, and ran until the end of the season of the same year. Of the two, "Captain Nice" was probably the best written and produced, while "Mister Terrific" was the most bizarrely original. Carter Nash (William Daniels) was a shy, mild-mannered, bespectacled scientist who discovered a secret formula while working as a chemist for the local crime lab. When he ingested the liquid, he was transformed into powerful superhero with super-strength and flight. Carter's mother (Alice Ghostley) thought he should use his newly-acquired powers to fight criminals, and stitched together a pajama-like costume, including tattered leotards, for him to wear. Despite his fear of heights, he flew off on his first adventure, and made history. Later, when questioned about his name and the initials C.N. on his signet ring, he makes up the

name "Captain…Nice?" On the show, he has a girlfriend who is a meter maid named Candy Kane (Ann Prentiss) and a boss named Chief Segal (Bill Zuckert). The television series ran for 15 episodes, and featured some of the finest comic actors of the period in cameo and guest roles. Unfortunately, as the ratings declined for "Batman," so did the ratings decline for all the shows inspired by it. "Captain Nice" ran until the end of the 1966-67 season, and then was canceled by the National Broadcasting Company. Not long after, William Dozier's "Batman" series was reduced to one night a week, and then finally canceled.

First Media Appearance: Captain Nice (also known as Carter Nash) took to the skies on January 9, 1967 in the episode titled, "The Man Who Flies Like a Pigeon." As part of NBC's promotion for its new television show, executives hired the legendary Jack Kirby to render an illustration that captured Captain Nice in action. This illustration was used in a number of promotional ads. And honestly, no one in the world of comics could have done Captain Nice better justice than Jack Kirby!

Trivial Matters: When Carter Nash first flies into his city as a superhero, he wears a ring with his initials, "CN." A bystander asks him what the "CN" stands for and, not wanting to give away his secret identity, he comes up with, "Captain... Nice?" The final episode, "Beware of Hidden Prophets," aired on May 1, 1967.

Fanboy Rating: Babes-2 Effects-2 Action-1 Brainwaves-2 Total=7

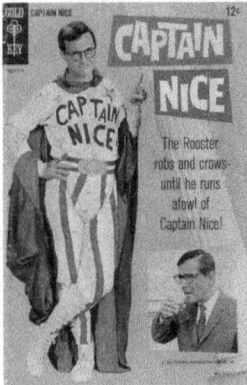

Captain Nice

Catwoman

Catwoman (2004). Warner Brothers, 104min. **Director:** Pitof. **Producers:** Denise Di Novi and Edward McDonnell. **Screenwriters:** Theresa Rebeck, John D. Brancato, and Michael Ferris. Based on characters created by Bob Kane. **Cinematographer:** Thierry Arbogast. **Film Editor:** Sylvie Landra. **Cast:** Halle Berry, Benjamin Bratt, Sharon Stone, Lambert Wilson, Frances Conroy, Alex Borstein, Michael Massee, Peter Wingfield.

First Comic Book Appearance: "Batman #1" (Spring 1940)
Origins: Selina Kyle, the first and most easily identifiable Catwoman, debuted in "Batman #1" (Spring 1940) as "The Cat." Created by Bill Finger and Bob Kane, the character was originally imagined as a cat burglar who fancied high-priced jewelry and other objects d'art. She carried a cat-of-nine-tails. Early in the comic book series, Catwoman was depicted as one of Batman's chief adversaries. But in "Batman #62" she attempted to reform her life of crime when she revealed that she had been a flight attendant who had suffered a blow to the head that had turned her into a criminal. Selina later admitted that she made the whole story up to appeal to Batman's sense of right and wrong. Eventually, she married Bruce Wayne, and the couple gave birth to Helena Wayne, better known as the Huntress. That whole storyline, however, took place in a parallel universe. The real Selina Kyle continued to commit crimes as the ex-wife of an abusive husband. In 1986, Frank Miller reintroduced Selina Kyle as a cat-loving prostitute who works as a dominatrix; when she sees Batman in action, she adopts the guise of a cat burglar to break out of her role as a prostitute. Over the years, her allegiances to Batman have kept shifting. In one storyline, "Batman #609-619" depicts the couple in a romantic relationship; in another, she is a murderess who must be brought to justice; and finally, in another, Selina Kyle retires as Catwoman, and trains Holly Robinson to take her place.
First Media Appearance: When William Dozier's campy, goofy "Batman"

series first aired on ABC in 1966, the Catwoman was played by Julie Newmar. She wore a black, skin-tight leather costume, not unlike the one worn by Diana Rigg as Emma Peel on "The Avengers," a black mask, and black, pointed cat ears. She was very sexy, and every fanboy's wet-dream. She was replaced by Earth Kitt on later episodes of the series and by Lee Meriwether in the big-screen spin-off.

Other Media Appearances: The Catwoman has also played a major role in all of the Batman animated series, starting in 1968 with "The Batman/Superman Hour." She was voiced by Adrienne Barbeau in the 1992 Saturday morning cartoon. Michelle Pfeiffer as Selina Kyle became Catwoman in Tim Burton's "Batman Returns" (1992) when she was thrown out of a high-rise window by Max Shreck (Christopher Walken) and fell to her death. Mysteriously revived by alley cats, she returns to seek revenge. Pfeiffer was so very sexy and appealing in the role as Catwoman that Warner Brothers planned a spin-off movie for the actress. However, as the years went by, Pfeiffer lost interest, and was eventually replaced by Oscar-winner Halle Berry.

The 2004 Movie Version: "Catwoman" was much reviled as a movie and failed miserably at the box office when it debuted in 2004. The primary reason for its failure was that the film's titular heroine bore almost no resemblance to the comic book figure or the character that was created in "Batman Returns." Patience Phillips (Halle Berry) becomes Catwoman, a superhero with cat-like powers, when the Egyptian goddess Bastet resurrects her from a horrible death that was planned by her employer, Laurel Hedare (Sharon Stone). Later, Ophelia Powers (Frances Conroy) shows up and explains that there have been other Catwomen over the ages, including (apparently) Selina Kyle from the Tim Burton movie. The Catwoman swings into action to get revenge on Laurel and stop her company's anti-aging drug from reaching the marketplace.

Trivial Matters: Halle Berry's first Catwoman costume is based on the one Eartha Kitt wore in the TV series. Michelle Pfeiffer bowed out of the project because of concerns about the costume's comfort level. Ashley Judd was next hired, but was replaced by Halle Berry. The preview featured a voice-over taken, word-for-word, from "The Crow" (1994).

Fanboy Rating: Babes-8 Effects-2 Action-2 Brainwaves-1 Total=13

Catwoman

Conan the Barbarian

Conan the Barbarian (1982). Universal Pictures, 129min. **Director:** John Milius. **Producer:** Buzz Feitshans and Raffaella De Laurentiis. **Screenwriters:** John Milius and Oliver Stone. Based upon characters created by Robert E. Howard. **Cinematographer:** Duke Callaghan. **Film Editor:** C. Timothy O'Meara. **Production Designer:** Ron Cobb. **Cast:** Arnold Schwarzenegger, James Earl Jones, Max Von Sydow, Sandahl Bergman, Ben Davidson, Gerry Lopez.

First Appearance: "The Phoenix on the Sword" *Weird Tales* (Dec. 1932)
First Comic Book Appearance: "Conan the Barbarian #1" (1970)
Origins: The character of Conan the Barbarian was born in the highly-gifted imagination of Robert E. Howard, who had also created Kull the Conqueror, Soloman Kane, and Red Sonja. Muscular, quick, incredibly ruthless, the thief who became king was the central figure in eighteen highly-popular heroic fantasies set against the distant, glittering Hyborian Age. With "The Phoenix and the Sword," first published in the December 1932 issue of *Weird Tales*, Howard launched the Sword and Sorcery genre. Stories, like "The Scarlet Citadel," "The Tower of the Elephant," "Black Colossus," and "Red Nails," not only helped expand the legend of Conan but created a fictional universe of Hyboria, set after the destruction of Atlantis and the rise of the known ancient civilization. Conan journeys from being a loner Barbarian to thief, outlaw, mercenary, pirate, and eventually King of Aquilonia. Despite his somewhat brutish appearance, Conan uses his brain as well as his brawn. He is a talented fighter, but also versed as tactician and strategist and a natural-born leader. He speaks several languages, and for all intents and purposes, Conan was the superhero of his day. Howard would have continued writing Conan adventures to this day had his semi-invalid mother not taken ill and fallen into a coma. Intensely devoted, the thirty year-old writer could not face a life without her, and committed suicide a few hours before she passed away. With his death in 1936, the Conan stories did not die away but rather inspired other

writers like L. Sprague de Camp and Lin Carter to keep the tradition alive through pastiches or completions of eight unfinished stories. In the mid-sixties, Conan reached a mass-market audience with the first paperback publications (featuring cover illustrations by artist Frank Frazetta). In the early seventies, the Cimmerian had become such a cult figure that Marvel Comics decided to release the comic series "Conan The Barbarian," illustrated by Barry Windsor-Smith, in 1970, and later "The Sword of Conan" graphic magazine.

First Media Appearance: Conan made his first media appearance outside the world of pulp magazines and comic books in the guise of world champion body-builder Arnold Schwarzenegger in "Conan the Barbarian" (1982). (See below.)

Other Media Appearances: Two years later, a less popular sequel was made, titled "Conan the Destroyer," also featuring Schwarzenegger. In 1997, a live-action television series, titled "Conan the Adventurer" and featuring German body-builder Ralf Moeller ran in syndication for twenty-two episodes. The series was such a major departure from the movies and original source material that most fans simply turned it off after only an episode or two. Two cartoon series, one titled "Conan the Adventurer" and the other titled "Conan and the Young Warriors," aired in 1992 and 1994, respectively.

The 1982 Film Version: "Between the time when the oceans drank Atlantis and the rise of the sons of Ayras, there was an age undreamed of . . . And unto this, Conan, destined to bear the jeweled crown of Aquilonia upon a troubled brow, came. Let me tell you of the days of high adventure . . ." In the small Cimmerian village, which is Conan's boyhood home, the Master (William Smith) forges a great sword for his young son, Conan (played by Jorge Sanz). When his peaceful village is overrun by a raiding party of Vanir Warriors, led by Thulsa Doom (James Earl Jones), he soon realizes the power that the mighty sword commands. His parents are murdered, and Conan is sold into slavery. Fifteen years' agony, first chained to the Wheel of Pain and then as a gladiator, forge a magnificent body and indomitable spirit. Though he becomes victorious as a "pit fighter" and gains great wealth and riches for his owner, he yearns for his freedom.

Conan

Freed miraculously one day by his owner, Conan wanders through his strange, Hyborian world in search of purpose and his own identity. Then, chased by wolves into a cave, he comes face to face with the skeletal body of his god Crom (which is actually the remains of some Atlantean king buried in a ceremonial tomb). All his life he has been told that Crom lives beneath the earth, and views his chance meeting with the deity as having great significance in his life. He approaches "the thing in the crypt" and takes the slumbering god's sword. With his newly acquired Atlantean steel, Conan sets out to destroy Thulsa Doom and his snake cult. Together with Valeria (Sandahl Bergman), Subotai (Gerry Lopez) and a wizard (Mako), they rescue the daughter of King Osric (Max Von Sydow) and face Doom. A rousing battle ensues, in which the three warriors stand up against a cavalry charge of twenty-five mounted riders among the ruins of the mounds. Slowly, deliberately, savagely, they take the raiders out one-by-one. Conan then follows the evil sorcerer back to his Mountain of Power and kills him, taking back his father's sword. The film was a huge hit when it debuted in the summer of 1982, and inspired a whole host of imitators, including "Sword and the Sorcerer" (1982). "Conan the Barbarian" also made Arnold Schwarzenegger a superstar.

Trivial Matters: While the story was concocted by John Milius and Oliver Stone, many of the key sequences and characters came from Robert E. Howard stories. The name "Valeria," for instance, comes from the heroine of the novella "Red Nails." The theft in Zamora is from "The Tower of the Elephant." The speech King Osric gives about the throne room becoming a prison echoes a similar passage in "The Mirrors of Tuzun Thune," a King Kull story. The scene where Conan is crucified and kills a vulture with his teeth is from "A Witch Shall Be Born." Finally, the scene where Valeria vows to come back from the dead to save Conan is from "Queen of the Black Coast."

Fanboy Rating: Babes-8 Effects-7 Action-8 Brainwaves-7 Total=30

Conan the Destroyer (1984). Universal Pictures, 103min. **Director:** Richard Fleischer. **Producer:** Edward R. Pressman. **Screenwriters:** Roy Thomas, Gerry Conway, and Stanley Mann. Characters created by Robert E. Howard. **Cinematographer:** Jack Cardiff. **Film Editor:** Frank Urioste. **Production Designer:** Pier Luigi Basile. **Cast:** Arnold Schwarzenegger, Grace Jones, Wilt Chamberlain, Mako, Tracey Walter, Sarah Douglas, Olivia D'Abo.

The 1984 Film Sequel: Scripted by Roy Thomas and Gerry Conway, two of the writers from the comic book series, "Conan the Destroyer" brought the titular character back to his pulp origins. Conan (Schwarzenegger) leads a ragtag group of adventurers, including Zula (Grace Jones), Bombaata (Wilt Chamberlain), Malak (Tracey Walter), Akiro (Mako), and Princess Jehnna (Olivia D'Abo), to find a magic crystal before the evil sorcerer Toth Amon (Pat Roach) can use it. He fails to realize the evil Queen Taramis (Sarah Douglas) has plans to use the crystal to destroy Jehnna and plunge the world into darkness. Schwarzenegger is in top form as the swashbuckling Hyborian, and probably should have done a third Conan movie before tackling the job of governor for the State of California. A story treatment titled "King Conan: Crown of Iron" had been written in the 1990s for Schwarzenegger.

Trivial Matters: "Conan the Destroyer" was filmed on many of the same sets and same locations as "Dune" (1984). David L. Lander was originally cast as Malak, but problems with his health forced him to withdraw, and Tracey Walter was cast. Roy Thomas and Gerry Conway were so displeased with the finished film that they turned their screen treatment into the graphic novel "Conan: The Horn of Azoth" in 1990. This film represented Wilt Chamberlain's one and only screen appearance.

Fanboy Rating: Babes-7 Effects-6 Action-7 Brainwaves-5 Total=25

Conan

Condorman

Condorman (1981). Walt Disney Productions, 90 min. **Director:** Charles Jarrott. **Producer:** Jan Williams. **Screenwriters:** Mickey Rose and Marc Stirdivant. Based upon the novel *The Game of X* by Robert Sheckley. **Cinematographer:** Charles F. Wheeler. **Film Editor:** Gordon D. Brenner. **Cast:** Michael Crawford, Oliver Reed, Barbara Carrera, James Hampton, Jean-Pierre Kalfon, Dan Elcar, Vernon Dobtcheff, Robert Arden.

First Appearance: The Game of X by Robert Sheckley (1965)
Origins: Condorman is a fictional comic book character that was loosely based on a character in Robert Sheckley's *The Game of X* and created and brought to life by Woody Wilkins (Michael Crawford) in the 1981 Disney comedy "Condorman" Like his counterpart Batman, Condorman employs an array of gadgets, including a winged costume that allows him to fly, in his battle with the forces of evil. His gadgets include a walking stick that is a machine-gun, a speed boat that has lethal weapons installed, and a James Bond-like sports car. What made Condorman different from all other comic book characters was Woody Wilkins' claim that he would never have Condorman do anything in the comic series that he had not already done in real life. So, no matter how outrageous it might have seemed on the printed page, Woody plans and executes all of his character's stunts in real life first. (Bash Brannigan creator Stanley Ford also made the same claim, and ran himself through all of the crime capers in reality before he put his artist's pen to page.) In one such instance, Woody straps on a makeshift winged Condorman costume and flies off the Eiffel Tower in Paris to prove that his comic book character could do it. So, when Woody Wilkins is asked by the C.I.A. to help a beautiful Russian spy defect from the Iron Curtain, it's actually Condorman to the rescue! While the character was originally created by Sheckley for his science fiction novel, the comic book character that emerges from the film bears virtually no resemblance to the character as envisioned.

First Media Appearance: Condorman made his one and only media appearance in the guise of Michael Crawford, who would later play the Phantom of the Opera, in the Disney comedy "Condorman" (1981), and has not resurfaced in over twenty-five years.

The 1981 Film Version: Walt Disney Productions did not want to get left behind in the superhero box office sweepstakes in the 1980s, and produced its own superhero in the character of "Condorman." Comic book artist and writer Woody Wilkins (Michael Crawford) is recruited by his friend Harry Oslo (James Hampton) who works for the C.I.A. to perform a simple courier operation. But when he successfully fends off hostile agents, he earns the respect of the beautiful Soviet agent Natalia (Barbara Carrera), who specifically requests his assistance for her defection. Woody agrees to this request, and asks the C.I.A. to create a number of the devices that his comic book character would use to save her. Then, donning the persona of Condorman and relying of a wide array of gadgets, he launches into an adventure to rescue her and keep her safe from the evil Krokov (Oliver Reed). The film was not widely received when it debuted in 1981, and has since been relegated to the back shelf at Blockbuster. Too bad! Crawford is terrific as the eccentric comic book creator, future Bond girl Carrera is ravishing, and Oliver Reed has rarely been better. Condorman's array of devices will remind you of Batman and James Bond.

Trivial Matters: Barbara Carrera, an ex-model born in Nicaragua, has played a variety of nationalities and ethnic identities, including Asian, Hispanic, Native American, and African; in "Condorman," she is Russian. Michael Crawford is most associated with the role of Eric in "The Phantom of the Opera" (1996).

Fanboy Rating: Babes-6 Effects-2 Action-2 Brainwaves-2 Total=12

Condorman

Congo Bill

Congo Bill (1948). Columbia Pictures, B&W, 220min., 12 chapters. **Directors:** Spencer Gordon Bennet and Thomas Carr. **Screenwriter:** Whitney Ellsworth. Characters created by **Cast:** Don McGuire, Cleo Moore, Jack Ingram, Stanford Jolley, Leonard Penn, Nelson Leigh, Charles King, Armida, Hugh Prosser, Neyle Morrow, Fred Graham.

First Comic Book Appearance: "More Fun Comics #56" (June 1940). *Origins:* Congo Bill was created by Whitney Ellsworth and artist George Papp in 1940 as an answer to King Features' comic strip "Jungle Jim," which was created by Don Moore and Alex Raymond. Bill and Jim dressed alike, with jodhpurs and pith helmets, and pursued many of the same kinds of adventures and dangers. Jim's jungle adventures took him to Southeast Asia, while Bill's took him to Africa. Congo Bill was never the breakout star that his newspaper comic strip rival was, and DC Comics relegated him to secondary status in most of the publications he appeared. For instance, he was the backup feature to the Spectre in "More Fun Comics" and Superman in "Action Comics." During his tenure in "Action Comics," Bill acquired Janu the Jungle Boy, a thinly disguised version of Tarzan, who had been living in the wilds since the death of his father. Janu became Bill's one and only sidekick. In 1954, Congo Bill had a comic book of his own, but that lasted for only seven issues. By then, stories about jungle adventurers seemed rather quaint and uninteresting to a public that hungered for stories about superheroes. In 1959, he met a rare golden gorilla that wore a magic ring. Congo Bill obtained a similar ring from a witch doctor, and used it to transfer his consciousness to that of a gorilla. The beast was known as Congorilla, but the concept never caught on with readers and it was left behind. More recently, Congo Bill has shown up in his own four-issue miniseries from Vertigo in 1999.

First Media Appearance: Congo Bill made his first appearance outside the universe of DC Comics in a 12-part movie serial from Columbia Pictures in 1948. (See below.)

The 1948 Film Version: Produced by Sam Katzman, the 12-part movie serial followed the adventures of Congo Bill (Don McGuire) as he attempts to find and rescue Ruth Culver (Cleo Moore) from the dangers of darkest Africa. The serial begins when Ruth is set to inherit a fortune, and her family charges the adventurer with the task to bring her back to civilization. Congo Bill follows a legend about some White Queen (Moore as Lureen), but he path is strewn with more obstacles than the average Saturday morning matinee. Eventually he finds her, and stops the man who will lose the fortune if she is found alive. By 1948, the popularity of the serial was beginning the wind down, but Katzman pulls out every stop to make this particular one memorable. Don McGuire is perfect as Congo Bill, and Cleo Moore chews up the scenery as the damsel-in-distress and the White Queen of Africa.

Trivial Matters: In 1957, after Cleo Moore had become a famous film star, the studio re-issued the serial for her fans to enjoy. As a comic book, "Congo Bill" has the distinction of being one of the longest running series in the history of DC Comics' titles.

Fanboy Rating: Babes-2 Effects-2 Action-4 Brainwaves-3 Total=11

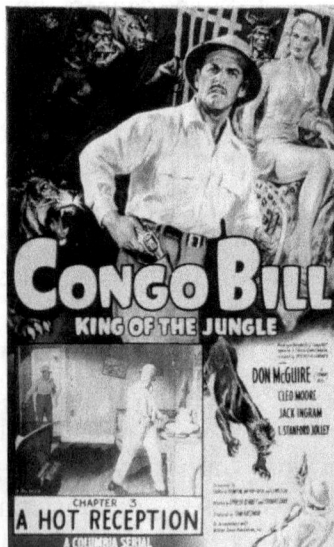

Congo Bill

Constantine

Constantine (2005). Warner Brothers, 121min. **Director:** Francis Lawrence. **Producers:** Lauren Shuler Donner, Akiva Goldsman, Lorenzo di Bonaventura. **Screenwriters:** Kevin Brodkin and Frank A. Cappello. Based upon characters created by Jamie Delano and Garth Ennis. **Cinematographer:** Philippe Rousselot. **Film Editor:** Wayne Wahrman. **Production Designer:** Naomi Shohan. **Cast:** Keanu Reeves, Rachel Weisz, Djimon Hounsou.

First Comic Book Appearance: "Saga of the Swamp Thing #37" (June 1985)
Origins: John Constantine, an ordinary man with supernatural powers, first appeared as a recurring character in the horror comic "Swamp Thing" (1985) as penned by Alan Moore and drawn by Stephen Bissette and John Totleben. He then made appearances in several other titles, including Neil Gaiman's "The Sandman" and "The Books of Magic." Constantine was also one of the few people who were aware of the "Crisis on Infinite Earths" (1985). In 1988, he headlined his own comic book, titled "Hellblazer," a horror/supernatural series. John Constantine was born in Liverpool, England, on May 10, 1953; while still in the womb, he strangled his twin brother with his own umbilical cord, and his mother Mary Anne died giving birth to John. His father Thomas never forgave him, and when John ran away from home in the 1960s, his father never came looking for him. In 1970, he became involved in occult circles in London and San Francisco, and met and dated Zatanna the Magician for a while. While traveling on tour with his punk rock band Mucous Membrane, he met a young woman who was possessed by Satan. He tried to exorcise the demon himself, but failed miserably. The demon took the young woman straight to Hell. He was haunted by the memory of what he had done for many years, and decided to devote himself to freeing souls from Satan's grasp. His chain-smoking led to terminal lung cancel which was slowly killing him. He knew the demons would eventually take his soul to Hell, and he hatched a plan to save himself by secretly selling his soul to two of

the three lords of Hell. They dared not risk a battle over his soul, and cured him of cancer instead. John Constantine continues to hunt demons and use his supernatural powers for good. In December 2004, the title of the 201st issue of "Hellblazer" was re-titled "John Constantine: Hellblazer."

First Media Appearance: John Constantine was portrayed by Keanu Reeves in the 2005 film "Constantine." In this first media appearance, Constantine is American, not British, and has been recast as a bitter man who once tried to commit suicide. For penance, he fights bloody demons trying to force their way onto the Earth. (See below.)

The 2005 Film Version: John Constantine (Reeves) is a supernatural detective who has been deporting demons back to Hell in an effort to get back on good terms with God, but as the Archangel Gabriel (Tilda Swinton) reminds him…suicide is the one sin that God refuses to excuse. So, Constantine is doomed to Hell, and heading there very quickly with lung cancer, despite all of his good deeds. When a skeptical policewoman Angela Dodson (Rachel Weisz) asks Constantine to look into the mysterious suicide of her twin sister (also played by Weisz), he comes face to face with a plan by demons to change the balance of power between good and evil. Together, Constantine and Angela battle the demons on earth and in the other realm. The movie adaptation was very well received in February 2005 when it came out, and has since suggested interest in a follow-up, featuring Reeves in the titular role.

Trivial Matters: Nicholas Cage was originally attached to the project to play John Constantine with Tarse Singh as director; Cage went on to play a different kind of superhero in 2007's "Ghost Rider." The Spear of Destiny is the same prop that was used in the "Hellboy" movie. The "holy hand grenade" is a reference to the "Holy Hand Grenade of Antioch" in "Monty Python & the Holy Grail" (1975).

Fanboy Rating: Babes-5 Effects-8 Action-4 Brainwaves-5 Total=22

Constantine

The Crow

The Crow (1994). Miramax, 102min. **Director:** Alex Proyas. **Producer:** Edward R. Pressman. **Screenwriters:** David J. Schow and John Shirley. Characters created by James O'Barr. **Cinematographer:** Dariusz Wolski. **Film Editor:** Dov Hoenig. **Production Designer:** Alex McDowell. **Cast:** Brandon Lee, Ernie Hudson, Rochelle Davis, Michael Wincott, Ling Bai, Sofia Shinas, David Patrick Kelly.

First Comic Book Appearance: "Caliber Presents #1" (January 1989). *Origins:* For as long as comic books have been published, there have been those characters who have returned from the dead to avenge their own murders. Jerry Siegel's the Spectre began in 1940 when Detective Jim Corrigan was murdered by gangsters and then turned away from Heaven because his death had gone un-avenged. Others like Deadman, Mr. Justice, and Nemesis have followed. In James O'Barr's "The Crow," which debuted in an anthology published by Caliber Press in 1989, Eric's recently-deceased soul is carried to the Land of the Dead by a crow. With the soul unable to find rest, the crow returns the soul to Earth to carry out revenge against those that killed Eric. Since he cannot use his own name, Eric uses the Crow as his identity. Apparently, Eric and his fiancée Shelley were assaulted by a street gang when their car broke down in the wrong part of town. He was shot in the head and later dies, and she was brutally beaten and raped by the gang members. She dies at the crime scene. One year later, Eric is resurrected, and seeks out vengeance on those that did it. O'Barr has since stated that he wrote the story as a means of getting over his girlfriend's senseless death at the hands of a drunk driver. Other influences from the lyrics in Techno music to Arthur Rimbaud's poetry are clearly visible in the work. In 1999, Image Comics published a comic series based upon the original comic. "The Crow" ran for ten issues, starting in January and ending in November of that year. Editor Ed Kramer also brought together a handful of science fiction writers and artists to produce work for *The Crow: Shattered Lives and Broken Dreams* (1999) for Random House.

First Media Appearance: Eric Draven was brought to life by actor Brandon Lee, son of the martial arts actor Bruce Lee, in the 1994 film adaptation of "The Crow." Unfortunately, tragedy struck on the 52nd day of the 60-day shoot when Lee was killed by a real bullet from a prop gun filled with blanks.

Other Media Appearances: Three sequels to the original "The Crow" have been made thus far, each with a different actor in the lead role. Vincent Perez played the titular character in "The Crow: City of Angels" (1996); Eric Mabius and Edward Furlong essayed the role of the Crow in "The Crow: Salvation" (2000) and "The Crow: Wicked Prayer" (2005), respectively. Mark Dacascos took over the lead role as Eric Draven in the short-lived Canadian television series, "The Crow: Stairway to Heaven" (1998). A fan made film, entitled "Wings of the Crow," featured a female Crow. All of the sequels have been both critical and commercial failures.

The 1994 Film Version: Most people remember the original "The Crow" (1994) as the film in which Bruce Lee's son Brandon was killed, a tragedy that reflected the earlier tragedy that had inspired the comic book series. At best, they recall that Eric Draven (Lee) and his girlfriend Shelly (Sofia Shinas) were attacked by a street gang; she was brutally raped and beaten, only to die thirty hours later in a hospital; he was shot and pushed out a window, left for dead. Exactly one year later, with the help of a crow, Eric wakes from the dead and takes revenge for his death and the death of the woman he was going to marry. He becomes an avenging angel, and one

The Crow

The Crow: City of Angels (1996). Miramax, 84min. **Director:** Tim Pope. **Producer:** Edward R. Pressman. **Screenwriter:** David S. Goyer. Characters created by James O'Barr. **Cinematographer:** Jean-Yves Escoffier. **Film Editors:** Michael Knue and Anthony Redman. **Production Designer:** Alex McDowell. **Cast:** Vincent Perez, Mia Kirshner, Richard Brooks, Iggy Pop, Thomas Jane, Thuy Trang.

by one, he kills off each of Top Dollar's (Michael Wincott) thugs. The film is extremely dark, shot as if it were being made by members of some Goth troop, with fantastical shots of the city and its seamier locales after the bewitching hour. The controversy over Brandon Lee's death played out in the press and limited ticket sales to those curious few.

Trivial Matters: Cameron Diaz was offered the role of Shelly, but declined to take the role because she didn't like the script. Brandon's father Bruce Lee also died under mysterious circumstances before completing "Game of Death" (1978). In that same movie, Lee's character is shot, presumably dead, and returns to get revenge on his adversaries.

Fanboy Rating: Babes-2 Effects-2 Action-2 Brainwaves-3 Total=9

The Crow: Salvation (2000). Miramax, 102min. **Director:** Bharat Nalluri. **Producer:** Edward R. Pressman. **Screenwriter:** Chip Johannessen. Characters created by James O'Barr. **Cinematographer:** Carolyn Chen. **Film Editors:** Luis Colina and Howard E. Smith. **Production Designer:** Maia Javan. **Cast:** Kirsten Dunst, Eric Mabius, Fred Ward, Jodi Lyn O'Keefe, William Atherton, K.C. Clyde.

The 1996 Film Sequel: "The Crow: City of Angels" (1996) tracks another man's revenge when he (Vincent Perez as Ashe Corven) is killed alongside his son by a gang of criminals. Just like the first movie, he is brought back to life by a supernatural crow, and given powers to kill his murderers one by one. Eventually, he comes face to face with the crime boss (Richard Brooks) who ordered his death, and learns that Judah Earl wants Ashe's powers for himself. The story was not particularly original, and failed to generate much interest at the box office. Even fans of the first film were disappointed by this pale carbon copy.

Trivial Matters: Rocker Jon Bob Jovi auditioned for the lead role, but lost out to established actor Vincent Perez. After the tragedy in the first film, Perez relied on stuntmen for most of his more dangerous stunts. The rhyme about crows comes from the original comic book and was written by James O'Barr.

Fanboy Rating: Babes-2 Effects-2 Action-2 Brainwaves-2 Total=8

The 2000 Film Sequel: The third installment in "The Crow" series offers very little in the way of original material to keep the franchise alive and fresh. Alex Corvis (Eric Mabius) is framed for his girlfriend's murder and is executed by a district attorney anxious to make a name for himself. Not surprisingly, Corvis is resurrected by a crow that maintains, "Love is stronger than death," as its motto. With the help of Lauren Randall's sister (Kirsten Dunst), the new Crow discovers the corrupt police force was behind his girlfriend's death. And one by one, he goes after the killers. Director Bharat Nalluri does what he can with the very limited material, but there's really not much to do that hasn't already been done in previous movies. O'Barr's one novel concept has devolved into a formula in which an innocent man is murdered and brought back to life to exact revenge on those responsible. Most film goers wanted a refund after they sat through yet another version of the same story.

Trivial Matters: Poor test screenings prior to the film's release doomed it to a direct-to-video release. The name Alex Corvis appears on the tombstone for the teaser "The Crow: City of Angels" (1996). Originally, rocker Rob Zombie was doing to write and direct, but he was fired due to creative differences with the producers. He probably told them they didn't have a script to shoot, and wanted to write one of his own.

Fanboy Rating: Babes-3 Effects-2 Action-2 Brainwaves-1 Total=8

The Crow: Wicked Prayer (2005). Miramax, 99min. **Director:** Lance Mungia. **Producer:** Edward R. Pressman. **Screenwriters:** Jeff Most, Sean Hood, Lance Mungia. Characters created by James O'Barr and Norman Partridge. **Cast:** Edward Furlong, Tara Reid, Emmanuelle Chriqui. Danny Trejo, and David Ortiz.

The 2005 Film Sequel: Five years after the poor reception of "The Crow: Salvation" (2000), the studio tried again with yet another revenge fable. In this one, Jimmy Cuervo (Edward Furlong) and his girlfriend Lily (Emmanuelle Chriqui) are murdered by Luc Crash (David Boreanaz), and Jimmy is resurrected to fight a Satanic gang of bikers who want to make their leader an immortal demon. How original! My brain hurts!

Trivial Matters: Most of the shots of the Crow were taken from previous Crow films. Dimension Films gave "The Crow: Wicked Prayer" a token release of one week in 2005 before sending it directly to video.

Fanboy Rating: Babes-2 Effects-2 Action-1 Brainwaves-0 Total=5

The Crow

Daredevil

Daredevil (2003). 20th Century-Fox, in association with Marvel Enterprises, 103min. **Director:** Mark Steven Johnson. **Producers:** Avi Arad, Gary Foster, Arnon Milchan. **Screenwriter:** Mark Steven Johnson. **Cinematographer:** Ericson Core. **Film Editors:** Armen Minasian and Dennis Virkler. **Cast:** Ben Affleck, Jennifer Garner, Colin Farrell, Michael Clarke Duncan, Jon Favreau, Ellen Pompeo, Kevin Smith, Frank Miller, Stan Lee.

First Comic Book Appearance: "Daredevil #1" (April 1964)

Origins: Daredevil, the man without fear, was created by Stan Lee, and brought to life in living color by artists Bill Everett and Jack Kirby in "Daredevil #1" (April 1964). Blinded by a radioactive substance while saving a blind man from the path of a runaway truck, Matthew Michael "Matt" Murdock learns to fine-tune his other four senses to compensate for the loss of his sight; in turn, he also develops a sonar-like ability to perceive objects without seeing them due to the radioactive exposure. He later studies martial arts and acrobatics under a mysterious man named Stick. His single father, a fading boxer known as "Battling Jack" Murdock, had always encouraged Matt not to fight; he wants him to go to college and study law, and knows nothing about Daredevil. While enrolled at the Columbia, Matt falls in love with Elektra Natchios, the daughter of a Greek diplomat. When Elektra and her father are kidnapped by terrorists, Matt dons a mask for the first time, and tries to rescue them. His rescue attempt fails, and Elektra's father is killed. She blames him, drops out of school and goes off to study martial arts in the East to become a high-priced assassin and Daredevil's chief nemesis. Later, when Matt's own father is killed by the mob for refusing to take a dive in a boxing match, he dons a yellow and black costume (made from his father's boxing robes) to exact revenge. Matt graduates from college and opens a law practice his college roommate "Foggy" Nelson. During the day, Matt is a blind attorney fighting for justice in the often corrupt legal system; at night, he becomes

Daredevil, a vigilante who seeks to even the scales of justice against mobsters and supervillains like Kingpin and Bullseye.

First Media Appearance: Daredevil made his first ever media appearance as Spider-Man's lawyer, Matt Murdock, on the 1981 animated television series, "Spider-Man and His Amazing Friends." In 1989, Rex Smith donned the Daredevil costume for a live-action appearance on "The Trial of the Incredible Hulk," opposite John Rhys Davies as the Kingpin. The Man without Fear also cameoed in Kevin Smith's "Jay and Silent Bob Strike Back" (2001), as Smith had previously written for the comic book series.

Film Development: In 1997, 20th Century Fox first acquired the rights to Daredevil from Marvel with Chris Columbus attached to direct. Disney later expressed an interest in the character, but let their option also expire. Mark Steven Johnson realized his life's ambition in 1999 when Marvel assigned the rights to Sony, and he was hired to write the screenplay. However, when Sony lost interest in the project, Johnson had to pitch himself all over again as the writer and director to New Regency, with Fox agreeing to distribute the 2003 release.

The 2003 Film Version: Blinded by toxic waste, Attorney Matt Murdock (Ben Affleck) becomes the avenging Daredevil when all of his other senses are heightened dramatically by the chemical accident. His first targets are the Kingpin (Michael Clarke Duncan), the biggest crime lord in New York City, and his assassin Bullseye (Colin Farrell). Along the way, he meets and falls in love with Elektra (Jennifer Garner), who is subsequently killed by Bullseye. He takes them both down, and feels justified for avenging not only Elektra, but also his father's death.

Trivial Matters: In the film, young Matt Murdock stops Stan Lee from crossing the street against traffic. Kevin Smith plays a lab assistant named Jack Kirby. Matt Damon, Guy Pearce, and Edward Norton were all considered for the role of Daredevil. Vin Diesel was the first choice for Bullseye, as was Jolene Blalock for Elektra.

Fanboy Rating: Babes-6 Effects-5 Action-7 Brainwaves-3 Total=21

Daredevil

Darkman

Darkman (1990). Universal Pictures, 99min. **Director:** Sam Raimi. **Producer:** Robert Tapert. **Screenwriters:** Sam Raimi, Ivan Raimi, Daniel Goldin, Joshua Goldin, and Chuck Pfarrer. Characters created by Sam Raimi. **Cinematographer:** Bill Pope. **Film Editors:** Bud Smith and David Stiven. **Production Designer:** Randy Ser. **Cast:** Liam Neeson, Frances McDormand, Colin Friels, Larry Drake, Ted Raimi, Nelson Mashita, Jessie Lawrence.

First Comic Book Appearance: "Darkman #1" (Marvel Comics, 1990)
Origins: For several years, director Sam Raimi was interested in adapting a comic book into a movie, and tried unsuccessfully to acquire the rights to "The Shadow" and "Batman." (Little could he have imagined back in 1990 that he would make one of the greatest superhero movies of all time with the blockbuster "Spider-Man," in 2002.) When all of his efforts failed, Raimi decided to create a superhero of his own. He drew his inspiration from *The Phantom of the Opera*, the story of the "Elephant Man," and of course "Batman" and "The Shadow." His Darkman was an amalgamation of everything he had ever read and remembered from devouring comic books as a child. He sold the project to Universal Pictures, based upon a short story treatment, and the studio gave Raimi $16 million to make his vision. The story of "Darkman" is a somewhat familiar one: Scientist Peyton Westlake (Liam Neeson) is working on a project to create synthetic skin to aid burn victims. The problem with his experiments is that the formula remains stable for only 99 minutes before disintegrating. His girlfriend, attorney Julie Hastings (Frances McDormand), has problems of her own. She has found documents which link crooked real estate developer Louis Strack (Colin Friels) with mob boss Robert G. Durant (Larry Drake), and asks Peyton to hide them for safekeeping. Unfortunately, Durant knows about the documents, and shows up at Peyton's laboratory with his goons demanding that he turn them over. A fight ensues, and Peyton's lab is blown up, with Peyton literally being blown away. He survives the

explosion, but is hideously burned and disfigured. Doctors at the hospital try a radical new procedure which means disconnecting the nerves to the pain center in his brain. The operation is a success and gives Peyton increased strength because he can no longer sense pain; the downside is that he is prone to violent outburst and huge mood swings. He rebuilds part of his lab, and uses the synthetic skin to hide his identity. In fact, the skin allows him to assume the identity of anyone, including Robert Durant. With his superhuman strength, he goes underground and seeks out those that caused his deformity.

First Media Appearance: The Darkman first appeared under the guise of Liam Neeson in the 1990 film of the same name. With bandages and a trenchcoat to cloak his identity, he looks not unlike Jack Griffith from "The Invisible Man" (1933).

Other Media Appearances: The popularity of the 1990 film inspired two direct-to-video sequels, one in 1994 and one in 1996, and the pilot to an unsold television series. Arnold Vosloo played Darkman in the two video sequels, and Christopher Bowen starred in the 30-minute television pilot. In all of the follow-ups, they maintained the integrity of Sam Raimi's origin story in the first movie.

Trivial Matters: Director Sam Raimi wanted Bruce Campbell for the role as Peyton Westlake/Darkman, but the producers didn't think he could handle the complex role and went with Gary Oldman, then finally Liam Neeson instead. Julia Roberts, Demi Moore, and Bridget Fonda were all considered for the role of Darkman's girlfriend. Richard Dreyfuss and James Caan both turned down the role of Louis Strack. Cameos in the film include walk-ons by director John Landis, Jenny Agutter, and Bruce Campbell. Sam Raimi wanted to direct a comic book adaptation, and twelve years after "Darkman," he made "Spider-Man" (2002), one of the greatest superhero epics on film.

Fanboy Rating: Babes-3 Effects-3 Action-5 Brainwaves-5 Total=16

Darkman

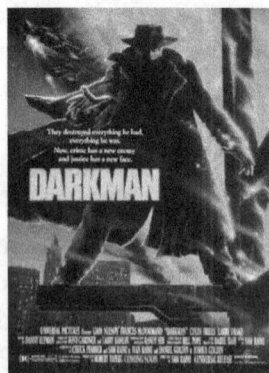

Dick Tracy

Dick Tracy (1990). Walt Disney, in association with Touchstone Pictures, 103min. **Director** and **Producer:** Warren Beatty. **Screenwriters:** Jim Cash and Jack Epps. Based upon characters created by Chester Gould. **Cinematographer:** Vittorio Storaro. **Film Editor:** Richard Marks. **Cast:** Warren Beatty, Madonna, Charlie Korsmo, William Forsythe, Glenne Headly, Al Pacino, Kathy Bates, Dustin Hoffman, Dick Van Dyke.

First Comic Strip Appearance: "Dick Tracy" (October 4, 1931)

Origins: Cartoonist Chester Gould created the character of Dick Tracy for the Chicago Tribune Syndicate, and his hard-hitting, fast-shooting, and highly intelligent police detective debuted as a newspaper comic strip on October 4, 1931. Gould continued to write and draw the strip until 1977. In the early strips, Dick Tracy was not portrayed as a superhero, even though he battled a rogue's gallery of strange and often grotesque super villains, like Flat Top and Prune Face. In 1946, Tracy adopted his trademark communications device, the 2-Way Wrist Radio, and the strip took on several elements of the fantastic in order to compete with pulp science fiction. With the advent of Sputnik and the "Space Race," Dick Tracy and his friends traveled to the Moon, and confronted a Moon Maid and humanoids living in "Moon Valley." He adopted a flying car, built a police force on the Lunar surface, and added an atomic laser beam to his arsenal. In 1964, Tracy for a megalomaniacal dictator bent on world domination – not unlike the villains that 007 routinely dispatched in the James Bond movies – and entered yet another phase. All the while, Tracy remained true to sweetheart Tess Trueheart. Upon retirement, Max Allan Collins and long-time assistant Rick Fletcher took over for Gould, and brought Tracy back down from space for more reality based stories. Dick Tracy focused his superior detective skills on dealing with organized crime.

First Media Appearance: In 1934, Dick Tracy made his first media appearance on the radio in a series of 15-minute episodes broadcast to New

England stations owned by NBC. Bob Burlen voiced the first radio Tracy, and was subsequently followed by Barry Thompson, Ned Wever, and Matt Crowley as the show moved to CBS and then ABC.

Other Media Appearances: Chester Gould's police detective proved to be a very popular character on the silver screen. Ralph Byrd was the first to play the titular hero in a handful of film serials made by Republic, starting with "Dick Tracy" in 1937. Byrd continued to play Tracy in "Dick Tracy Returns" (1938), "Dick Tracy's G-Men" (1939), and "Dick Tracy Versus Crime Inc." (1941). In these serials, Dick Tracy was an FBI agent (or G-Man), and worked out of San Francisco rather than the large Midwestern city that resembled Chicago in the comic strip. After the war, RKO made four feature films, starting with "Dick Tracy, Detective" in 1945. Morgan Conway played Tracy in the first two films, while Ralph Byrd returned for the final two to reprise his interpretation of the great detective. RKO tried to spin-off its popular film series on television, with Ralph Byrd in the lead, but the live-action series ran less than two years (the final season in syndication). Tracy then became an animated figure for Saturday morning cartoons in two different series. In 1967, William Dozier, the producer responsible for the "Batman" television series, produced a pilot for a live-action show, but that never went anywhere.

The 1990 Film: For many years, Warren Beatty had flirted with the idea of producing and directing a big-budget, Hollywood spectacular, but lost interest each time he moved to the pre-production stage. Finally, in 1990, he created a surreal motion picture that was composed entirely of primary colors, like that of a comic strip. While he is trying to battle Big Boy Caprice's (Al Pacino) syndicate of mobsters, the comic strip detective finds his life vastly complicated by the advances of beautiful but deadly Breathless Mahoney (Madonna). Beatty's film was beautifully rendered, but a commercial failure.

Trivial Matters: 16 villains from the comic strip were incorporated into the film, using Chester Gould's original sketches. Robert DeNiro and Jack Nicholson were initially considered for the role of Dick Tracy; Michelle Pfeiffer and Kim Bassinger were early favorites for the role of Breathless Mahoney. Sean Young, cast as Tess Trueheart, was fired after only a few days of shooting.

Fanboy Rating: Babes-6 Effects-5 Action-7 Brainwaves-3 Total=21

Dick Tracy

Doc Savage

Doc Savage (1975). Warner Brothers, in association with George Pal Productions, 112min. **Director:** Michael Anderson. **Producer:** George Pal. **Screenwriter:** Joe Morhaim. Based upon characters created by Lester Dent. **Cinematographer:** Fred J. Koenekamp. **Film Editor:** Thomas J. McCarthy. **Cast:** Ron Ely, Paul Gleason, William Lucking, Michael Miller, Eldon Quick, Darrell Zwerling, Paul Wexler, Janice Heiden, Pamela Hensley.

First Appearance: "Doc Savage Magazine #1" (March 1933)

Origins: Like the Shadow, Doc Savage was a fictional hero that emerged from the pulp magazines published by Street & Smith. Created by Henry Ralston and John Nanovic to capitalize on the Shadow's success, the character came to life in the prose of Lester Dent. Doc Savage was a physician, surgeon, scientist, adventurer, inventor, explorer, researcher and musician — a renaissance man in the truest sense of the term. Born Clark Savage Jr., he was trained from birth by a team of scientists (assembled by his father) to achieve near-superhuman-like abilities. He had great strength and endurance, a photographic memory, and an encyclopedic knowledge that surpassed most libraries. He was a master of disguise and an accomplished mimic. Dent described his hero as having the deductive reasoning of Sherlock Holmes, the physical prowess of Tarzan, the scientific smarts of Craig Kennedy, and the goodness of Abraham Lincoln. Savage lived on the 86the floor of the Empire State Building, maintained a fleet of cars, planes and boats in a secret hangar on the Hudson River, and kept a retreat in the Arctic, known as the Fortress of Solitude. (Doc Savage's retreat actually predates Superman's similar hideout by several years.) In the early stories, Doc Savage battled one-dimensional villains bent on world domination; in the later ones, the stories focused on more supernatural and science-fictional foes. He also later became known as "the Man of Bronze" for his beautifully-tanned skin.

First Comic Book Appearance: Doc Savage appeared as the back-up

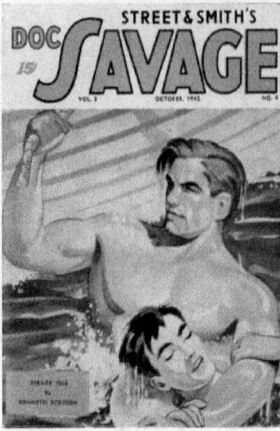

story in a number of the Shadow comic books, starting with "Shadow Comics#1" (1940). He later appeared in his own book, titled "Doc Savage Comics." In the fifth issue, Doc Savage was turned into a genuine superhero when he crashed in Tibet and found a mystical gem that transformed him. These stories departed greatly from the ones being published in the pulps. The comic series ran until 1943. Doc Savage has subsequently appeared in Gold Key (1966, one issue), Marvel Comics (1970s), DC Comics (1987-1990), Millennium Comics (1991-1992), and Dark Horse (1995).

First Media Appearance: In much the same way that his counterpart, the Shadow, debuted on radio, Doc Savage made his first media appearance on a radio show in 1943, which was based on the story of the mystical gem he discovered in Tibet.

The 1975 Film Version: Sci-Fi Producer George Pal attempted to bring Lester Dent's superhero to life in 1975 with the highly-touted "Doc Savage: Man of Bronze," but failed miserably with the unintentionally campy motion picture. In the film, Savage (played by the former Tarzan, Ron Ely) and the Amazing Five (a reference to the team of heroes often employed by Savage in the pulps) trace the disappearance of the Doc's father to the wilds of South America. They uncover a horde of Incan gold, and battle the maniacal Captain Seas (Paul Wexler) for control of the world. Director Michael Anderson chose to set the picture in the 1930s and borrows the same tricks the Saturday morning serial directors used to keep the action moving along at a fast pace. Regrettably, the story is terribly dated, and the pulp characters are not very believable.

Trivial Matters: "Doc Savage: Man of Bronze" was the final film of George Pal, who had come to greatness with "Destination Moon" (1950), "When Worlds Collide" (1951), and "War of the Worlds" (1953). Supposedly, a sequel was filmed in the Lake Tahoe area at the same time principal photography for the first Doc Savage movie was shooting, but was never completed due to the poor box office reception for the first film.

Fanboy Rating: Babes-1 Effects-0 Action-2 Brainwaves-0 Total=3

Doc Savage

Dr. Strange

Dr. Strange (1978). Universal, in association with Marvel Enterprises, 93min. **Director** and **Screenwriter:** Philip DeGuere. **Producer:** Alex Beaton. Based upon characters created by Stan Lee and Steve Ditko. **Cinematographer:** Enzo Martinelli. **Film Editor:** Christopher Nelson. **Cast:** Peter Hooten, Clyde Kusatsu, Jessica Walter, Anne-Marie Martin, Philip Sterling, John Mills, June Barrett, Larry Anderson.

First Comic Book Appearance: "Strange Tales#110" (July 1963)
Origins: Doctor Strange, the master of mystical arts and superhero, was created by Stan Lee and illustrated by Steve Ditko. He first appeared in "Strange Tales#110" (July 1963), and used his supernatural abilities to battle evil magicians, night stalkers and other demons of the lowest order. He proved to be so popular with comic book fans that "Strange Tales" was renamed "Doctor Strange" with Issue#169, and he appeared in numerous crossover stories with the Fantastic Four, Nick Fury, the Avengers, and other groups. Born Stephen Strange in 1930, he grew up in the Midwest, and later became an accomplished but arrogant surgeon. When he suffers neurological damage as the result of an automobile accident in 1963, he travels to the Himalayas in search of an old mystic known as the Ancient One to cure him. The Ancient One offers to make Strange his new apprentice, but Strange refuses, selfishly seeking only a cure to his disorder. Later, after confronting the evil Baron Mordo, he has a change of heart, and studies magic under the Ancient One for seven years before returning to the United States in 1970. Strange takes a mansion in New York City's Greenwich Village, and from his "sanctum sanctorum," he uses his new abilities to fight the forces of evil. His first foe was the Nightmare. When his mentor dies, sacrificing himself to prevent the demonic Shuma-Gorath from crossing over, Dr. Strange inherits the mantle and power of Sorcerer Supreme.
First Media Appearance: The Sorcerer Supreme made his first media

appearance in the 1978 made-for-television movie, titled "Dr. Strange," on CBS. Directed by Phil DeGuere, the low-budget telefilm was more faithful to the original character than previous Marvel Comics adaptations of the period, like "The Incredible Hulk." Psychiatrist Steven Strange (Peter Hooten) receives a visit from Thomas Lindmer (John Mills), the last Sorcerer Supreme whose powers are beginning to fail him. He enlists Dr. Strange's help to battle an evil Sorceress from the past, named Morgan LeFay (Jessica Walter). (Historically, Morgan LeFay was the sorceress who opposed Merlin, and gave birth to the knight who killed King Arthur.) Now, she seeks to conquer the world with her new found media fame as the inventor of the LeFay Method, a self-help system that unlocks potential powers within. The three magicians fight it out for supremacy, and only Strange is left standing.

Trivial Matters: The starburst insignia that Dr. Strange wears on his costume was borrowed from fellow Marvel Comics hero, Captain Marvel; the comic book figure wears no such insignia. The creature that Morgan serves was visually inspired by Dr. Strange's arch-nemesis, Dormammu, although unnamed in the film. Michael Ansara, who played a wizard on "I Dream of Jeannie" while married to Barbara Eden, voices the Ancient One. And Ted Cassidy, the familiar character actor who played Lurch, supplies the voice for the Demon Balzaroth. Both of their vocal roles went uncredited.

Other Media Appearances: In 1992, Full Moon Entertainment tried to revive Dr. Strange as the magician-turned-superhero, and shot nearly the entire film with Jeffrey Combs as the titular hero. Unfortunately, the rights to the character and his name were lost. The movie was reworked as "Doctor Mordid." The real Dr. Strange did make house calls on several

cartoon series, "Spider-Man: the Animated Series" (1996), "Spider-Man and His Amazing Friends" (1996), "The X-Men" (1996), and "The Incredible Hulk" (1997). He also appeared on a direct-to-DVD from Marvel Entertainment. Plans to make a big-budget Hollywood motion picture are still being discussed.

Fanboy Rating: Babes-2 Effects-3 Action-3 Brainwaves-2 Total=10

Dr. Strange

Electra Woman

Electra Woman and Dyna Girl (1976). Sid and Marty Krofft Productions, 15min, 16 episodes. **Directors:** Chuck Liotta, Walter C. Miller, Jack Regas. **Producers:** Sid and Marty Krofft. **Screenwriters:** Duane Poole, Dick Robbins, Joe Ruby and Ken Spears et al. Characters created by Joe Ruby and Ken Spears. **Cast:** Deidre Hall, Judy Strangis, Norman Alden, Michael Constantine, Susan Lanier, Marvin Miller, Jane Elliot, H.B. Haggerty, Sid Haig, Andrea Hall.

First Comic Book Appearance: None.

Origins: Electra Woman and Dyna Girl were the creations of Sid and Marty Krofft, and the weekly action-adventures of the two gorgeous superheroes debuted on September 11, 1976, as part of ABC's Krofft Supershow on Saturday mornings. They starred in 8 two-part adventures that were aired as 15-minute segments. The show lampooned the campy, zany "Batman" series from the 1960s, while mining many of its other jokes from the fact that these two superheroes were gorgeous babes in skin-tight spandex. The premise was not very sophisticated, but then, it didn't have to be sophisticated because Sid and Marty Krofft had intended their show for kids. They never imagined that it would become the must-see weekly show of fanboys all over the world! In their secret identities as Lori (Deidre Hall) and Judy (Judy Strangis), they worked as writers for *Newsmaker* magazine, but when trouble dialed their number, they would don their skin-tight spandex (in a bright flash of light called a "Electra-Change"), hop into their Electracar, and use an arsenal of technological gadgetry to thwart criminals…just in time to get back to have their nails manicured. They didn't actually have any superpowers. They operated out of a secret underground base, known as Electrabase, headed by Frank Heflin (Norman Alden). Heflin was also responsible for designing and building most of the heroines' sophisticated equipment. (Most of the equipment seemed to be inspired by devices that Batman and Robin had used on that earlier television series.) In the course of their adventures, Electra Woman and Dyna Girl matched wits with an eccentric collection of supervillains that included the Sorcerer (Michael Constantine), Glitter Rock (Susan Lanier), Ali Baba (Malchi Throne), Princess Cleopatra (Jane Elliot), the Pharaoh (Peter Mark Richman), and the Empress of Evil (Claudette Nevins). Regrettably, the show only lasted one season, but in the thirty years since the show aired, fans have kept the spirit of Electra Woman and Dyna Girl alive with fan fiction, websites, and hand-made costumes.

First Media Appearance: Electra Woman and Dyna Girl made their first media appearance on September 11, 1976, on the first episode of the Krofft Supershow in the guise of Deidre Hall and Judy Strangis. The series lasted only 16 weeks.

The 2001 Television Pilot: The WB commissioned a pilot for a new version of "Electra Woman and Dyna Girl" to air on its new network in 2001. The pilot featured Markie Post as Electra Woman and Anne Stedman as Dyna Girl, and was set twenty-five years after the original series so that a retired Electra Woman could be brought back into the action by her number one fan, Dyna Girl. By contrast, the new Electra Woman is angry and bitter, and wants to turn in her cape and spandex. Directed by David Grossman and written by Elisa Bell, the sixty-minute pilot was shot but then never aired or picked up by the WB as a series.

Fanboy Rating: Babes-9 Effects-1 Action-2 Brainwaves-2 Total=14

Electra Woman

Elektra

Elektra (2003). 20th Century-Fox, in association with Marvel Enterprises, 97min. **Director:** Rob Bowman. **Producers:** Avi Arad, Gary Foster, Arnon Milchan. **Screenwriters:** Zac Penn, Stu Zicherman, and Raven Metzner. **Cinematographer**: Bill Roe. **Film Editor:** Kevin Stitt. **Production Designer:** Graeme Murray. **Cast:** Jennifer Garner, Goran Visnjic, Kristen Prout, Will Yun Lee, Cary-Hiroyuki Tagawa, Terence Stamp.

First Comic Book Appearance: "Daredevil #168" (January 1981)
Origins: Created by Frank Miller, Elektra Natchios made her first appearance as the deadly ninja assassin, known for her twin sais, in "Daredevil #168" (January 1981); subsequently, the supervillianous has made other appearances in various Marvel Comics for the last quarter century. She was born on a Greek island in the Aegean Sea, and named after the classical heroine Electra, daughter of Agamemnon and Clytemnestra. She came to the United States at age 19 when her father Hugo Natchios was appointed the Greek ambassador to the United Nations, and attended Columbia University where she met Matt Murdock (Daredevil). When she and her father were kidnapped by terrorists, Daredevil tried to rescue them; but unfortunately, he failed, and her father was shot and skilled. Elektra quit Columbia, and traveled to the East to study martial arts under Stick, the master who had trained Daredevil. She later turned to the Hand, a sect of mystical ninja, and trained as an assassin. When her training was complete, she left the Hand and went to work for the Kingpin, but was fatally stabbed by Bullseye with one of her own sais in a battle over turf. Elektra was eventually resurrected by the Hand, and later worked as a ally with Wolverine and Agent Nick Fury of S.H.I.E.L.D. She has switched allegiances many times, and to this day, no one is really certain as to which side she is really on.
First Media Appearance: Portrayed by Jennifer Garner, the character of Elektra Natchios appeared for the first time in the 2003 "Daredevil" film

as the titular hero's love interest. For many years, Elektra had blamed Daredevil for her father's death. She has trained herself in martial arts, and prepared for the day when she can kill him with her deadly sais. However, when she finally confronts Daredevil, Elektra learns that it was Bullseye who really murdered her father. But she is too late. The Kingpin's assassin slits her throat and impales her on her own sai. Elektra dies in Daredevil's arms.

Film Development: The "Daredevil" movie had proved to be such as disappointment to New Regency and 20th Century-Fox, despite the fact that it made over $100 million, that any discussions of a sequel were quickly tabled. However, most critics who hated the film loved Jennifer Garner as Elektra. And the buzz reached a fever-pitch, less than one year later, when Rob Bowman was handed the reigns of the "Daredevil" spin-off, "Elektra." Garner filmed the movie during her summer hiatus from the television series, "Alias," in which she also played a spy and assassin.

The 2003 Film Version: Elektra (Jennifer Garner) is resurrected by Stick (Terence Stamp), and trained in the martial arts in the Way of the Kimagure (with powers to control time and the future as well as life and death). She soon abandons this force for good, and works as a paid assassin for the Hand. Kirigi (Will Yun Lee) and the Order of the Hand send Elektra on a mission to kill the widower Mark Miller (Goran Visnjic) and his daughter Abby (Kristen Prout). She befriends the Millers, seeing something very special in Abby, and decides to defend them from Kirigi's ninja assassins. In time, Elektra learns that Abby has the power to tip the scales in favor of good or evil, and fights to the death to protect her young charge.

Trivial Matters: Ben Affleck filmed a cameo, reprising his role as Daredevil, but that scene was cut from the final film. The opening sequence with Bauer and DeMarco was taken nearly scene for scene from "Elektra #23," written by Robert Rodi. 20th Century-Fox associated "Elektra" with the "X-Men" movie, and totally ignored any connection to "Daredevil" in its promotional campaign.

Fanboy Rating: Babes-7 Effects-3 Action-6 Brainwaves-2 Total=18

Elektra

Fantastic Four

> **Fantastic Four** (1994). New Horizons, 90min.
> **Director:** Oley Sassone. **Producer:** Roger Corman.
> **Screenwriters:** Craig Nevius and Kevin Rock. Char-
> acters created by Stan Lee and Jack Kirby. **Cinema-
> tographer:** Mark Parry. **Film Editor:** Glenn Gar-
> land. **Production Designer:** Mick Strawn. **Cast:**
> Alex Hyde-White, Jay Underwood, Rebecca Staab,
> Michael Bailey Smith, Joseph Culp, Kat Green, Carl
> Ciarfalio.

First Comic Book Appearance: "Fantastic Four #1" (November 1961)
Origins: Created by Stan Lee and Jack Kirby, the Fantastic Four was the first comic book superhero team from Marvel Comics. At the time, DC Comics was busy reviving the superhero genre from the 1940s with all-new versions of the Flash and Green Lantern; the comic book giant had also launched the first successful superhero team, the Justice League of America, and that title was doing extremely well. Martin Goodman, the publisher of Marvel Comics, recommended that Stan Lee, who served as editor-in-chief and art director, create a superhero group for its comics, and the Fantastic Four was born. Even though the make-up of the group has changed temporarily from time to time, the original group was made up of Dr. Reed Richards, a handsome young scientist; Benjamin Grimm, his best friend and test pilot; Susan Storm, Reed's girlfriend, and Johnny Storm, her teenaged brother. Without proper authorization, Reed and his friends take an untested and poorly-shielded space craft up into space and accidentally fly through a storm of cosmic rays. They return to the Earth with superpowers. Reed discovers that he has the ability to stretch, like Plastic Man, and adopts the name "Mister Fantastic." Ben's body becomes grotesquely warped and distorted, but he gains tremendous strength as "The Thing." Sue learns that she has the power to become invisible and create force fields, and takes on the name "The Invisible Girl." And Johnny discovers that he can surround himself with flames and fly, like "The Human Torch." (The Human Torch was a Marvel character

that had first appeared in 1939, as created by Carl Burgos.) Together, this team of four superheroes battled villains like the Sub-Mariner (Issue #4) and Dr. Doom (Issue #5) and teamed-up with characters like Spider-Man and the Black Panther from their headquarters in the Baxter Building in New York City. With "Fantastic Four #48," they became aware of other civilizations spread throughout the galaxy, and were introduced to the Watcher, the Silver Surfer and Galactus. Reed and Sue married in "Fantastic Four Annual #3" (1965), and had a child with superhuman abilities named Franklin Benjamin Richards in "Fantastic Four Annual #6" (1968). Writer and artist John Byrne took the Fantastic Four back to the basics with "FF #232," and wrote what many critics and fans alike consider the best run of the series since the departure of Lee and Kirby in the late 1960s. Other characters like She-Hulk, Ms. Marvel and Ant-Man joined the team as replacements when one or more of the lead characters took time off or simply disappeared. Johnny Storm as the Human Torch and Ben Grimm as the Thing made solo appearances in other books and limited series. More recently, Marvel Comics' "Civil War" crossover series has found the Fantastic Four disbanded, more like torn apart, because of differing views on the Superhuman Registration Act. But have no fears…the Fantastic Four is one group that will last forever.

First Media Appearance: The Fantastic Four appeared for the first time outside of the comic book universe in a Saturday morning animated series produced by Hanna-Barbera Productions for ABC. The action-adventure show aired 20 episodes from September 9, 1967, to September 28, 1968, and featured the vocal talents of Gerald Mohr, Jo Ann Plug, Jack Flounders, and Paul Frees. The show was hugely popular for its dramatizations of some of the comic's famous stories, including "The Coming of Galactus," "The Menace of the Mole Men," and the origin of Dr. Doom.

Other Media Appearances: In 1975, the Fantastic Four were brought to life in a short-lived radio show that featured the voice of Bill Murray as Johnny Storm. DePatie-Freleng teamed up with Marvel Comics Animation in 1978 to produce another animated television series. Unfortunately, the character of Johnny Storm as the Human Torch was written out, for

Fantastic Four

fear that children may imitate his actions with fire, and replaced by a robot named H.E.R.B.I.E. Ted Cassidy, Mike Road, Dick Tufeld, and Ginny Tyler-Hilton provided the voices. Most fans hated the political correctness of the show, and it lasted only 13 episodes. In 1994, Marvel Productions syndicated yet another animated show that featured direct recreations of the episodes from the original 1960s animated series. Brian Austin Green voiced the role of Johnny Storm; Lori Alan was Susan Storm; Beau Weaver was Reed Richards, and Chuck McCann played Ben Grimm. And finally, in 2006, the Fantastic Four debuted in another animated television series on the Cartoon Network. The series featured fabulous computer animation, and guest-starred many of Marvel's superheroes, including the Hulk, Iron Man, and Henry Pym.

The 1994 Film Version: In 1994, with its rights to the property soon to revert back to Marvel Entertainment, Roger Corman's New Horizons company produced a low-low budget film that was never intended for release. Corman merely wanted to establish his legal rights, even though he was not prepared to make a big-budget version. His "ashcan copy" blocked Chris Columbus from making his film adaptation. The "Fantastic Four" movie is available on the secondary market and through dealers at sci-fi conventions, but don't expect anything substantial. The screen story is the typical origin story, with Reed Richards (Alex Hyde-White) befriending Victor Von Doom (Joseph Culp) in college and then watching him become disfigured in an experiment gone wrong. Years later, Reed, his girlfriend Sue (Rebecca Staab), her brother Johnny (Jay Underwood), and Ben Grimm (Michael Bailey Smith) test-pilot an experimental space craft that gets hit by cosmic rays. After they crash-down on Earth, the four discover that they have superhuman abilities, and decide to use those abilities to fight crime. Meanwhile, Dr. Doom has kidnapped Alicia (Kat Green), Ben's girlfriend, and stolen a huge diamond to power a laser cannon that will destroy New York City. The Fantastic Four spring into action, and battle Dr. Doom and his robots at a castle in Latveria. The film was never released to theaters or home video, and has languished in limbo.

Trivial Matters: The character of the Jeweler (Ian Trigger) was re-written when Corman and company discovered they had not purchased the rights to the character of the Mole Man from the original comic book. This adaptation actually shows the four astronauts getting bombarded with cos-

mic rays when they test-pilot an experimental space craft; in the 2005 film, the four are aboard a space station when bombarded with cosmic rays, along with Dr. Doom.

Fanboy Rating: Babes-2 Effects-1 Action-4 Brainwaves-4 Total=11

Fantastic Four (2005). 20th Century-Fox, 109min. **Director:** Tim Story. **Producers:** Avid Arad, Ralph Winter, and Bernd Eichinger. **Screenwriters:** Mark Frost and Michael France. Characters created by Stan Lee and Jack Kirby. **Cinematographer:** Oliver Wood. **Film Editor:** William Hoy. **Production Designer:** Bill Boes. **Cast:** Ioan Gruffudd, Jessica Alba, Chris Evans, Michael Chiklis, Julian McMahon, Kerry Washington, Laurie Holden.

The 2005 Film Version: After several years in development hell, 20th Century-Fox's big budget version of the "Fantastic Four" told a very familiar tale with a few contemporary twists of its own. Reed Richards (Ioan Gruffudd), who has recently lost girlfriend Sue Storm (Jessica Alba) to rival Victor Von Doom (Julian McMahon), agrees to go forward with tests aboard a brand new space station launched by Doom's military-industrial complex. Ben Grimm (Michael Chiklis) and Johnny Storm (Chris Evans) are also present when the space station goes off course and gets exposed to cosmic radiation. Each of them, including Dr. Doom, discovers that they've gained superpowers. Sue gains the ability to turn invisible and create force fields; her younger brother Johnny Storm gains the ability to control fire, including covering his own body with flame; Ben Grimm is turned into a super-strong rock creature, and Reed gains the ability to stretch his body. Dr. Doom keeps his powers of magnetism to himself. United, the Fantastic Four return to Earth to rid the planet of evil, and ultimately foil the evil plans of the corporate giant, Victor Von Doom. The film's story deviates from the original comic book, but once it gets going, the actions of the four central characters seem to overwhelm all manner of logic and story-plotting.

Fantastic Four

Fantastic Four

Trivial Matters: Chris Columbus, Raja Gosnell, Peyton Reed, Steven Soderbergh and Sean Astin were all interested in directing the movie, at one time or another. Similarly, George Clooney and Brendan Fraser were considered for the part of Reed Richards, and Julia Stiles, Kate Bosworth, Elizabeth Banks, KaDee Strickland, and Rachel McAdams were all considered for the role of Sue Storm. Paul Walker read for the part of Johnny Storm; Tim Robbins was briefly considered as Dr. Doom, and James Gandaolfini was an early choice for Ben Grimm. This was actually the second "Fantastic Four" movie made.

Fanboy Rating: Babes-8 Effects-7 Action-4 Brainwaves-4 Total=23

Fantastic Four: Rise of the Silver Surfer (2007). 20th Century-Fox, 109min. **Director:** Tim Story. **Producers:** Avid Arad, Ralph Winter, and Bernd Eichinger. **Screenwriters:** Mark Frost and Don Payne. Characters created by Stan Lee and Jack Kirby. **Cinematographer:** Larry Blanford. **Film Editors:** William Hoy, Peter Elliot, and Michael McCusker. **Production Designer:** Kirk Petruccelli. **Cast:** Ioan Gruffudd, Jessica Alba, Chris Evans, Michael Chiklis, Julian McMahon, Doug Jones.

The 2007 Film Sequel: Having just defeated the plans of Dr. Doom (McMahon) (at the end of the first movie), the Fantastic Four (Gruffudd, Alba, Evans, and Chiklis) square off against the powerful Silver Surfer (Doug Jones) and the planet-eating Galactus. The screen story is based on the three-part story arc, "The Coming of Galactus" from "Fantastic Four #48-50" (1966). The Silver Surfer was originally Norrin Radd, a young astronomer of the planet Zenn-La. He agreed to serve as the herald of a god-like being, known as Galactus, in order to save his home world. He was given enormous cosmic powers, and sent out to find other worlds that Galactus could consume. When he comes to Earth, he meets the Fantastic Four and ultimately betrays Galactus, who

dooms him to exile on Earth. If the film looks anything like the trailer, expect a story that far eclipses that of the first film.

Trivial Matters: Of all of the supervillains that the Fantastic Four have met over the years, the characters of Galactus and the Silver Surfer were chosen for their cinematic potential. Fox and other studios have been trying to launch a Silver Surfer franchise for years. The success of the 2007 film could pave the way for a standalone "Silver Surfer" movie. We can only hope and pray.

Fanboy Rating: Babes-? Effects-?
Action-? Brainwaves-? Total=??

Fantastic Four

The Flash

The Flash (1990). Warner Brothers, 94min. **Director:** Robert Iscove. **Producers:** Steven Long Mitchell and Craig W. Van Sickle. **Screenwriters:** Danny Bilson, Paul De Meo and Denise Skinner. Characters created by Gardner Fox. **Cinematographer:** John Newby and Sandi Sissel. **Film Editor:** Frank Jimenez. **Cast:** John Wesley Shipp, Amanda Pays, Alex Desert, Robert Hooks, Biff Manard, M. Emmet Walsh, Richard Belzer, Tim Thomerson, Priscilla Pointer.

First Comic Book Appearance: "Flash Comics #1" (January 1940)
Origins: The Flash, also known as Jay Garrick, raced out of the pages of "Flash Comics #1" in January 1940, and into the hearts of millions of loyal readers during an era when superhero comics were tops. Created by Gardner Fox and illustrated by Harry Lambert, Jay Garrick was an all-American college student who gained his super-speed powers when he accidentally inhaled heavy water (radioactive) vapors. He wore a winged helmet, much like the mythological Roman god Mercury, and a red shirt with a yellow lightning bolt in the center. Garrick never bothered with a mask because he felt he could maintain his secret identity by continually vibrating his body (and face) in public. He fought criminals in Keystone City as the Flash. Since he was among DC Comics' early hits, he inspired other speedsters, including the Whizzer at Marvel, Quicksilver at Quality Comics, and DC's own Johnny Quick. Garrick was a founding member of the Justice Society of America, and fought supervillains alongside Green Lantern and Wonder Woman. In 1949, after superhero comics had run their course, Jay Garrick retired as the Flash with Issue 104. The character of the Flash was revived in 1956 in the guise of Barry Allen, a police chemist who was the victim of an accidental lightning strike on dangerous chemicals. When he discovered that he could run super-fast, he donned a set of red tights with a lightning bolt, and named himself after his childhood hero in the comic books, Jay Garrick. He stored his costume in a special ring which could be compressed or ejected at will. The Flash was the first

of a new Silver Age of superheroes which regarded the Golden Age heroes as fictional. However, in 1961, Gardner Fox gave Barry Allen a device which allowed him to travel between parallel Earths so that he could meet Jay Garrick, in a story titled "Flash of Two Worlds." The comic book story was a hit, and allowed for other journeys to parallel Earths as well as time travel to the past and future. Wally West eventually replaced Barry Allen (who was killed in "Crisis on Infinite Earths," 1985) as the Flash, and was in turn replaced by Bart Allen, Barry's grandson. Much like his childhood hero, Barry Allen's Flash also joined and became a leading member of the Justice League of America. He teamed often with Batman, Green Lantern, and Superman; in fact, a series of comic books featured races between Superman and the Flash in order to determine who was the fastest man alive.

First Media Appearance: In his first ever media appearance, Barry Allen's Flash appeared as a guest on "The Adventures of Aquaman," an animated television show, in 1968.

Other Media Appearances: From 1973 to 1985, the Flash appeared as a regular on the "Super Friends" animated series. The live-action "Legends of the Superheroes" specials featured actor Rod Haase as Barry Allen (aka the Flash) in a 1977 episode. The Flash earned his own television series in 1990, with John Wesley Shipp in costume as the Scarlet Speedster. Kenny Johnston played the Flash in a live-action pilot called "The Justice League of America" for CBS that never aired. The Flash has also been featured on the "Superman" animated series (1996) and the "Justice League" animated series (2001). Bart Allen as the Flash made a guest appearance on the television series "Smallville" (2004); in the fourth season episode, Allen was played by Kyle Gallner, who easily outdistances Tom Welling's Clark Kent.

The 1990 Film Version: "The Flash" television series was launched by a 94-minute television movie, directed by Robert Iscove, in 1990. In the

original pilot, a laboratory accident endows police scientist Barry Allen (John Wesley Shipp) with the ability to move at superhuman speed. With the help of S.T.A.R. Labs scientist Tina McGee (Amanda Pays), he develops his powers, and modifies a prototype deep sea diving suit to withstand the tremendous pressures of speed as his Flash costume. After his brother Jay Allen (Tim Thomerson), a motorcycle cop, is murdered by a menacing gang

The Flash

of bikers, Barry uses his new found powers to bring the gang to justice. Subsequent episodes in the television series found the Flash fighting a "rogues gallery" of colorful, costumed supervillains, including the Trickster (Mark Hamill), Captain Cold (Michael Champion), and Mirror Master (David Cassidy). The pilot film and television series were huge hits with fans and critics alike, but stiff competition from NBC's strong Thursday night lineup meant certain death for the series. "The Flash" television series ran for 21 episodes and was canceled by CBS on May 18, 1991.

Trivial Matters: The pilot film and subsequent television series is replete with references to the comic books and their creators. The police captain is named Julius Schwartz; several streets are named Garrick Avenue or Gardner Road; a hotel is named after Carmine Infantino, and several of the comic book villains, including Professor Zoom and Gorilla Grodd, appear to threaten the life and livelihood of the Flash.

Fanboy Rating: Babes-4 Effects-4 Action-7 Brainwaves-5 Total=20

The 2002 Film Version: In 2002, a low-low budget, unauthorized version of "The Flash" was produced by Waterworks Entertainment in association with Tuxedo Company Productions. This independent production, which was made like a "Blair Witch" docudrama, was supposedly released, but no one this author contacted or consulted had ever seen the finished product. Waterworks Entertainment is best known for its docudramas about "Bigfoot" and "Sasquatch 2." But it's really hard to judge a film about the Scarlet Speedster based on the production values of two docudramas about the discovery of some mythological creature. A sequel, titled "The Flash 2," was supposed to have been released two years later, but was never completed due to creative differences among the cast and crew.

The Flash (2008). Warner Brothers, in association with DC Comics, 120min. **Director:** Shawn Levy. **Producers:** TBA. **Screenwriter:** David S. Goyer. Characters created by Gardner Fox and Harry Lambert. **Cinematographer:** TBA. **Film Editor:** TBA. **Cast:** Ryan Reynolds. This motion picture is still under pre-production, and will not be released until 2008.

The 2008 Film Version: While the project was still in its early pre-production stages at the time of this writing, Warner Brothers announced that it was going to produce a big budget version of "The Flash" for possible release in 2008. David Goyer, the man who had written the "Blade" trilogy and "Batman Begins" (2005), was assigned to write and direct the new movie. No cast was announced, but rumors that Ryan Reynolds will play the Flash continue to appear.

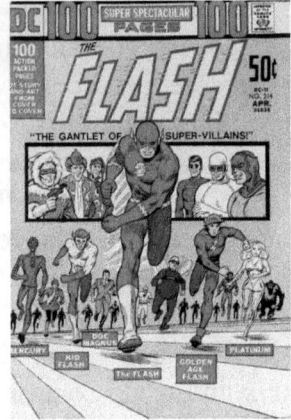

The Flash

Flash Gordon

Flash Gordon (1936). Universal Pictures, B&W, 245min, 13episodes. **Director:** Frederick Stephani. **Producer:** Henry MacRae. **Screenwriters:** Ella O'Neill, George Plympton, Basil Dickey. Based on the comic strip by Alex Raymond. **Cinematographers:** Jerome Ash and Richard Fryer. **Film Editors:** Sam Goodkind, Louis Sackin, Alvin and Edward Todd. **Cast:** Buster Crabbe, Jean Rogers, Charles Middleton, Priscilla Lawson, Frank Shannon, Richard Alexander.

First Comic Strip Appearance: "Flash Gordon" (January 7, 1934)
First Comic Book Appearance: "King Comics #60" (1941)
Origins: In 1934, writer Don Moore and artist Alex Raymond created a superhero named "Flash Gordon" for a daily comic strip in King Features in order to compete with the huge audience that was reading "Buck Rogers in the 25th Century" in rival newspapers. The series debuted on January 7, 1934, with a full page, including its topper, and packed a punch with each of its comic strip panels. In almost no time at all, "Flash Gordon" surpassed the popularity of "Buck Rogers" and gave America a new hero who had no real superpowers, but had all of the grit and determination of an American. Flash Gordon, a renowned polo player, is forced to parachute from a commercial aircraft when it is struck and damaged by a falling meteor. Both Flash and the beautiful Dale Arden, whom he managed to grasp in his arms on his way out the plane's door, land near an launch site where Dr. Hans Zarkoff plans to rocket into space for the runaway planet Mongo. Zarkoff cannot stop the countdown, nor does he have time to argue with his two new guests. With mere seconds before the rockets on his spaceship turn the launch site into a fiery inferno, he takes Flash and Dale aboard his ship. They rocket to the planet Mongo, which is on a collision course with Earth, and try to plead with Mongo's warlord Ming the Merciless to turn away from his destructive course. Ming takes an immediate liking for Dale, and sends Zarkoff to work with fellow scientists. But he wants only to destroy Flash Gordon. For the next ten years,

Ming tried every means at his disposal to get rid of Flash, while Flash Gordon and the others became involved with Mongo's improbable inhabitants in a string of memorable adventures. Those adventures included encounters with Prince Vultan of the Hawk Men, Prince Thun of the Shark Men, Prince Barin and Ming's own daughter Princess Aura. The daily comic strip ended in 1944, when Alex Raymond enlisted in the Army, and was revived in 1951. The Sunday comic strip has been run nearly continuously since its debut in 1934.

First Media Appearances: In 1935, the strip was adapted into "The Amazing Interplanetary Adventures of Flash Gordon," a twenty-six episode radio serial that followed the storyline of the early comic strip. Not long after the comic strip debuted in 1934, Universal Pictures produced a 13-part serial in 1936 with Buster Crabbe in the titular role as "Flash Gordon." It was the first of three serials based on the comic strip series from Alex Raymond.

Other Media Appearances: Buster Crabbe played Flash Gordon in two additional serials in 1938 and 1940. When television began adapting popular serials for the small screen, "Flash Gordon" was among its first television series. Steve Holland played Flash Gordon from 1954 to 1955 in thirty-nine episodes. Ironically, the series was filmed in West Berlin, less than a decade after World War 2. A pornographic parody, titled "Flesh Gordon," debuted theatrically in 1974, and became a cult favorite among sci-fi fans. In 1979, two years after the phenomenal success of "Star Wars" (1977), Filmation Studios released "The New Adventures of Flash Gordon" as a made-for-television movie of the week. When NBC saw the finished work, the executives so liked what they saw that they spun the animated movies into a Saturday morning cartoon. The weekly adventures followed Flash and his friends on their fateful trip to Mongo and his various encounters with Thun, Barin, Vultan, and of course Ming the Merciless. "The New Adventures of Flash Gordon" was set in the late 1930s as a period piece, and featured Ming consulting with Hitler and other evil rulers on their use of new technology. One year later, Dino De Laurentiis unveiled his over-budgeted, bloated camp classic "Flash Gordon" (1980) with Sam J. Jones stepping lively as the titular character to the music of

Flash Gordon

Queen. More recently, Stephen Sommers, director of "Van Helsing" and the "Mummy" movies for Universal, has announced that he will make a more respectful version of the classic comic strip for a 2007 or 2008 release. Just imagine Brendan Fraiser or Hugh Jackman as Flash Gordon!

The 1936 Film Serial: The serial, which was the most expensive of them all, told of Flash's first journey to Mongo and his struggle with Ming the Merciless (Charles Middleton). Jean Rogers played Dale Arden and Frank Shannon played Dr. Alexis Zarkov. In episodes that seemed to be inspired by the comic strip, Flash first catches the eye of Princess Aura (Priscilla Lawson), and then plummets down into the tunnel of terror with her where he faces dinosaurs. Later, he is captured by the Shark Men, and befriends Prince Thun (James Pierce). Flash battles a sea beast, participates in a gladiatorial tournament of death, fights a fire dragon, and then get caught in the claws of the Tigron. Finally, he defeats Ming the Merciless, and unites the planet of Mongo with Prince Barin (Richard Alexander) and King Vultan (Tiny Lipson) sharing power. Even though the serial was shot in less than six weeks with the cast working fourteen-hour days, the high production values and sincerity of the actors makes the 245min serial look far better than it had a right to be. A great deal of credit must also be extended to former Olympian Buster Crabbe who embodies the character of Flash Gordon and director Fred Stephani who turns in an A-list feature on a B-movie budget. The serial was a huge success for Universal, which was already riding a wave of blockbuster successes with its string of handsomely-produced horror films.

Trivial Matters: The serial re-cycled many sets from other Universal films, including the laboratory from "The Bride of Frankenstein" (1935), the opera house interiors from "The Phantom of the Opera" (1925), and the cathedral walls from "The Hunchback of Notre Dame" (1923). By re-cycling many of these sets, the serial saved money that could be spent on special effects or other production costs. Still, the serial was the most costly of any serial at that time; its budget of $360,000 was three times more than what was given for a serial. The production also borrowed music that had been made famous in some of Universal's horror films, including Franz Waxman's great scores. An edited version played on television in the 1950s with the title "Rocketship."

Fanboy Rating: Babes-5 Effects-5 Action-7 Brainwaves-5 Total=22

Flash Gordon's Trip To Mars (1938). Universal Pictures, B&W, 300min, 15episodes. **Directors:** Ford Beebe and Robert F. Hill. **Producer:** Barney Sarecky. **Screenwriters:** Norman S. Hall, Wyndham Gittes, Herbert Dalmas and Ray Trampe. Based on the comic strip by Alex Raymond. **Cinematographer:** Jerome Ash. **Editors:** Joseph Gluck, Sam Goodkind, Louis Sackin, Alvin Todd. **Cast:** Buster Crabbe, Jean Rogers, Charles Middleton, Anne Gwynne, Frank Shannon.

The 1938 Film Sequel: The huge success of the first "Flash Gordon" serial encouraged Universal to produce a sequel, featuring many of the same actors and crew in key roles. No sooner do Flash (Crabbe), Dale (Rogers) and Zarkov (Shannon) return from their adventures on the planet Mongo, they learn that Ming the Merciless (Middleton) has taken refuge on Mars. He plans to use a new deadly ray to reign evil and destruction down on our planet. Earth's only hope is Flash Gordon! He and his friends blast off for Mars, where they and stowaway Happy Hapgood (Donald Kerr) battle Ming's new ally, Queen Azura (Beatrice Roberts). She has a way of turning her enemies into Clay People, and we all know what that means. The sequel was expanded to 15 chapters, and featured deadly perils for Flash and his friends week after week. Once again, Universal struck gold with its above-average serial.

Trivial Matters: The serial is based, in large part, on the comic strip storyline from "Flash Gordon and the Witch Queen of Mongo." The bullet car utilized by the Clay people is the same one Buck Rogers used in his one and only serial (in 1939). With this serial, Jean Rogers left as Dale Arden, and was replaced by Carol Hughes. The music is borrowed from Universal's "Bride of Frankenstein" (1935) and "The Invisible Man" (1933). A vastly edited ver-

Flash Gordon

sion of the serial played on television in the late 1950s with the title "Space Soldiers' Trip to Mars."
Fanboy Rating: Babes-4 Effects-5 Action-6 Brainwaves-5 Total=20

Flash Gordon Conquers the Universe (1940). Universal Pictures, B&W, 220min, 12episodes. **Directors:** Ford Beebe and Ray Taylor. **Producer:** Henry MacRae. **Screenwriters:** George Plympton, Basil Dickey, and Barry Shipman. Based on the comic strip by Alex Raymond. **Cinematographers:** Jerome Ash and William Sickner. **Editors:** Sam Goodkind, Louis Sackin, Alvin Todd, and Joseph Gluck. **Cast:** Buster Crabbe, Carol Hughes, Charles Middleton.

The 1940 Film Sequel: Once again, the box office returns on "Flash Gordon's Trip to Mars" (1938) encouraged Universal to produce a third and final serial. When a mysterious plague, known as the Purple Death, ravages the Earth, Dr. Zarkov (Shannon) discovers a spaceship from the planet Mongo dropping dust in the atmosphere. Ming is back (!) and deadlier than ever. So Flash (Crabbe), Dale Arden (Carol Hughes), and Zarkov blast off for Mongo in Zarkov's rocket. Upon arrival, they meet up with Prince Barin (Roland Drew) of Arboria and enlist a few new allies from the frozen northern land of Frigia, where, it so happens, an antidote to the plague is found. But Ming will use all his evil powers to keep our heroes from thwarting his plans to conquer the universe. The third serial was also successful.
Trivial Matters: The serial is based, in large part, on the comic strip storyline from "Flash Gordon and the Queen of Frigia." Costumes in the serial were re-cycled from several historical epics that Universal produced. Universal also borrowed footage from the German film "White Hell of Pitz Palu" for the exciting mountain catastrophe and rescue. Ming's rule of the disparate regions of Mongo was modeled after Hitler's rule of several European countries. An edited version played on television in the 1950s with the title "Space Soldiers Conquer the Universe."
Fanboy Rating: Babes-4 Effects-5 Action-6 Brainwaves-5 Total=20

The 1980 Film Version: When George Lucas first envisioned "Star Wars," he wanted to make a space opera not unlike the "Flash Gordon" serials of the 1930s. In fact, he first pitched Universal on a remake of "Flash Gordon," but the rights had already gone to Dino De Laurentiis. The success of "Star Wars" prompted Laurentiis to launch his own space opera, and hired Lorenzo Semple Jr. who had written the 1966 "Batman" television series. Instead of a science fiction film that paid deference to its source material, Semple's script played the material like high camp. Regrettably, the story winks at its own attempts to be serious and laughs at its own attempts to be funny, and the characters are all made out of cardboard, rather than flesh and blood. Flash Gordon (Sam J. Jones), now a football player, and Dale Arden (Melody Anderson) are kidnapped by mad doctor Hans Zarkov (Topol) on his way to the planet Mongo. Once there, the three battle the Emperor Ming the Merciless (Max Von Sydow) and his legions. Prince Barin (Timothy Dalton) is Flash's rival for the attentions of Aura (Ornella Muti), and Prince Vultan (Brian Blessed) is a comical buffoon. Ming's obsession with Dale Arden is also pushed to absurd improbabilities. Ultimately, the final battle is played out against the music of Queen, as Flash leads the forces of good against Ming. "Flash! Ah-Ah! He'll save everyone of us!" He just couldn't save the box office.

Trivial Matters: Arnold Schwarzenegger and Kurt Russell were early forerunners to play Flash Gordon; in the end, Sam J. Jones was cast when De Laurentiis' mother-in-law saw him on an episode of "The Dating Game."

Fanboy Rating: Babes-7 Effects-5 Action-5 Brainwaves-2 Total=19

Flash Gordon

Flash Gordon (1980). Universal, 111min. **Director:** Mike Hodges. **Producer:** Dino De Laurentiis. **Screenwriters:** Lorenzo Semple Jr. Characters created by Alex Raymond. **Cinematographer:** Gil Taylor. **Film Editor:** Malcolm Cooke. **Cast:** Sam J. Jones, Melody Anderson, Max Von Sydow, Topol, Ornella Muti, Timothy Dalton, Brian Blessed, Richard O'Brien.

G-Girl

My Super Ex-Girlfriend (2006). 20th Century-Fox, 95 min. **Director:** Ivan Reitman. **Producers:** Gavin Polone and Arnon Milchan. **Screenwriter:** Don Payne. **Cinematographer:** Don Burgess. **Film Editors:** Wendy Greene Bricmont and Sheldon Kahn. **Production Designer:** Jane Musky. **Cast:** Uma Thurman, Luke Wilson, Anna Faris, Rainn Wilson, Eddie Izzard, Wanda Sykes.

First Comic Book Appearance: None.

Origins: G-Girl, also known as Jenny Johnson, was created by Don Payne for the 2006 film, "My Super Ex-Girlfriend," directed by Ivan Reitman. She has many of the same superpowers as Supergirl, including super strength, invulnerability, flight, super speed, heat vision, super hearing, super vision, and super breath. Like the Silver Age Supergirl (also known as Linda Lee Danvers), Jenny dons a brown wig and glasses to hide her identity. According to the back story, Jenny Johnson gained her superpowers in her junior year of high school. She had befriended a fellow geek named Barry, and then, one night, decided to consummate their relationship in the back seat of his car. Their romantic interlude was interrupted by a meteor that streaked through the sky and crashed in the woods near their parked car. When Jenny got out of the car to investigate and subsequently reached down to touch the glowing meteorite, it exploded, knocking her to her feet. Barry was also knocked down by the explosion. Moments later, he catches his first sight of the new Jenny. The geeky girl with the horned-rim glasses and brunette hair has been transformed into a beautiful and voluptuous blonde. In the days and weeks and months that followed this event, Jenny Johnson became one of the most popular girls at school, and in turn, left her friend Barry fall further and further behind her. He resented her popularity, and gradually sunk lower and lower into a depression that lasted for years. He eventually became her arch nemesis Professor Bedlam. Meanwhile, Jenny attended college, and learned to

hide her identity as G-Girl behind the guise of a geeky museum curator. As the superhero G-Girl, she protects the City of New York from all manner of human and natural disaster. In 2006, Professor Bedlam tried to strip G-Girl of her superpowers by arranging to have her exposed to another meteor. Instead of succeeding with his plan, he inadvertently created a sidekick for G-Girl out of passerby Hannah Lewis. The incident taught him a big lesson, and allowed him to forgive her and repair their strained relationship. Professor Bedlam has rehabilitated and is now dating Jenny Johnson.

First Media Appearance: G-Girl made her one and only media appearance in the 2006 comedy, "My Super Ex-Girlfriend."

The 2006 Film Version: When Matt Saunders (Luke Wilson) meets Jenny Johnson (Uma Thurman) on the New York subway, he thinks he's found the perfect girl…only she won't give him the time of day. Circumstances provide Saunders with an opportunity to play hero to Jenny, and suddenly, she realizes that she has found the perfect guy. After a few dates and some very hot sex, Jenny decides to tell Saunders the truth about her super identity as G-Girl. He flips out because, in his mind, that's better than dating a Victoria Secret model. Unfortunately, Jenny becomes too needy and controlling, and when she spots Saunders with another woman (Anna Faris as Hannah Lewis), she looses all sense of reality. Matt Saunders suggests that they take a break from their relationship, and starts dating Hannah. Jenny Johnson's jealousy gets the better of her, and as G-Girl, she uses her superpowers to get back at him (including throwing a great white shark into bed with he and Hannah). Professor Bedlam (Eddie Izzard) takes advantage of the lovers' spat in order to strip G-Girl of her superpowers. Instead of succeeding with his plan, he inadvertently turns Hannah into a superhero. He asks for Jenny's forgiveness, and the two rebuild their former relationship. In turn, Matt Saunders has exchanged one super girlfriend for another, but hopefully also learned his lesson. The Ivan Reitman comedy was not well received at the box office, and left the theaters after only a week in release. Hopefully, home video will allow viewers to catch up this pleasant little romantic comedy.

Trivial Matters: Uma Thurman played supervillainess Poison Ivy in "Batman and Robin" 1997.

Fanboy Rating: Babes-9 Effects-6 Action-4 Brainwaves-4 Total=23

G-Girl

Ghost Rider

Ghost Rider (2007). Columbia Pictures, 120min. **Director:** Mark Steven Johnson. **Producers:** Avi Arad, Gary Foster, and Steven Paul. **Screenwriter:** Mark Steven Johnson. **Cinematographers:** Russell Boyd and John Wheeler. **Film Editor:** Richard Francis-Bruce. **Production Designer:** Kirk Petruccelli. **Cast:** Nicolas Cage, Eva Mendes, Raquel Alessi, Wes Bentley, Laurence Breuls, Peter Callan, Sam Elliott, Donal Logue, Peter Fonda.

First Comic Book Appearance: "Marvel Spotlight #5" (August 1972). *Origins:* Several previous comic books were published using the title "The Ghost Rider." One that first appeared in 1949, and was created by Vincent Sullivan, Ray Krank, and Dick Ayers for Magazine Enterprises, featured a Western gunslinger named the Calico Kid. He later revealed himself to be federal marshal Rex Fury, who relied on his alter ego the Ghost Rider to scare confessions out of outlaws. In 1967, Marvel Comics swiped the whole story, and slapped on the new identity of Carter Slade on the Western lawman who road the horse Banshee and appeared as the Ghost Rider. He was later renamed Night Rider and then the Phantom Rider. When Marvel decided to update a number of its books in the early 1970s, the Ghost Rider was brought into the 20th Century by Roy Thomas and Mike Ploog riding a motorcycle instead of a horse. Johnny Blaze was an ordinary stunt rider who, because of his dealings with Mephisto, had become fused with the soul-eating demon Zarathos. At night, he'd change into a demon with a flaming skull that road the streets on a flaming motorcycle. Blaze eventually learned to control the demon within, and discovered that he could project hellfire, a kind of supernatural flame which burned the soul but not the victim's body. With a new lease on life, Johnny Blaze decided to fight evil on the highways and byways of the country…while still fighting the evil of the demon within him. The character received his own comic book series in 1973, and that ran until 1983 for 81 issues. In the final issue, Zarathos fled Blaze's body, and gave him back a normal life. In 1990, Danny Ketch, Johnny Blaze's long-lost brother, became the new Ghost Rider when a new demon took control. He fought supernatural meanies for eight years, and Johnny Blaze returned in a short-lived series.

First Media Appearance: The Ghost Rider made his first media appearance outside the world of comic books on the 1994 episode of the animated "Fantastic Four" titled "When Calls Galactus." Richard Grieco provided the voice. Ironically, Richard Grieco also directed a 2007 movie titled "The Ghost Riders," in which a group of outlaws in the 1880s are killed and come back to terrorize a small Western town.

Other Media Appearances: Johnny Blaze in the guise of his alter ego the Ghost Rider later appeared opposite the Hulk in an episode of the "Incredible Hulk" animated series on the UPN network in 1996. Eleven years later, Nicolas Cage strapped on the leather gear of Johnny Blaze in the 2007 live-action film "The Ghost Rider."

The 2007 Film Version: Nicolas Cage has been a fan of comic book superheroes most of his life, and in fact changed his name from Coppola to Cage out of deference to Marvel superhero Luke Cage. He has been attached to several live-action comic adaptations, including Superman, but he finally got his chance to play a comic book character in Mark Steven Johnson's "Ghost Rider" (2007). In the film version, young stunt cyclist Johnny Blaze (Matt Long) sells his soul to Mephisto (Peter Fonda) to save his dying father. The bargain also means that he looses his love, pure-hearted young Roxanne (Raquel Alessi). Years later, Johnny (Cage), now a great stunt performer, crosses paths with Roxanne (Eva Mendes) who is a television reporter. Mephisto also offers Johnny Blaze another bargain. He will release Johnny's soul if, and only if, Johnny agrees to become the fabled, fiery Ghost Rider – a supernatural agent of justice. Mephisto needs Ghost Rider to defeat Blackheart (Wes Bentley) before the demon's son can displace his father and make a new, more terrible place of Hell.

Trivial Matters: Jon Voight was attached as Johnny's father at one point but dropped out. Most of the film's indoor motorcycle sequences were filmed in Melbourne, Australia. The shotgun used in the movie is a Model 1887 Winchester lever-action shotgun.

Fanboy Rating: Babes-6 Effects-6 Action-4 Brainwaves-4 Total=20

Ghost Rider

Greatest American Hero

The Greatest American Hero (1981). Stephen J. Cannell Productions, 60min, 43 Episodes. **Director:** Rod Holcomb et al. **Producers:** Frank Lupo and Stephen K. Cannell. **Screenwriter:** Stephen J. Cannell. **Cinematographer:** Andrew Jackson. **Film Editor:** Christopher Nelson. **Production Designer:** John D. Jefferies Sr. **Cast:** William Katt, Robert Culp, Connie Sellecca, Don Cervantes, Michael Pare, William Bogert, Jesse Goins, Faye Grant, Brandon Williams.

First Comic Book Appearance: None
Origins: Created by Stephen J. Cannell, "The Greatest American Hero" was a television series that was launched by a two-hour pilot on March 18, 1981, and ran for three seasons (or 44 episodes) on ABC. The show was billed as a superhero comedy-drama, and introduced the world to the Greatest American Hero, or so the title would suggest. (Many still believe that Superman or Captain America is the greatest american hero.) The premise of the series followed the misadventures of school teacher Ralph Hinkley (William Katt) as he tried to master a superhero costume that was left to him and Special FBI Agent Bill Maxwell (Robert Culp) by aliens. The special bright red suit endowed him with superhuman abilities, like flight, super strength, invulnerability, invisibility, precognition, telekinesis, super speed, and X-ray vision, but unfortunately, on the night when the aliens left him the suit, he lost the instruction booklet. Together with Maxwell and his girlfriend Pam Davidson (Connie Sellecca), Ralph fumbled and bumbled his way through one crisis after another, all the time trying to make the world a safer place to live. The theme song, "Believe It or Not," which was composed by Mike Post and written by Stephen Gever, pretty much summed up the improbability of an average man that is suddenly endowed with superpowers than asked to save the world. Cannell had initially wanted the show to be about how Ralph dealt with typical human flaws like envy and hypochondria, but the ABC network pushed for more kiddie faire with Ralph saving the world from some sort of calamity every

week. Unfortunately, the show degenerated fast, and became more a comedy show for kids than a dramatic show for adults. Warner Brothers filed a lawsuit against "The Greatest American Hero" and ABC, charging that the show was a blatant rip-off of its big budget "Superman," but the lawsuit was eventually dismissed. Indeed, the show had borrowed many key elements from DC Comics' "Green Lantern," but not Superman. Green Lantern's powers are given to him by aliens in order to fight evil.

First Media Appearance: The television series debuted on ABC on March 18, 1981, as a two-hour pilot, with William Katt in the title role.

Other Media Appearances: In 1986, the original cast reunited for a pilot film for a new NBC series, titled "The Greatest American Heroine," but when the new series was rejected by executives, the pilot was never broadcast on television. Apparently, several years after the final episode of "The Greatest American Hero," Ralph Hinkley revealed his secret identity to the public. The aliens who first gave him the suit were upset, and demanded that he find a replacement. Ralph finds a young woman (Mary Ellen Stuart) who is an idealist just like him, and gifts her with new powers. Bill Maxwell then takes over and begins to train her in how to use the suit. This pilot was edited down and added to the syndication package.

The 1981 Television Film: The two-hour pilot told the origin story of the Greatest American Hero and set the tone for the rest of the series. Teacher Ralph Hinkley (William Katt) is taking his high school students on a field trip when suddenly the school bus that he is driving takes over and mysteriously drives itself out into the desert. At the same time, Special FBI agent Bill Maxwell (Robert Culp) swerves to miss the bus, and ends up in the same locale. Out in the Southern California desert, at night, they are visited by "little green men" who give them a special red suit that was designed for Ralph. Ralph becomes a reluctant hero as Maxwell goads him on to use the superhero costume for good against the evil forces of the world. If only he hadn't lost the instruction booklet! Since the series ended in 1983, several attempts have been made to make a feature film. Disney tried in 2002, and more recently, a big screen version was announced to be in the planning stages in 2004.

Trivial Matters: Ralph's last name was changed from Hinkley to Hanley during the first season when John Hinckley tried to kill Ronald Reagan; the executives didn't want to use the name because of its negative connection; fans objected to the change, and Ralph's name was changed back in the second season. Beautiful Faye Grant became a resistance leader on "V."

Fanboy Rating: Babes-6 Effects-3 Action-4 Brainwaves-5 Total=18

Greatest Am. Hero

The Green Hornet

The Green Hornet (1940). Universal, B&W, 258min, 13 episodes. **Directors:** Ford Beebe and Ray Taylor. **Producer:** Henry MacRae. **Screenwriters:** George Plympton, Basil Dickey, Morrison Wood, Lyonel Margolies. Based upon characters by Fran Striker. **Cinematographers:** Jerome Ash, William Sickner. **Film Editors:** Joseph Gluck, Irving Birnbaum, Alvin Todd. **Cast:** Gordon Jones, Wade Boteler, Anne Nagel, Keye Luke.

First Appearance: "The Green Hornet" radio show (January 31, 1936)
First Comic Book Appearance: "Green Hornet Comics #1" (Dec. 1940)
Origins: The character of the Green Hornet first appeared on WXYZ radio station in Detroit, Michigan, on January 31, 1936, and was created by station manager George W. Trendle, who had also created "The Lone Ranger," and written by Fran Striker. Britt Reid whose alter ego was the Green Hornet was also the nephew of John Reid, the Lone Ranger. Like his predecessor, the Green Hornet fought crime wearing a green mask and carrying a gas gun instead of a six-shooter; he drove the Black Beauty instead of riding Silver and had a sidekick in Filipino-born Kato (not Japanese-born) in place of Native American Tonto. His theme music was Rimsky-Korsakov's "Flight of the Bumble Bee" instead of the "William Tell Overture." And very much in keeping with the Lone Ranger's opening prologue ("A fiery horse with the speed of light, a cloud of dust and a hearty Hi-Yo Silver…"), the Green Hornet opened each night with a voice decrying, "With his faithful valet Kato, Britt Reid, daring young publisher, matches wits with the underworld, risking his life that criminals and racketeers within the law may feel its weight by the sting of the Green Hornet." The debonair newspaper publisher by day and crime-fighter at night faced all manner of menace from 1936 to 1952 when the radio show was finally cancelled. "The Green Hornet" first featured Al Hodge, then Donovan Frost, Robert Hall, and Jack McCarthy in the title role. Naturally, the show was so popular that it was also adapted to comic books and film.

Other Media Appearances: Following the radio drama as his first media appearance, the Green Hornet went on to headline two serials for Universal. He also appeared in his first comic book, published by Helnit (later Harvey), in December 1940. In 1967, along with a three-issue series produced by Gold Key Comics, the Green Hornet appeared as a co-star on "Batman," then headlined his own series. More recently, Kevin Smith has produced a screenplay which he hopes to make with Jet Li as Kato and Jake Gyllenhaal as the Green Hornet. The start date is unknown.

The 1940 Film Serial: Universal produced a thirteen-part film serial in 1940 based upon the popular radio drama. Intrepid newspaper publisher Britt Reid (Gordon Jones) watches helplessly as the crime rate rises and racketeering increases. He realizes that he must do something about it. Donning a disguise, the Green Hornet becomes a crime fighter when the sun sets at night. With his brilliant Korean manservant Kato (Key Luke), who is also an inventor and martial arts master, the two vigilantes fight a never-ending battle against an infamous racket that is menacing their city. The serial jettisoned most of the background story from the popular radio show, but maintained the Hornet's gas gun and, of course, the Black Beauty. It was not one of the best serials ever produced by Universal, but still packed a punch for those who showed up every Saturday afternoon.

Trivial Matters: The character of Kato was made Korean because of World War 2. When Green Hornet's Black Beauty moves on screen, the soundtrack contains the sound of a buzzing hornet.

Fanboy Rating: Babes-1 Effects-2 Action-2 Brainwaves-2 Total=7

The 1967 Television Series: The Green Hornet was reborn as a spin-off of ABC's campy "Batman" television series with Van Williams in the title role and Bruce Lee as Kato. Unlike "Batman," however, the television series was played straight. Each adventure placed our heroes in grave danger in which they had to rely on their wits and skills as crimefighters to resolve. The larger-than-life villains were kept to a minimum, and action was emphasized over camp. The series made Bruce Lee a star, and launched his career as a martial artist. The other star of the show was the Green Hornet's Black Beauty, a 1965 Chrysler Imperial customized by Dean Jeffries. The series was canceled after only one season.

Fanboy Rating: Babes-3 Effects-3 Action-5 Brainwaves-5 Total=16

Green Hornet

Hellboy

Hellboy (2004). Columbia/Sony Pictures, 122min. **Director:** Guillermo del Toro. **Producers:** Lawrence Gordon, Lloyd Levin, and Mike Richardson. **Screenwriters:** Guillermo del Toro and Peter Briggs. Characters created by Mike Mignola. **Cinematographer:** Guillermo Navarro. **Film Editor:** Peter Amundson. **Production Designer:** Stephen Scott. **Cast:** Ron Perlman, John Hurt, Selma Blair, Rupert Evans, Karel Roden, Jeffrey Tambor, Doug Jones, Brian Steele.

First Comic Book Appearance: "SDCC Comics #2" (July 1993)

Origins: Hellboy was first brought to life by cartoonist Mike Mignola in a four-page story that ran in "San Diego Comic-Con Comics #2, given out at the 1993 San Diego Comic Book Convention. The four-page story was presented to promote a four-issue mini-series from Dark Horse Comics, titled "Hellboy: Seed of Destruction." Heavily influenced by H.P. Lovecraft, Edgar Allan Poe, and Jack Kirby, the origin story told how Hellboy was brought into the real world by Nazi occultists. In 1944, Hitler orders a mysterious man named Grigori Rasputin with a background in the occult to use all of his powers to come up with a solution that will reverse the tide of the war. He gathers a team of Nazi occultists on Tarmagant Island, a small island just off the coast of Scotland, to summon a demon named Anung Un Rama to fight on the side of Germany, but the experiment they perform on December 23rd produces nothing, or so they think. 100 miles away, in East Bromwich, England, a demon-child suddenly appears to Professor Trevor Bruttenholm who gave the red-skinned, horned demon a home and the name "Hellboy." Bruttenholm discovers that, while Hellboy may appear to be a demon, he is not actually an evil creature. He knows the difference between right and wrong, and chooses to do right. Allied forces subsequently rescue Bruttenholm and the demon, and bring them to the United States' Bureau for Paranormal Research and Defense. For the next half-century, Hellboy grew up and became a chief operative of the BPRD. Together with Elizabeth Sherman and Abraham Sapien, two

other gifted agents, they function as a team of superheroes who fight the forces of evil and combat occult threats of the supernatural. Hellboy actually gains honorary human status, as granted by the United Nations, in 1952. While the extent of Hellboy's powers are unclear, he does posses super strength, particularly in his right hand which is made of red stone. He can also endure more physical pain than most, and has an uncanny sense of when evil is near. He also carries a large pistol known as the Samaritan. In one of the early stories, Grigori Rasputin returns, and tries to influence Hellboy, but he fails to turn our hero bad.

First Media Appearance: Hellboy made his one and only media appearance in the guise of Ron Perlman in Guillermo del Toro's 2004 film "Hellboy," and has yet to resurface.

The 2004 Film Version: To director Guillermo del Toro, "Hellboy" was as a dream project that he had wanted to make ever since he read the comic book back in 1993. He endowed the film with a great deal of energy and fun that most fans appreciated. Unfortunately, the film debuted opposite "The Passion of the Christ," and suffered miserably at the box office for no other reason than its provocative title. In the film version, Hellboy's origin is established in the opening minutes, and then he is teamed with geeky new agent John Myers (Rupert Evans) for the boy's first assignment. Hellboy (Ron Perlman) teaches the boy the ropes, and in between, he takes time to romance the love of his life Liz Sherman (Selma Blair), a pyro-telekinetic. When Rasputin (Karl Roden) returns once again, accompanied by the maniacal, undead assassin Kroenen (Ladislav Beran) and monks faithful to his lover Ilsa (Biddy Hodson), Hellboy springs into action. Perlman is delightful in the title role, and Selma Blair does a star turn as Liz. Del Toro announced a follow-up movie for 2008.

Trivial Matters: Ron Perlman has become the new master of a thousand faces, with turns as the Beast in the "Beauty and the Beast" television series, Reinhardt in "Blade 2," Johner in "Alien: Resurrection," and "Hellboy" (2004). The studio wanted Vin Diesel to play Hellboy, and Del Toro had to convince them that Ron Perlman was the better choice.

Fanboy Rating: Babes-4 Effects-5 Action-7 Brainwaves-5 Total=21

Hellboy

He-Man

Masters of the Universe (1987). Cannon, 106min. **Director:** Gary Goddard. **Producers:** Yoram Globus and Menahem Golan. **Screenwriters:** David Odell and Donald F. Glut. **Cinematographer:** Hanania Baer. **Film Editor:** Anne V. Coates. **Production Designer**: William Stout. **Cast:** Dolph Lundgren, Frank Langella, Meg Foster, Billy Barty, Courtney Cox, Robert Duncan McNeill, Jon Cypher, Christina Pickles.

First Comic Book Appearance: "Masters of the Universe" (Dec. 1982) *Origins:* He-Man, Skeletor, Teela, and the other Masters of the Universe were actually part of a line of toys designed by Roger Sweet and produced by Mattel Toys in 1982. At first, Mattel had wanted to produce toys for the "Conan" movie, but when the company saw the film's violent and often bloody content, they turned to Sweet to create a whole new line. These few characters, a Castle Grayskull playset, and a dozen other separately-sold items were launched as part of a grand publicity campaign in a short-lived 1982 DC Comics series, titled "Masters of the Universe," and an animated television series from Filmation that premiered in 1983 and ran for 130 episodes until 1985. The show was set on the extra-dimensional world of Eternia, which borrows elements from medieval and barbarian worlds, and featured all sorts of prehistoric creatures and high-tech weapons and vehicles. The premise was a simple one: In the aftermath of a great war that has devastated all of the kingdoms of Eternia, He-Man wanders the wasteland in search of a purpose for his being. He is, in fact, Prince Adam, the son of King Randor of Eternia and Queen Marlena of Earth, the last rulers of Eternia, but his secret identity is not revealed until much later in the series. The Sorceress of Castle Grayskull endows He-Man with special powers and weapons, so that he can defend the Castle against the evil villain Skeletor. By holding a magic sword above his head and proclaiming, "By the power of Grayskull, I have the power," He-Man is transformed into a mighty warrior. His pet tiger Cringer also

transforms from a cowardly animal into a fierce-some Battle Cat. Later, He-Man was given a powerful and strong-willed girlfriend in Teela, the female Captain of the Royal Guard, and teamed with other allies to fight the forces of evil. He also learned that he had a twin sister named Adora, who became She-Ra, Princess of Powers. The series was well received, and eventually spawned a whole industry of products, shows, and one big-budget, feature film.

First Media Appearance: He-Man first appeared as a toy action figure from Mattel Toys for the 1982 Christmas season.

Other Media Appearances: He-Man later headlined a long-running animated series from Filmation Studios, with John Erwin providing the voice. In 1987, the barbarian hero was played by Dolph Lundgren in a live-action film. He-Man re-surfaced in "The New Adventures of He-Man," with Cary Chalk providing the voice, in the 1989 animated series. A third animated series, with Cam Clarke as He-Man, debuted in 2002 series.

The 1987 Film Version: In 1987, Cannon Films snapped up the rights to the Mattel character, and produced a somewhat hastily assembled feature film with Dolph Lundgren in the role as He-Man. Skeletor (Frank Langella) has finally managed to seize Castle Grayskull, source of He-Man's power on the planet Eternia, and plans to bring the rest of the planet to its knees with a cosmic key that the Thenorian locksmith Gwildor (Billy Barty) has developed. But first, he delights in torturing the Sorceress (Christina Pickles) as he waits for the Great Eye of the Universe to bestow god-like powers on him. He-Man and his friends break into Grayskull, free Gwildor, and race to save the Sorceress when they are surrounded by Skeletor's superior forces. Gwildor triggers the cosmic key, and teleports He-Man and his friends to Earth so they can escape. Skeletor and his minions, including Evil Lyn (Meg Foster), follow. On Earth, He-Man teams with a pair of teenagers (Courtney Cox and Robert Duncan McNeill) in an effort to rally support to defeat Skeletor once and for all. The film was savaged by fans and critics alike, and even Lundgren was embarrassed by it.

Trivial Matters: After the final credits, Skeletor's head pops back up, and decries, "I'll be back!" which supposedly set the stage for a sequel that was never produced. Instead the script was re-written for Jean-Claude Van Damme and became "Cyborg" (1989). Much of the film was filmed in Whittier, California.

Fanboy Rating: Babes-5 Effects-5 Action-5 Brainwaves-1 Total=16

He-Man

Heroes

Heroes (2006). NBC/Universal Television, 60min, 22 Episodes. **Directors:** Greg Beeman and Allan Arkush. **Producer:** Tim Kring. **Screenwriters:** Tim Kring and Natalie Chaidez. **Cinematographer:** John B. Aronson. **Production Designer:** Curtis Schnell. **Cast:** James Kyson Lee, Hayden Panettiere, Masi Oka, Sandil Ramamurthy, Ali Larter, Adrian Pasdar, Milo Ventimiglia, Jack Coleman, Tawny Cypress, Greg Grunberg, Santiago Cabrera, Ashley Crow, Jimmy Jean-Louis.

First Comic Book Appearance: "Heroes #1" (Online, September 2006)
Origins: "Heroes" is the brainchild of Tim Kring, who had earlier written for a show about superheroes, titled "Misfits of Science." The series, which premiered on September 25, 2006, on NBC television, tells the story of a handful of ordinary people from different walks of life that discover they have extraordinary powers. Cheerleader Claire Bennet (Hayden Panettiere) has the ability to spontaneously regenerate tissue, and is therefore invulnerable. Isaac Mendez (Santiago Cabrera) can paint future events during precognitive trances, and his comic book series, titled "9th Wonders!," is a chronicle of future history. Hiro Nakamura (Masi Oka) has the ability to manipulate the time-space continuum, while Matt Parkman (Greg Grunberg) can hear other people's thoughts. Nathan Petrelli (Adrian Pasdar) can fly, and his brother Peter (Milo Ventimiglia) has the ability to mimic the powers of others. Niki Sanders (Ali Larter) has an alternate personality that exhibits superhuman strength. Her son Micah (Noah Gray-Cabey) is a child prodigy, and her estranged husband D.L. Hawkins (Leonard Roberts) can phase through solid objects. None of them know how they came by their superpowers, but with the help of Mohinder Suresh (Sendhil Ramamurthy), a genetics professor from India, these people soon realize that they have a role to play in preventing a catastrophe and saving mankind. The first few episodes, which were advertised with the tagline "Ordinary people discovering extraordinary abilities," focused on how each of them discovered their powers, and Mohinder's discovery that his father

may have been tracking them for years. The show also introduced Claire's adoptive father (Jack Coleman) as an agent for an organization that tracks and abducts people with superhuman abilities. The next few episodes, which carried the slogan "Save the cheerleader, save the world," detailed how some of them came together to save Claire from Sylar (Zachary Quinto), a serial killer who ingests the powers of other superheroes. The final few episodes, which had a new tagline ("Are you on the list?"), followed them to New York and the great catastrophe (New York City nuked!) ahead. Fan favorite Hiro Nakamura was also forced to steal an ancient Japanese sword from Mr. Linderman (Malcolm McDowell) in order to reclaim his "mojo." A slight detour to a dystopian future revealed that Sylar had taken Nathan's identity as President of the United States and was rounding up the remaining heroes with the help of Parkman and Suresh. Only Tim Kring knows where the story is ultimately headed, but he claims that he has enough material for the show to go five seasons.

First Media Appearance: A special 72-minute version of the pilot was first screened to a large audience at the 2006 San Diego Comic Book Convention, and the heroes of "Heroes" first became media sensations.

Other Media Appearances: At the NBC website for the show, visitors have the opportunity to read pages from "9th Wonders!," the meta-fictional comic book series that is a part of the "Heroes" television show. In the show, it is written, illustrated, and self-published by Isaac Mendez, but in reality, it is the work of comic book veteran Tim Sale. Sale is best known for his work on DC Comics' "Batman: The Long Halloween."

Trivial Matters: Hiro, Ando, Niki and Nathan all visit the Montecito hotel/casino in the early episodes of the first season; the Montecito is actually the fictional casino featured on the NBC television series "Las Vegas" (2003). During one conversation between Hiro and Ando, Ando warns Hiro not to step on any butterflies when he is time-traveling. This is a reference to Ray Bradbury's short story "A Sound of Thunder." George Takei who played Sulu on "Star Trek" was hired as Hiro Nakamura's wealthy father.

Fanboy Rating: Babes-9 Effects-2 Action-7 Brainwaves-9 Total=27

Heroes

Howard the Duck

Howard the Duck (1986). Universal/Lucasfilm, 111min. **Director:** Willard Huyck. **Producer:** Gloria Katz and George Lucas. **Screenwriters:** Willard Huyck and Gloria Katz. Characters created by Steve Gerber. **Cinematographer:** Richard Kline. **Film Editors:** Michael Chandler and Sidney Wolinsky. **Production Designer:** Peter Jamison. **Cast:** Lea Thompson, Jeffrey Jones, Tim Robbins, Ed Gale, Chip Zien, Timothy Rose, Paul Guilfoyle.

First Comic Book Appearance: "Adventure into Fear #19" (Dec. 1973). *Origins:* Howard the Duck accidentally slipped through a dimensional warp in the 19th issue of Marvel Comic's "Adventure into Fear" comic, and ended up in a world where superheroes ruled instead of funny animals. Howard was the creation of Steve Gerber, and while initially the idea of a cartoon duck (like Daffy Duck or Donald Duck) in the fictional world of Spider-Man and the Fantastic Four must have seemed like a good idea at the time, the idea began to wear thin very quickly. At first, he appeared opposite the Man-Thing; then, in January 1976, Marvel gave him his own comic book. Disney threatened to sue Marvel, and then creator Steve Gerber sued Marvel, claiming his ownership made Howard a property he could take to rival Eclipse Comics. Marvel won both suits, and continued to publish "Howard the Duck" comics. Howard's somewhat irreverent approach to situations made him popular with intellectuals who normally would not have read comic books, but his character did not sit well with the mainstream comic fan. His series' tagline, "Trapped in a world he never made…" appealed to those existentialist readers who knew exactly what Gerber was trying to do with his most unorthodox figure. After his comic was finally canceled, Howard the Duck continued to appear in team-ups with "The Defenders" and other Marvel characters. He might have disappeared altogether had it not been for the first class turkey of a film that George Lucas made after "Star Wars" (1977), and alas, he has remained in the public's eye ever since.

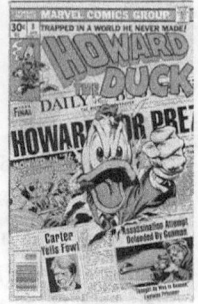

First Media Appearance: Howard the Duck made his one and only media appearance in the guise of Ed Gale with the voice of Chip Zien in the big-budget flop "Howard the Duck" (1986), and thankfully has not resurfaced in over twenty years.

The 1986 Film Version: What possessed George Lucas to team up with Universal Pictures to produce this 1986 turkey is still a matter of speculation and rumor! In the film, Howard is transported to the city of Cleveland by a laser experiment gone wrong by Dr. Walter Jenning (Jeffrey Jones). The sarcastic duck isn't the only being pulled to Earth by Jenning's experiments. The Dark Overlord of the Universe, whose only intent was to destroy peaceful planets like the Earth, is also summoned. Beverly Switzler (Lea Thompson), who is a rock singer, finds Howard and tries to get him back home. But of course he has to help us poor humans deal with the Dark Overlord before he is allowed to return home. The film was widely panned when it was released in 1986, and remains as one of the worst films ever made.

Trivial Matters: Howard the Duck landed on Earth on September 8, the date in 1966 that "Star Trek" (1966) premiered on NBC. Phoebe Cates and Tori Amos were considered for the role of Beverly Switzler, a character from the comic book, before Lea Thompson won the part. George Lucas spent $2 million on the Howard the duck suit, and eight different actors worked inside the costume. When the film bombed at the box office, Lucas blamed the live-action duck, and launched a new CGI animation division to produce special effects that could be integrated with live action.

Fanboy Rating: Babes-1 Effects-0 Action-1 Brainwaves-0 Total=2

Howard Duck

The Hulk

The Incredible Hulk (1977). Universal, 120min. **Director:** Kenneth Johnson. **Producer:** Kenneth Johnson. **Screenwriter:** Kenneth Johnson. Based upon characters created by Stan Lee and Jack Kirby. **Cinematographer:** Howard Schwartz. **Film Editors**: Alan Marks and Jack W. Schoengarth. **Cast:** Billy Bixby, Lou Ferrigno, Susan Sullivan, Jack Colwin, Susan Batson, Mario Gallo, Charles Siebert.

First Comic Book Appearance: "The Incredible Hulk #1" (May 1962)
Origins: Before Stan Lee and Jack Kirby created "The Fantastic Four" and launched the Silver Age of comic book superheroes at Marvel, they created a handful of monsters with goofy names like Rommbu, Fin Fang Foom, and Googam, Son of Goom that appeared in "Tales of Suspense" and "Strange Tales." The Hulk was the last of their monsters who, in turn, became one of the team's earliest superheroes. "The Incredible Hulk #1," which debuted in May 1962, told the story of how scientist Robert Bruce Banner rescued Rick Jones from the detonation of an experimental gamma bomb but still absorbed a full dose of gamma radiation. That first night, Banner undergoes the first of many transformations into the super-strong brute known as the Hulk; the Hulk was colored gray in his first comic book appearance, but later changed to the signature green because of a problem with the printer. The only person who knows about the Hulk's human identity is Rick Jones. The comic series only lasted six issues, and was canceled, but in those six issues, the whole backstory was created. For instance, many early Hulk stories featured General Thaddeus "Thunderbolt" Ross trying to capture or destroy the Hulk with his U.S. Army troops. Ross's daughter Betty loves Banner, and while she does not know about his secret identity, she derides her father for trying to kill the Hulk. Other details included having Bruce Banner change into the Hulk at sunset each day, but that was later changed to when the scientist became angry or upset. After the book was canceled, the Hulk made regular appear-

ances in "The Avengers," "Fantastic Four," and "Tales to Astonish." "Tales to Astonish" was eventually re-titled "The Incredible Hulk," and the green monster continued to headline that comic book until 1999. Several writers have tinkered with the Hulk story, making him the victim of multiple personalities or linking him to some supernatural force. Banner's cousin Jennifer Walters has also been added as the She-Hulk. But after all of the dust has settled, the Hulk remains a mutation created when Bruce Banner received a high dose of gamma radiation while saving a teenager. Banner's Jekyll and Hyde relationship with the Hulk has continued to make the comic book series a very real one.

First Media Appearance: Like Captain America, Iron Man, Thor and the Sub-Mariner, the Hulk made his first media appearance on the Marvel Super Heroes animated television series in 1966.

Other Media Appearances: In 1977, Kenneth Johnson developed the Hulk into a weekly series for CBS that featured Bill Bixby as Dr. David Banner and Lou Ferrigno as the Hulk. (See below.) The series ran for five seasons on CBS and inspired three television movies. After the Hulk appeared on an episode of "Spider-Man and His Amazing Friends" (1991), Marvel Studios and Saban Entertainment created an animated series, titled "The Incredible Hulk" (1996), which featured the voice of Lou Ferrigno as the Hulk. Academy Award-winning director Ang Lee brought his enormous talents to bear on a big budget "Hulk" movie with Eric Bana in the titular role as Bruce Banner and the Hulk. Finally, the Hulk appeared in both of the animated "Ultimate Avengers" movies (in 2006). At the San Diego Comic Con in 2006, Louis Leterrier announced that a second live-action "Hulk" movie was being prepared for a 2008 release.

The 1977 Television Series: "The Incredible Hulk" television series was launched in 1977 by a two-hour television movie produced, written and directed by Kenneth Johnson. It featured Bill Bixby as David (not Bruce) Banner, and bodybuilder Lou Ferrigno as his alter ego, the Hulk. When his wife dies in a tragic car accident that he was helpless to present and save, David Banner begins researching how to tap the hidden powers of strength that he believes are in all of us. He interviews and examines many people who have displayed this kind of super strength, and determines

The Hulk

that the unknown factor is gamma radiation. Convinced that he is right, he deliberately overdoses himself with gamma radiation. He does not notice an immediate effect, but later, when he injures himself while changing a car tire in the rain, the rage and frustration transform him into a massively powerful green giant known as the Hulk. He eventually changes back, and realizes that he has experienced something both wondrous and frightening. He enlists the aide of a fellow scientist, Dr. Elaina Marks (Susan Sullivan), but when she is killed in a freak accident, he becomes a fugitive. Reluctantly, David Banner leaves his home behind to wander the country in search of a cure, with Jack McGee (Jack Colvin), an investigative reporter, always on his trail. The series was patterned after "The Fugitive" (1963), the Roy Huggins series that featured David Janssen as Dr. Richard Kimble, a fugitive running from the law. And each week, like "The Fugitive," David Banner met a new guest star who needed his help. This premise was popular enough that it gave the series an unusually long lifespan.

Trivial Matters: At first, the casting directors sought Arnold Schwarzenegger for the role of the Hulk, but Kenneth Johnson didn't think he was tall enough. They then cast Richard Kiel, who played Jaws in "Moonraker" (1979), but Johnson didn't think he was bulky enough for the role. Finally, they settled on Lou Ferrigno. The haunting theme song played at the end of the episodes was "Superheroes" from "The Rocky Horror Picture Show," written by Richard O'Brien.

Fanboy Rating: Babes-2 Effects-3 Action-3 Brainwaves-3 Total=11

The Incredible Hulk Returns (1988). Universal, 100min. **Director:** Nicholas Corea. **Producer:** Bill Bixby. **Screenwriter:** Nicholas Corea. Based upon characters created by Stan Lee and Jack Kirby. **Cinematographer:** Chuck Colwell. **Film Editors**: Janet Ashikaga and Briana London. **Cast:** Billy Bixby, Lou Ferrigno, Jack Colwin, Lee Purcell, Charles Napier, Tim Thomerson, Eric Kramer.

The 1988 Television Movie Sequel: When Universal packaged several of its episodes as movies for release to the European market and then released the balance of the episodes in syndication in the United States, "The Incredible Hulk" demonstrated an incredible vitality that was lacking in most series of the day. Under the guidance of Nicholas Corea, Univer-

sal produced several made-for-the-television movies. The first, "The Incredible Hulk Returns," takes place two years after the Hulk disappeared at the end of the television series. (Yes, we know that six years have actually passed!) Dr David Bruce Banner (Bixby) needs the Gamma Transponder, a device which he helped to create, to finally cure himself of the Hulk. At the same time, Thor's (Eric Kramer) hammer has been stolen and found its way into the hands of Don Blake (Steve Levitt), a former colleague of Banner's. The hammer is a mystic weapon capable of summoning the god of war to do anyone's bidding. When the Gamma Transponder is nearly stolen and Banner's girlfriend Maggie Shaw (Lee Purcell) is kidnapped, Banner is forced to give up his plans of being cured and rely on the Hulk and Thor to save the day. Naturally, Jack McGee (Colvin) is there to hound Banner every step of the way. The television movie was good but not great; however, it did do big business in the overseas market, and spawned two additional sequels.

Trivial Matters: Universal had hoped the television movie would serve as a pilot for a proposed "Thor" television series, but failed to generate much interest. The character of Thor bears very little resemblance to the comic book character.

Fanboy Rating: Babes-2 Effects-1 Action-2 Brainwaves-2 Total=7

The Trial of the Incredible Hulk (1989). Universal, 100min. **Director:** Bill Bixby. **Producer:** Bill Bixby. **Screenwriter:** Gerald Di Pego. Based upon characters created by Stan Lee and Jack Kirby. **Cinematographer:** Chuck Colwell. **Film Editor**: Janet Ashikaga. **Cast:** Billy Bixby, Lou Ferrigno, Rex Smith, John Rhys-Davies, Nancy Everheard, Joseph Mascolo.

The 1989 Television Movie Sequel: This second of three made-for-the-television movies found David Banner (Bixby) on trail for a crime that he didn't commit while traveling through the city. His court-appointed attorney is the blind Matt Murdock (Rex Smith), who is also the superhero

The Hulk

Daredevil. Murdock doesn't believe Banner is guilty, and strives to show that the city's resident crime lord, the Kingpin (John Rhys-Davies), is responsible. Murdock does to see a woman (Nancy Everhard) to change her story, but she is far too afraid. Later, when she is alone in her room, someone tries to kill her, but Daredevil comes to the rescue. In time, we learn that Matt Murdock had a very similar accident with radioactive materials, and that left him blind but with very heightened senses of smell, hearing, taste and touch. Together, Daredevil and the Hulk (Ferrigno) work to expose the Kingpin for who he truly is. While this one was grittier and more dynamic than the first, the ratings for these made-for-the-television movies had begun to drop off substantially. If it hadn't been for the overseas market, Universal may have ended with this second movie.

Trivial Matters: Daredevil's costume in the movie is black, despite the fact that his costume is dark-red in the comics. John Rhys-Davies may have had the girth to play Kingpin, but with a full head of hair and beard, he looked nothing like the character from the comic book series. Hulk appears in his trademark purple pants for the first and only time.

Fanboy Rating: Babes-1 Effects-2 Action-2 Brainwaves-2 Total=7

The Death of the Incredible Hulk (1990). Universal, 95min. **Director:** Bill Bixby. **Producer:** Bill Bixby. **Screenwriter:** Gerald Di Pego. Based upon characters created by Stan Lee and Jack Kirby. **Cinematographer:** Chuck Colwell. **Film Editor**: Janet Ashikaga. **Cast:** Billy Bixby, Lou Ferrigno, Elizabeth Gracen, Philip Sterling, Barbara Tarbuck, Anna Katarina.

The 1990 Television Movie Sequel: In this third, and final, television movie, David Banner (Bixby) falls in love with the Eastern European spy Jasmin (Elizabeth Gracen) who has destroyed his laboratory during a critical experiment. She tells Banner that she did it because her sister (Anna Katarina) is being held by Jasmin's superiors. Together, Banner and Jasmin escape enemy agents, and try to rescue her sister. Unfortunately, the film ends with the Hulk taking a fatal fall from an aircraft.

Trivial Matters: A fourth television movie, alternately titled "Rebirth of the Incredible Hulk" or "Revenge of the Incredible Hulk," was planned, but Bixby's death in 1993 ended any further discussion.

Fanboy Rating: Babes-2 Effects-2 Action-2 Brainwaves-2 Total=8

The 2003 Film Version: Eric Bana took over his role as the long-suffering scientist, Bruce Banner. Directed by Ang Lee, the film told a greatly altered origin story. Geneticist Bruce Banner suffers a terrible accident in the lab that leaves his extraordinary mind in an altered state of consciousness. He begins to see people and places that are not really there, and learns that his father David Banner (Nick Nolte) was following a very similar experiment that left him debilitated. Anger turns to rage, and when Banner is unable to control the rage, he transforms into the brute known as the Hulk. Betty Ross (Jennifer Connelly) wants to care for him, but her father, General Thaddeus "Thunderbolt" Ross (Sam Elliott), only wants to destroy the Hulk. Ultimately, his father's rage turns him into an evil monster that turns everything it touches to evil (including two Hulk dogs), and the Hulk must now save the world and its people from his out of control rages. The added psychological dimension adds far more gravitas to Lee's retelling of the Hulk origin, but overall, most fans criticized the over use of CGI effects in telling the story. A sequel, titled "The Incredible Hulk," is planned for a 2008 release with Edward Norton and Liv Tyler.

Trivial Matters: Lou Ferrigno cameos as a security guard opposite Stan Lee while he is leaving the BioTech Institute. Steve Buscemi, Billy Crudup, David Duchovny, Jeff Goldblum, Tom Cruise, Johnny Depp were all originally considered for the role that went to Eric Bana. The Hulk doesn't show up in his full form until 42 minutes into the movie.

Fanboy Rating: Babes-7 Effects-4 Action-3 Brainwaves-3 Total=17

The Hulk (2003). Universal, 138min. **Director:** Ang Lee. **Producer:** Avi Arad, Larry Franco, Gale Anne hurd. **Screenwriters:** James Schamus, John Turman, Michael France. Characters created by Stan Lee and Jack Kirby. **Cinematographer:** Frederick Elmes. **Film Editor:** Tim Squyres. **Production Designer:** Rick Heinrichs. **Cast:** Eric Bana, Jennifer Connelly, Sam Elliott, Josh Lucas, Nick Nolte, Paul Kersey.

The Hulk

The Incredibles

The Incredibles (2004). Disney and Pixar Animation, 115min. **Director:** Brad Bird. **Producer:** John Walker. **Screenwriter:** Brad Bird. **Cinematographers:** Andrew Jimenez, Patrick Lin, and Janet Lucroy. **Film Editor:** Stephen Schaffer. **Production Designer:** Lou Romano. **Cast:** Craig T. Nelson, Holly Hunter, Samuel L. Jackson, Jason Lee, Dominique Louis, Sarah Vowell, Spencer Fox.

First Comic Book Appearance: "The Incredibles #1" (November 2004) *Origins:* Created by Brad Bird, who had worked as a director on "The Simpsons" (1989), the 2004 Academy Award-winning animated feature film from Pixar Animation Studios, "The Incredibles," was a loving tribute, parody and pastiche of superhero movies. In a parallel universe where superheroes are real, the government is forced to crack down and ban all superhero activity because of a wave of lawsuits resulting from destruction of private property and other reckless acts of endangerment. Mr. Incredible/Bob Parr (Craig T. Nelson), his wife Elastigirl/Helen (Holly Hunter), and his friend Frozone/Lucius (Samuel L. Jackson) are banned from saving the world. Fifteen years later, Bob works as an insurance claims adjuster for an immoral insurance company, and has three children with Helen, including fourteen-year-old Violet (Sarah Vowell) who has invisibility and force-shield powers, ten-year-old Dash (Spencer Fox) who has incredible speed, and baby Jack-Jack (Eli Fucile) whose powers have yet to emerge. Bob and Lucius still secretly moonlight as superheroes, fighting crime, but more often than not, that angers Helen who wants them to live as a normal family. (She still relies on her elastic powers to control her children, however.) When Bob is approached by Mirage (Elizabeth Pena) to perform a secret mission for an unnamed government agency, he pumps himself back into shape and sets off on the mission. He disappears on an unknown island, while trying to destroy an out-of-control robot called the Omnidroid. Helen knows that something is wrong, and consults with Edna

Mode (Brad Bird), a former costume designer for superheroes. She confesses that she's made Bob a new costume, and Helen takes a new one home for her and her kids. Meanwhile, Bob has learned that Buddy Pine (Jason Lee), a former, would-be sidekick, has killed most of the other superheroes as part of an evil plan as Syndrome to rule the world. His plans to kill Mr. Incredible are thwarted when Helen and her two oldest children show up, but Buddy gets away. United as a family, the Incredibles must stop Buddy and save the world one more time. Bird's fondness for superheroes provides him with a unique opportunity to pay tribute to the comic books that he loved as a kid as well as make some biting, satirical comments about our world and its desire for political correctness.

Parallels to Other Superheroes: The most obvious parallel is with Marvel Comics' "The Fantastic Four." Elastigirl shares the same superpowers as Mister Fantastic; Violet's powers are identical to those used by the Invisible Woman, and Dash moves with the kind of speed that is exhibited by the Human Torch, minus of course the flame. Mr. Incredible shows the incredible brute strength of the Thing. Even baby Jack-Jack remind us of young Franklin Richards. Both teams wear similar costumes, and they are both a family. Syndrome is not unlike Dr. Doom, while the Underminer recalls Mole Man, the villain the FF faced in their first issue. Aside from the Fantastic Four, many other parallels abound. The Incredibles live in a world where superheroes have been outlawed by political and economic forces that parallel the storyline in "The Watchmen." Dash has the super speed of the Flash and Quicksilver; like Plastic Man, Elastigirl can transform into any shape imaginable; Mr. Incredible recalls both Superman and the Hulk, and Frozone's powers seem borrowed from Iceman. And finally, the whole spy theme seems influenced by Nick Fury.

Other Media Appearances: Dark Horse Comics released a limited series of comic books based on the movie that was timed as a promotional product, but the comic books were definitely secondary to the film's release. As part of the DVD extras, a Mr. Incredible cartoon, titled "Mr. Incredible and Pals," suggests the Pixar animated film was actually based on an earlier series that aired on Saturday morning in the late 1960s.

Trivial Matters: Composer Michael Giacchino borrowed heavily from Henry Mancini and John Barry to create the jazz-inspired, secret agent-infused music for the film. The theme music from the James Bond film "On Her Majesty's Secret Service" (1969) was used in all the preview trailers for the film. Syndrome's Kronos Project is named for the movie "Kronos."

Fanboy Rating: Babes-6 Effects-6 Action-7 Brainwaves-7 Total=26

The Incredibles

Inspector Gadget

Inspector Gadget (1999). Walt Disney Productions, 78min. **Director:** David Kellogg. **Producers:** Roger Birnbaum, Andy Heyward, and Jordan Kerner. **Screenwriters:** Dan Olsen, Kerry Ehrin, and Zak Penn. Characters created by Andy Heyward, Jean Chalopin, and Bruno Bianchi. **Cinematographer:** Adam Greenberg. **Cast:** Matthew Broderick, Rupert Everett, Joely Fisher, Michelle Trachtenberg, Andy Dick, Richard Kiel, Mr. T.

First Comic Book Appearance: None

Origins: For DiC Entertainment, Andy Heyward, Jean Chalopin, and Bruno Bianchi created "Inspector Gadget" as an animated television series for syndication, and the first episode aired on September 10, 1983. Don Adams, who had previously provided the voice for "Tennessee Tuxedo," voiced Inspector Gadget, but it was Adams' bumbling secret agent Maxwell Smart on "Get Smart!" (1965) that supplied the inspiration for this clumsy, absent-minded, and oblivious new cartoon figure. Inspector Gadget was not a superhero with secret powers, but rather an ordinary human (a detective) with extraordinary gadgets built into his anatomy. With these gadgets, he battled Dr. Claw, the leader of an evil organization known as MAD (an acronym for Mean and Dirty). DiC Entertainment used the cartoon series to merchandize Inspector Gadget toys, in much the same way that Mattel had marketed its He-Man toys through the "He-Man and the Masters of the Universe" cartoon series. Throughout its original run, from 1983 to 1986, the eighty-six episodes imagined all manner of gadgets for its titular inspector. The gadgets included very common ones, like binoculars, cuffs, umbrella-parachute, phone and spring, and uncommon ones, like a respirator, siren, skis, sail, and Swiss-Army knife built into his fingers. Inspector Gadget also relied on a tricked-out car, like the Batmobile. He never appeared in a comic book, but he did star in a Little Golden Book, titled *Inspector Gadget in Africa.*

The 1999 Film Version: Walt Disney Productions umpteenth attempt to create a superhero franchise was a hit with the young and young-at-heart, but did not reach the mass market the studio had hoped. In the story, security guard John Brown (Matthew Broderick) longs to be a member of the police force, but he simply doesn't fit the profile of the modern cop. After a fight with a cyberthief leaves him critically injured, Brown is given a second chance at life when Dr. Brenda Bradford (Joely Fisher) offers to make him into a robotic cybercop known as Inspector Gadget. Together, they battle the Claw (Rupert Everett), an evil industrialist who hungers for Brenda's technological secrets. He is also intent upon destroying Gadget once and for all. The plot borrows its main premise not from the cartoon series, but from Paul Verhoeven's 1987 "Robocop," in which Officer Alex J. Murphy is killed, then resurrected as a robotic cybercop known as Robocop. A direct-to-video sequel featured French Stewart in the lead role as Inspector Gadget.

Trivial Matters: Don Addams who provided the voice for the cartoon character cameos in voice only as Brian the dog. The "Dragnet" theme is played when Gadget first talks to Chief Quimby (Dabney Coleman), who starred in the "Dragnet" remake in 1987. Drs. Howard and Fine are summoned on the hospital's PA system; this is a reference to the Three Stooges and one of their classic bits.

Fanboy Rating: Babes-2 Effects-2 Action-2 Brainwaves-2 Total=8

Inspector Gadget

Iron Man

Iron Man (2008). Paramount Pictures, 120min. **Director:** Jon Favreau. **Producers:** Avi Arad and Kevin Feige. **Screenwriters:** Arthur Marcum, Matt Holloway, Mark Fergus, Hawk Ostby. Characters created by Stan Lee, Larry Lieber, Jack Kirby, and Don Heck. **Cinematographer:** Matthew Libatique. **Film Editor:** Dan Lebental. **Production Designer:** J. M. Riva. **Cast:** Robert Downey Jr, Gwyneth Paltrow, Jeff Bridges, Leslie Bibb, Terence Howard.

First Comic Book Appearance: "Tales of Suspense #39" (March 1963) *Origins:* In 1963, the character of Iron Man (also known as Tony Stark) was created by Stan Lee, Larry Lieber, Don Heck, and Jack Kirby in "Tales of Suspense #39." He was originally imagined with bulky gray armor, but his costume was re-imagined in golden armor in the second issue; ultimately, his familiar, sleek red-and-golden armor appeared several issues later. Iron Man relies on the powered armor for his super strength, invulnerability, and array of weaponry. The armor was invented by American industrialist, billionaire and military contractor Tony Stark when he was a prisoner of the Vietnamese during the Vietnam War. At age 21, Stark inherited his father's company when his parents were killed in a car crash, and he decided to fly around the world in an effort to take stock of how the company's products were being used. While on a visit to Vietnam to see how mini-transistors were being employed to win the war effort, he was captured by a warlord named Wong Chu. Chu forces Stark to work with fellow prisoner Yin Sen, a famed physicist, and together they hatch a plan for escape which requires building a powered suit of armor. Stark fights his way free of the prison camp, and saves Jim Rhodes, a wounded American helicopter pilot, from the North Vietnamese. Upon his return, Stark continues to work on the armor, making improvements that will allow him to become Iron Man. Throughout the early issues, Stark maintains that Iron Man is actually a personal bodyguard because they are often seen in the same locale – but never at the same time. Six months after his first appearance, Iron Man joined the Avengers as a founding member (along with Thor, Ant Man, the Wasp and the Hulk), and he also worked with Nick Fury's S.H.I.E.L.D. In 1968, Iron Man got his own title, and he has been published continuously since then. Tony Stark battled alcoholism in the 1980s, and the addiction caused him to have such radical personality changes that the Avengers turned their back on him. Since he has since sobered up, Tony Stark has had to battle his own armor which gained sentience and deal with a couple of heart attacks.

First Media Appearance: Iron Man made his first media appearance outside the world of comic books in the 1966 animated television series "Marvel Super Heroes," with John Vernon providing his voice.

Other Media Appearances: In 1981, Iron Man appeared on an episode of "Spider-Man and His Amazing Friends," with the vocal talents of William Marshall, and in the 1990s, he was a regular on "The Avengers" animated series on Fox. With Robert Hays providing the voice, he had his own "Iron Man" animated series as part of the Marvel Action Hour. He has also been featured in the "Ultimate Avengers" (2006), a direct-to-video production by Marvel Entertainment and Lion's Gate Films.

The 2008 Film Version: Several times, Iron Man has been considered as the subject of a big-screen film version, but each time, the news was premature. In 1993, just prior to Bill Bixby's death, Iron Man was going to be featured in "The Rebirth of the Incredible Hulk," but the film project ended when the main star died. New Line Cinema announced that it was producing an "Iron Man" movie with Nick Cassavetes as director and a November 2005 release date, but then the film was rescheduled to 2006 and then 2007. Finally, the studio's rights expired, and went back to Marvel.

At the San Diego Comic-Con in 2006, Jon Favreau talked with fans about his film version that he was making for Paramount Pictures. Based on a script by Arthur Marcum and Matt Holloway, Favreau also indicated the villain would be the Mandarin, and that "the suit would be more like a weapons platform than a flying suit." Robert Downey Jr. plays Tony Stark, with Terrence Howard as Jim Rhodes, Gwyneth Paltrow as Pepper, and Jeff Bridges at Obadiah Stane. The film has a release date of May 2, 2008. Like most fans, we look forward to what the future brings.

Iron Man

Isis

Isis (aka The Secret of Isis) (1975). Filmation Associates, 30min, 22 episodes. **Directors:** Earl Bellamy, Arnold Laven, Hollingsworth Morse. **Producer:** Arthur H. Nadel. **Executive Producer**: Lou Scheimer. **Screenwriters:** Russell Bates, Kathleen Barnes, Peter and Sara Dixon, Norman Cameron et al. Characters created by Marc Richards. **Cinematographer:** Robert F. Sparks. **Cast:** Joanna Cameron, Brian Cutler, Joanna Pang, Albert Reed, Ronald Douglas.

First Comic Book Appearance: "Shazam! #25" (Sept-Oct. 1976).
Origins: Created by Marc Richards, the character of Andrea Thomas and her alter ego Isis was developed by Filmation Associates to share an hour-long time spot with Captain Marvel as a live-action Saturday morning show. "The Shazam!/Isis Hour" debuted on CBS on September 6, 1975, and ran for two years. In "The Secrets of Isis," which aired during the second part of the hour, Andrea Thomas (Joanna Cameron) was a high school science teacher who found an amulet while on an archeological dig in Egypt. The amulet was a mystical one that once belonged to an ancient Egyptian Queen, and now had the power to give the wearer super strength, flight, telekinesis, control over the elements, and super speed. Researching the amulet's past, she discovers its secret powers. Andrea decides to use these powers to fight crime and help those that are in trouble and adopts the name Isis for her superhuman persona. So, whenever she needed to transform into her superhero, she dons the amulet and chants, "Oh Might Isis." Isis often intoned rhythmic, rhyming chants to activate her powers, like "Oh zephyr winds which blow on high, lift me now, so I can fly," which helped her to fly or do whatever the chant called for. Throughout the 22 episodes that were produced for the show, Isis used her powers for good by capturing criminals, righting wrongs, and helping those in danger. Rick Mason (Brian Cutler) was another teacher at her school, while Cindy Lee (Joanna Pang) and Renee Carroll (Ronalda Douglas) were her students. The series was spun-off into a comic book, produced

by DC Comics and adapted by Denny O'Neil, Jack C. Harris, and Mike Vosburg. Although Isis is often wrongly cited as a creation of DC, she was in fact created specifically for the television series. Shortly after the live-action series ended, Isis returned as an animated character on "The Freedom Force," a segment of Filmation's "Tarzan" show in 1980. In 2006, DC re-introduced the character of Isis as Andriana Tomaz, an ancient goddess with hidden powers.

First Media Appearance: With the debut of "The Shazam!/Isis Hour" on CBS on September 6, 1975, Isis and her secret identity of Andrea Thomas made her first media appearance in the guise of Joanna Cameron.

Other Media Appearances: During the initial run of "The Shazam!/Isis Hour," Isis guest-starred on three episodes with Captain Marvel. In 1977, "The Secret of Isis" was given its own timeslot, and seven new episodes were broadcast alongside reruns of the 15 shows from the first two seasons. Later, Filmation incorporated the character of Isis, now in cartoon form, in "The Freedom Force."

The 1975 Unaired Pilot: When Marc Richards was first developing "Isis" for television, he imagined Andrea Thomas as a forensic criminologist who worked with Dr. Elias Barnes and Rick Slocum headquartered at MidState University in California. Barnes, an old-line "Sherlock Holmes"-type investigator, hired Thomas and Slocum to do most of the footwork for him. Thomas is fairly young, somewhat naïve, but anxious to learn all that she can, and Slocum is a computer technician and profiler with far more experience. During one investigation, Andrea Thomas unearths an amulet that once belonged to a past queen of Egypt, and later discovers that the amulet enables her to become the goddess Isis with the powers to control the elements. Throughout the series, she would be called to use her powers to save Rick and bring criminals to justice. Richards' pilot was good, but not great…

Trivial Matters: Isis was one of the few superheroes on television and at the movies not derived from a comic book. According to Lou Scheimer, the series executive producer, the character was created as a counterpart to Captain Marvel. Joanna Cameron hated working with the black raven and asked producers to write the bird out of the script.

Fanboy Rating: Babes-8 Effects-2 Action-3 Brainwaves-4 Total=17

Isis

Judge Dredd

Judge Dredd (1995). Hollywood Pictures, 96min. **Director:** Danny Cannon. **Producers:** Charles Lippincott and Beau Marks. **Screenwriters:** William Wisher, Steven E. de Souza, and Michael De Luca. Characters by John Wagner and Carlos Ezquerra. **Cinematographer:** Adrian Biddle. **Film Editors:** Harry Keramidas and Alex Mackie. **Production Designer:** Nigel Phelps. **Cast:** Sylvester Stallone, Diane Lane, Armand Assante, Rob Schneider, Jurgen Prochnow.

First Comic Book Appearance: "2000 AD #2" (February 1977)
Origins: Created by John Wagner and Carlos Ezquerra, "Judge Dredd" was first imagined as a "Dirty Harry" of the future, and debuted in the second issue of IPC's "2000 AD" comic magazine in Great Britain. In 1977, Pat Mills was tasked with developing content material for the brand new comic magazine, which was to be printed on newspaper stock. He wanted a dark, gritty feel to the 'zine, and his former writing partner Wagner to develop some characters for these near-future stories. Mills had also created a horror strip called "Judge Dredd," but knew that it was all wrong. However, Wagner liked the name for his futuristic lawman. He gave artist Ezquerra an advertisement for the film "Death Race 2000," and the die was cast for their strip. In Mega City One, a vast, sprawling city that covers the entire Eastern portion of the United States, Dredd works as one of the "judges" who are tasked to maintain order. These "judges" are uniformed police officers who function as enforcers, judges, and juries for the criminal perpetrators they track down. Once apprehended, the criminals face summary judgment, and then are put on ice (suspended animation) for the rest of their lives. Since the world is imagined as a totalitarian state, the role of the judges is purposely fascist. Judge Dredd is particularly ruthless in executing the law, and includes nearly everyone, even those involved in victimless crimes, in his summary judgment. Later in the series, we learn that Judge Dredd is actually one of a number of clones of Chief Judge Fargo, the most famous of all of the judges that run Mega City One.

Dredd drives a motorcycle which has an arsenal of lethal weapons and an A.I. for driving itself. He also carries a "Lawgiver" handgun which is programmed to fire six different types of bullets, based upon the situation, and he wears a helmet that obscures most of his identity. Catch phrases, like "I am the Law" and "Democracy is not for the people," are typically spoken in a monosyllabic tone by our titular hero. Since Dredd is a clone, he was forced to turn on his "brother" Rico, and sent him up for twenty years for criminal activity. Dredd's criminal pursuits have taken him to other parts of a polluted world and to Luna City on the Moon. A penal colony for rogue judges has been established on Titan, one of Saturn's moons. Several of the storylines have featured robots, time travel, and the Apocalypse War.

In 1983, Eagle Comics reprinted most of the IPC storylines, and than in 1994, when DC Comics licensed the character, he made of number of crossovers with DC characters, including Batman.

First Media Appearance: Judge Dredd made his one and only media appearance in the guise of Sylvester Stallone for the 1995 big-screen version, and has yet to resurface in the last dozen years.

The 1995 Film Version: Very loosely based on the comic book series, "Judge Dredd" was a huge disappointment for fans who had long dreamed of a movie adaptation. Part of the reason for its failure was that the screen story by William Wisher and Michael De Luca jettisoned much of the mythology behind the comic. The bare bones plot had Dredd (Stallone) convicted for a crime that he did not commit, while his murderous counterpart Rico (Armand Assante) remains free. With the help of a prisoner (Rob Schneider) who he himself convicted, Dredd sets out to clear his name and leaves a wake of destruction in his path. The fact that Dredd and Judge Hershey (Diane Lane) develop a love affair, which was forbidden in the comics, and that Stallone appears without his trademark helmet throughout most of the film , angered fans even more. The film was named as one of the worst of the year 1995.

Trivial Matters: Arnold Schwarzenegger was first offered the role of Judge Dredd, but turned it down because he didn't want to wear a helmet for most of the movie. The role of Fergie was first offered to Joe Pesci, and then Rob Schneider. The Coen brothers, Richard Donner, Renny Harlin, Peter Hewitt, and Richard Stanley were all offered the chance to direct the film, but turned it down.

Fanboy Rating: Babes-4 Effects-2 Action-3 Brainwaves-2 Total=11

Judge Dredd

Kiss

KISS Meets the Phantom of the Park (aka Attack of the Phantoms) (1978). Hanna-Barbera Productions, 96 min. **Director**: Gordon Hessler. **Producer**: Terry Morse. **Screenwriters:** Jan Michael Sherman and Don Buday. **Cinematographer:** Robert Caramico. **Film Editor**: Peter Berger. **Cast:** Anthony Zerbe, Peter Criss, Ace Frehley, Gene Simons, Paul Stanley, Carmine Caridi, John Dennis Johnston, John Lisbon Wood, Lisa Jane Persky, John Chappell.

First Comic Book Appearance: "Kiss" One-Shot (Marvel, 1977).
Origins: Gene Simmons, Paul Stanley, Peter Criss, and Paul "Ace" Frehley comprised the original rock band KISS, which had its origins in a New York City-based rock-and-roll band called "Wicked Lester." Simmons and Stanley founded the band in 1971, but with the additions of Cross and Frehley, they abandoned Wicked Lester in favor of a new name. Stanley came up with the name KISS, and Frehley created its now-iconic logo with the double "s" shaped like lightning bolts or the insignia of the Nazi SS. Some believe the band's name is an acronym for "Knights in Satan's Service," but the band members have vehemently denied this. In order to distinguish themselves from other bands performing the same kind of eclectic rock-and-roll, they donned outrageous costumes and make-up, and assumed the personas of comic book characters. Simmons was the Demon; Stanley was the Star Child; Frehley was the Space Ace, and Cross was the Cat Man. The band's first performance was in Queens, New York, on January 30, 1973, and not long after they signed a record contract with Emerald City Records. On December 31, 1973, Simmons accidentally set his hair on fire with a fire-breathing stunt, and totally electrified their audience. In the months that followed, every one of their concerts was sold out, and "Let Me Go, Rock-n-Roll" was headed up the music charts. They continued to perform outrageous stunts on stage, and then their first live album, titled "Alive!," achieved quadruple platinum status. KISS broke through and broke out, and soon everyone wanted a piece of their suc-

cess. In 1977, Marvel Comics issued a one-shot, super special comic book featuring the band members of KISS as superheroes. The first issued published actually contained ink mixed with blood donated by the group. Less than one year later, they appeared as superheroes in "KISS Meets the Phantom of the Park." Produced by Hanna-Barbera, the movie aired on NBC on October 28, 1978, and then was released as a theatrical movie in 1979, with the title "Attack of the Phantoms." The world can breathe a little easier knowing that the members of the rock band KISS are superheroes in disguise.

The 1978 Film Version: When the rock band KISS comes to do a concert at a popular theme park, they run afoul of the Phantom (Anthony Zerbe as Abner Devereaux). Devereaux has found a way to clone humans into robots in his underground laboratory at the park, and he plots to use the KISS concert as a launching platform for revenge against the unscrupulous partner who has stolen the park from him. Debonair, charming, and utterly frustrated that Melissa (Deborah Ryan), the girl of his dreams, fails to notice his overtures, the Phantom becomes enraged, and turns her boyfriend into his electronic zombie. She, in turn, enlists the help of the rock group, and KISS must use their special powers to stop him. Scripted by Jan Michael Sherman, one of the creative talents behind "The Rocky Horror Picture Show" (1975), "Kiss Meets the Phantom of the Park" was one of the highest-rated television movies of the year. Unfortunately, the film's poor acting and semi-comedic script make the action seem like it's borrowed from the "Batman" tele-vision series. Each member of the rock band gets to play a superhero with special powers, and the featured songs include "Rock and Roll All Night," "Shout It Out," and "Beth."

Trivial Matters: Cartoon-like music was added to the fight scenes so that younger members (re: kids) would be allowed to see the movie. Band members did not memorize the script, but rather were given their lines during shooting.

Fanboy Rating: Babes-4 Effects-2 Action-3 Brainwaves-2 Total=11

A MARVEL COMICS SUPER SPECIAL!

KISS

Forty pages of full-color comics. Plus never-before-published photos and features. Printed in real KISS blood.

Kiss

Kull the Conqueror

Kull the Conqueror (1997). Universal Pictures, 95 min. **Director:** John Nicolella. **Producer:** Raffaella De Laurentiis. **Screenwriter:** Charles Edward Pogue. Characters created by Robert E. Howard. **Cinematographer:** Rodney Charters. **Film Editor:** Dallas Puett. **Production Designer:** Benjamin Fernandez. **Cast:** Kevin Sorbo, Tia Carrere, Thomas Ian Griffith, Litefoot, Roy Brocksmith, Harvey Fierstein, Karina Lombard.

First Appearance: "The Shadow Kingdom" *Weird Tales* (August 1929)
First Comic Book Appearance: "Kull the Conqueror" (1971)
Origins: The character of Kull the Conqueror was born in the highly-gifted imagination of Robert E. Howard, who had also created Conan the Barbarian, Soloman Kane, and Red Sonja. According to Howard's short stories, Kull was born in Atlantis well before the great cataclysm that destroyed the great island-nation, and lived with a barbarian tribe in the Tiger Valley until it was wiped out by a flood. As a young warrior, he set out to explore his world, but was subsequently captured and sold as a galley slave. He gained his freedom during a mutiny, became a pirate, then an outlaw, and finally a gladiator in Valusia. Muscular, quick-witted, incredibly ruthless, the gladiator served as a mercenary and soldier, and eventually won his own kingdom and became King Kull. With "The Shadow Kingdom," first published in the August 1929 issue of *Weird Tales*, Kull became a forerunner of Conan and all of the other barbarian warriors that followed in the Sword and Sorcery genre. Stories, like "The Curse of the Golden Skull," "The Mirrors of Tuzun Thune," "By This Axe, I Rule," and "Exile of Atlantis," not only helped expand the legend of Kull but also established the kingdoms of Thuria, Lemuria, and Atlantis and pitted him against adversaries like Thulsa Doom and King Borna. Most of Howard's Kull stories were not written or published with a clear chronology in mind, and sometimes the character appeared in 100,000 BC ("Kings of the Night") and then later in 20,000 BC, still many years before the sinking of

Atlantis and Conan's Hyborian Age. Speculation gave rise to the notion that Kull was actually immortal or simply long-lived. So, when Marvel Comics began publishing Kull stories in 1971, he was an immortal figure fighting both barbarian and supernatural forces.

First Media Appearance: Kull made his one and only media appearance in the guise of Kevin Sorbo, who had earlier played Hercules, in the 1997 action-adventure "Kull the Conqueror," and the character has not re-surfaced in the media in the last ten years.

The 1997 Film Version: After Arnold Schwarzenegger had passed on reprising his role as Conan in the third entry titled "Conan the Conqueror," De Laurentiis quickly re-titled the movie "Kull the Conqueror" and hired the latest incarnation of Hercules, Kevin Sorbo, to place the title role. The screenplay by Charles Edward Pogue finds a barbarian named Kull (Sorbo) unexpectedly becoming king when the old king Borna (Sven Ole Thorsen), whom Kull has just slain, gives him the crown. But direct heirs of the king disagree with their father's choice, and try to topple Kull and regain the throne. A direct assault fails, so they bring an old witch-queen Akivasha (Tia Carrere) back to life to bewitch Kull. That plan also fails when Akivasha double-crosses them and resurrects a whole army of demons to rule the kingdom with her. The only thing that stands between her and the throne is Kull! Fans were not fooled by the title, and stayed away from the film in great numbers. The movie was a major box office disappointment.

Trivial Matters: Akivasha's line, "I am altering our bargain. Pray I don't alter it any further!" is a rip-off of Darth Vader's "I am altering the deal. Pray I don't alter it any further!" from "The Empire Strikes Back" (1980). The final line of the movie, "With this axe, I rule," was taken from one of Howard's Kull stories, just as the character of Akivasha was taken from "The Hour of the Dragon."

Fanboy Rating: Babes-3 Effects-2 Action-4 Brainwaves-3 Total=12

Kull

Lady Death

Lady Death (2004). ADV Films, 80min. **Director:** Andrew Orjuela. **Producer:** Kevin Corcoran. **Screenwriters:** Carl Macek and Brian Pulido. **Film Editors:** Joey Goubeaud and Andy Orjuela. **Cast:** Christine Auten, Mike Kleinhenz, Andy McAvin, Rob Mungle, Mike MacRae, Chris Patton, Dwight Clark, Maureen McCullough.

First Comic Book Appearance: "Evil Ernie #1" (December 1991)
Origins: Brian Pulido and Steven Hughes created the character of Lady Death as a "bad girl," endowed her with highly improbable physical attributes, and dressed her in an incredibly skimpy, dominatrix costume to appeal to the market of adolescent boys who buy comic books. They also imagined a comic book figure who was light years removed from those female characters at Marvel and DC. According to her backstory, she is the daughter of Matthias, whose direct ancestors some 666 generations back were among Lucifer's fallen angels, and Marion, a virtuous woman whose lineage went all the way to Heaven. She was given the name Hope, back in the early 13th century when she was still passing for human. When her mother dies, she goes to live with her father, but is never able to make a home with him. She feels drawn to Hell, and ends up ruling the place after dealing with all of the petty jealousies and rivalries and conspiracies. She destroys Lucifer by throwing him through Heaven's Gate; in his final act, Lucifer cursed her to live in Hell. Hope wants to return to Earth, but as long as one living soul is left there, she cannot return and live a normal life. So, instead, she returns as Lady Death. The story shifts between Medieval Sweden and the modern world, and is incredibly detailed with lots of material drawn from *The Bible* and Milton's *Paradise Lost*. The comic book was first published by Eternity Comics, then Chaos! (in 1994), CrossGen, and finally Avatar Press. In 1999, she had a crossover with comicdom's other bad girl, Vampirella.

First Media Appearance: Lady Death made her one and only media appearance in Carl Macek's 2004 direct-to-video movie with Christine M. Auten in the title role.

The 2004 Film Version: Carl Macek purposely set out to make the "Lady Death" movie like Japanese animae, and succeeded with a product that is far better than it had any right to be. In 15th Century Sweden, Lucifer's daughter (Auten) is burned at the stake for witchcraft, and she returns to plot revenge against him in an elaborate scheme that will ultimately make her Lady Death.

Trivial Matters: To streamline the screen story, Lady Death becomes Lucifer's daughter, instead of Matthias and Marion's daughter. The animated film was first screened for fans at the San Diego Comic Book Convention in 2004.

Fanboy Rating: Babes-8 Effects-4 Action-4 Brainwaves-4 Total=20

Lady Death

The League

The League of Extraordinary Gentlemen (2003). 20the Century-Fox, 110min. **Director:** Stephen Norrington. **Producers:** Trevor Albert and Don Murphy. **Screenwriter:** James Robinson. Characters created by Alan Moore and Kevin O'Neill. **Cinematographer:** Dan Laustsen. **Film Editor:** Paul Rubell. **Production Designer:** Carol Spier. **Cast:** Sean Connery, Naseeruddin Shah, Peta Wilson, Tony Curran, Stuart Townsend, Shane West.

First Comic Book Appearance: "The League of Extraordinary Gentlemen #1" (January 1999)

Origins: Alan Moore and Kevin O'Neill's clever comic book series, "The League of Extraordinary Gentlemen," re-introduces us to some of Victorian literature's most famous characters, and posits them as members of a very unique superhero team that is called together by Campion Bond on the British Secret Service to fight an evil menace that threatens the peace of the civilized world. The League, which is led by Miss Wilhelmina Murray (from Bram Stoker's 1897 novel *Dracula*), includes Captain Nemo, Allan Quatermain, Dr. Henry Jekyll and Mr. Edward Hyde, and Hawley Griffin (better known as "the Invisible Man"). In Volume One, they are tasked with finding an unknown menace who has taken a sample of cavorite from the British Museum; cavorite is the substance that allows Dr. Cavor to travel to the Moon in H.G. Wells' *First Men in the Moon*. With Captain Nemo's *Nautilus* submarine, they head to Paris to consult with Poe's C. Auguste Dupin, and charge after Fu Manchu who has actually stolen the sample. Upon their return, they discover that Professor Moriarty has been hiding out at British Intelligence, and he plans to use the cavorite to launch a flying machine to bomb London. In Volume Two, Mycroft Holmes learns from John Carter and Lt. Gulliver Jones of Mars that the Martians are planning to attack. When the Martians land, the League is waiting for them, and with the help of Dr. Moreau, they turn the tide of battle. Wilhelmina's League, however, was not the first league of superheroes assembled to deal with the world's problems. In the 17th Century, Prospero's League gathered Caliban, Ariel, Christian, and Captain Robert Owe-Much under the command of Shakespeare's sorcerer Prospero. In the 18th Century, the Pirate League was comprised of Long John Silver, Captain Blood, Captain Hook, Captain Pissgums, and Captain Slaughterboard. In the late 18th Century, Lemuel Gulliver gathered Dr. Syn, the Scarlet Pimpernel and his wife, Natty Numppo, and Fanny Hill as Gulliver's League. Thus far, only two volumes have been published by Moore and O'Neill, but it is likely that many more will follow with the same attention to detail and in-jokes that the originals had. Moore and O'Neill's concept for "The League" was probably inspired by John Myers 1949 novel, *Silverlock*, in which every character is lifted from the pages of another fictional work.

First Media Appearance: Members of the League of Extraordinary Gentlemen first appeared outside the comic book in the 2003 film adaptation, but have yet to surface again in any other form of media.

The 2003 Film Version: In an alternate Victorian Age, the "Fathom" plots to plunge the civilized nations of the world into a World War, and has been using highly superior weapons against both sides in an effort to trigger the first shot. M (Richard Roxburgh), the head of British Intelligence, gathers Allan Quatermain (Sean Connery), Captain Nemo (Naseeruddin Shah), Mina Harker (Peta Wilson), Invisible Man Rodney Skinner (Tony Curran), Dorian Gray (Stuart Townsend), American Secret Agent Tom Sawyer (Shane West), and Dr. Henry Jekyll (Jason Flemyng) together into one team to fight the "Fantom" and prevent a world war. The film was such a major departure from the comic books that Moore and O'Neill disowned it.

Trivial Matters: Portraits of members from other teams, including one that features the Four Musketeers and another one that features Robin Hood, Ivanhoe and Black Arrow, appear on the walls of the headquarters. The character of Campion Bond was supposed to have been played by Roger Moore, but was dropped before filming.

Fanboy Rating: Babes-5 Effects-2 Action-4 Brainwaves-5 Total=16

The League

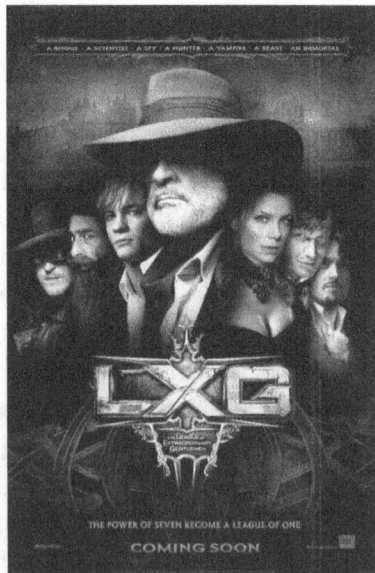

THE POWER OF SEVEN BECOME A LEAGUE OF ONE
COMING SOON

Man-Thing

Man-Thing (2005). Artisan Entertainment, 105min.
Director: Brett Leonard. **Producer:** Avi Arad.
Screenwriter: Hans Rodionoff. Characters created by
Steve Gerber. **Cinematographer:** Steve Arnold. **Film
Editor:** Martin Connor. **Production Designers:** Tim
Ferrier and Peter Pound. **Cast:** Matthew Le Nevez,
Rachael Taylor, Jack Thompson, Rawiri Paratene, Alex
O'Loughlin, Steve Bastoni, Robert Mammone, Steve
Gerber.

First Comic Book Appearance: "Savage Tales #1" (May 1971)
Origins: Like DC Comics' "Swamp Thing" (1971), which came out one
month later, "Man-Thing" was imagined as a horror comic by Roy Thomas, Gerry Conway, and Gray Morrow that eventually evolved into something completely different. "Savage Tales #1" was a magazine-sized comic
book, like *Mad* magazine and "Vampirella," that was part of an experiment by Marvel Comics to see if adults would read a larger format and
thus expand the comic book's basic adolescent demographic. The format
failed, but the character of Man-Thing lived on in "Adventures of Fear"
and then its own title. In the series, biochemist Ted Sallis is betrayed by his
girlfriend Ellen Brandt, while on the run from Advanced Idea Mechanics
(AIM) who wanted his formula as a miracle drug, and drowns in a swamp
in the Florida Everglades, not far from the Seminole reservation at Lake
Okeechobee. Toxic waste, exotic chemicals, and festering viruses in the
swamp combine with Sallis' formula and bring him back to life as a shambling, disgusting, quasi-human form that is largely vegetation. His brain
turns to mush as well, and he lives on with only a sketchy knowledge of
what he once was. When Steve Gerber took over writing the "Fear" comic
with "Issue #11," he embroidered the story somewhat linking the Man-
Thing character to supernatural forces, bringing Daredevil and Black Widow
into one storyline, and a duck named Howard. In 1974, "Man-Thing"
was Marvel's top, non-superhero title. Since Man-Thing's swamp just so
happened to contain the Nexus of All Realities, writers were given a great

deal of latitude in developing any kind of adventure they wanted. The Fountain of Youth, the Cult of Entropy, pirates, mad Vikings, and an evolutionary war were all central ideas that played out in the pages of "Man-Thing" comic.

First Media Appearance: The Man-Thing's one and only media appearance in the 2004 direct-to-video release, titled "Man-Thing."

The 2004 Film Version: When agents of an oil-rich tycoon vanish while exploring the Florida Everglades for a play to drill, the local sheriff (Matthew Le Nevez) investigates. He learns from the local Seminole Indians about a legend that has come to life in the nearby swamps. The Man-Thing is a shambling swamp-monster whose touch burns those who feel fear. The film was slated for a theatrical release, but when a test screening for the movie was held, half of the audience walked out before the movie ended. Those plans were scrapped, and the film was sold to the Sci-Fi Channel as an original movie that aired in the Spring of 2005. It was release on video that summer.

Trivial Matters: The characters of Steve Gerber (William Zappa) and Mike Ploog (Robert Mammone) are references to the comic creators by the same names who developed the "Man-Thing" comic book in the 1980s, establishing the "nexus of all realities" and other distinctive features of the comic. Filming was scheduled for New Orleans, but then re-located to Australia to keep down the costs of production.

Fanboy Rating: Babes-2 Effects-2 Action-2 Brainwaves-2 Total=8

Man-Thing

The Mask

The Mask (1994). New Line Cinema, in association with Dark Horse Entertainment, 97min. **Director:** Charles Russell. **Producer:** Bob Engelman. **Screenwriter:** Mike Werb. Characters created by Michael Fallon and Mark Verheiden. **Cinematographer:** John Leonetti. **Film Editor:** Arthur Coburn. **Production Designer:** Craig Stearns. **Cast:** Jim Carrey, Peter Riegert, Peter Greene, Amy Yasbeck, Richard Jeni, Cameron Diaz, Johnny Williams, Nancy Fish.

First Comic Book Appearance: "Dark Horse Presents #10" (1987)
Origins: "The Mask" was the brainchild of Randy Stradley and Mike Richardson, the two publishers who founded Dark Horse Comics, and Mike Badger. When they first conceived it, the comic debuted in "Dark Horse Presents #10" as "The Masque," and printed in black and white. Later, John Arcudi and Doug Mahnke fleshed the concept out in a four-issue miniseries that started in "Mayhem #1" as "The Mask," and that title has stuck with the comic ever since. In the series, the Mask is not actually a person but an ancient artifact that came from Africa, and ended up in an antique store. Meek, mild-mannered Stanley Ipkiss, who is clearly at the bottom of the totem pole of life, purchases the Mask as a gift for his girlfriend Kathy. What he doesn't know is that the wooden mask has magical abilities that strip away all inhibitions and endow the wearer with almost limitless powers. Before presenting it to her, Stanley tries it on, and is instantly transformed from the pathetic person that he is into a hyper-frenzied superhero with a green head, a large set of teeth, and the unlimited powers of a Tex Avery cartoon character. With his inhibitions gone, Stanley Ipkiss decides to get even with those people who had made fun of him or wronged him in the past, and goes on a rampage, killing and maiming. The media refer to the killer as Big Head. Of course, when Stanley removes the mask, he returns to his feeble-minded self. In time, Kathy puts the mystery together, and shoots and kills Big Head to save her own life. The Mask then passes to Kathy who gives it to Lt. Kellaway for safekeeping.

He uses it to take down some crime lords who have evaded capture. But unfortunately the power of the Mask turns Kellaway violent, and he gives it away as well. The Mask then passes on to several criminals, at least one dog, and several characters in other comic books, like DC's Joker.

First Media Appearance: The Mask as worn by Jim Carrey's Stanley Ipkiss made its first media appearance on July 29, 1994, when the feature film version opened at theaters.

Other Media Appearances: Following the enormous popularity and success of the movie, an animated cartoon series aired in syndication with Rob Paulsen providing the voice for Stanley Ipkiss/The Mask. John Arcudi, a former writer of the comic book, penned several of the episodes. In 2005, with Jim Carrey unavailable, New Line Cinema produced a watered-down version of the original featuring Tim Avery (Jamie Kennedy) as an aspiring cartoonist who becomes the owner of the Mask. The film was called "Son of the Mask," and failed miserably at the box office.

The 1994 Film Version: Under the direction of Chuck Russell, New Line sanitized the violence and downbeat ending of the comic book series, and presented a highly enjoyable and comedic version of Stanley Ipkiss' story in "The Mask." Meek, mild-mannered Stanley Ipkiss (Jim Carrey) works as a clerk at the biggest bank in Edge City. Because he is a nice guy – perhaps too nice – he gets pushed around a lot by everyone, and can't seem to handle confrontations very well. After one of the worst days of his life, Stanley stumbles across a mask which bears the likeness of Loki, the Norse god of mischief. (Loki is the god that burned down Valhalla.) He tries the mask on, and is suddenly transformed into a maniacal, hyperactive cartoon character with a green face. As "the Mask," he is outrageous, funny, charismatic and irreverent. He easily steals Tina Carlyle (Cameron Diaz) from gangster Dorian Tyrell (Peter Greene) and upsets Tyrell's plans to climb the Mafia ladder to become the head boss. Eventually, Tyrell gets his hands on the mask, and Stanley must face him, with help of his dog Milo, and save the woman of his dreams. The movie

The Mask

was a huge hit for New Line Cinema, and turned Jim Carrey from a talented comic into a big star.

Trivial Matters: "The Mask" was Cameron Diaz's first movie role. The nightclub Stanley frequents is named Coco Bongo. That's the name of the bar that Jim Carrey's Peter Appleton goes to after losing his job in "The Majestic" (2001).

Fanboy Rating: Babes-7 Effects-6 Action-7 Brainwaves-5 Total=25

Men in Black

Men in Black (1997). Columbia Pictures, 98min. **Director:** Barry Sonnenfeld. **Producer:** Walter F. Parkes. **Screenwriter:** Ed Solomon. Characters created by Lowell Cunningham. **Cinematographer:** Donald Peterman. **Film Editor:** Jim Miller. **Production Designer:** Bo Welch. **Cast:** Tommy Lee Jones, Will Smith, Linda Fiorentino, Vincent D'Onofrio, Rip Torn, Tony Shalhoub.

First Comic Book Appearance: "Men in Black #1" (January 1990)
Origins: One of the most successful feature films based on a comic book, "Men in Black" (1997) started as a black-and-white series from Aircel Comics. The three-issue miniseries was created by a young writer hoping to break into the business named Lowell Cunningham and illustrated by Sandy Carruthers, a graphic designer. The story borrowed its initial premise from UFO mythology and the belief that men dressed in black suits, claiming to be government agents, would harass and confound UFO witnesses. While no credible evidence has ever been presented to confirm or deny this theory, plenty of unverified reports link them to government operatives (often in black suits) who have taken part in a conspiracy of disinformation. Cunningham felt there was a wealth of story ideas buried in the folklore about flying saucers and Men in Black, and created two agents of his own who would function as the protagonists in each of his books. Kay was imagined as the by-the-book man, not unlike Dragnet's Joe Friday who refused to see anyone else's side but his own. Jay was the new guy who sought to learn everything that Kay had to teach him. Together, they fought unseen alien forces that were attempting to subvert the United States of America. In 1991, Aircel published a second miniseries by Cunningham and Carruthers, and then, after the 1997 big screen adaptation was released, Marvel Comics put out three one-shot comics by Cunningham.
First Media Appearance: Tommy Lee Jones and Will Smith lent their likenesses to Kay and Jay for the Men in Black's first media appearance on July 2, 1997, when "Men in Black" was released.

Other Media Appearances: In 1997, Sony Pictures turned "Men in Black" into an animated television show with Ed O'Ross as Kay and Keith Diamond as Jay. A thrill ride inspired by the movies opened at Universal Studios Orlando. The year 2002 saw the release of a sequel.

The 1997 Film Version: Columbia Pictures struck it rich with one of the most successful films made (up to that point) from a comic book, earning an estimated $326 million worldwide. Directed by Barry Sonnenfeld, the screen story ushered NYPD officer James Edwards (Smith) into the MIB agency as Agent J, and teamed him with Agent K (Jones). Together, they investigate the sudden appearance of an alien (Vincent D'Onofrio) in the back woods of New York, and try to thwart his plan to steal a tiny galaxy that is contained in an ornament hanging around the neck of a royal cat from Orion. Their mission is further complicated by a dippy medical examiner (Linda Fiorentino) who has a thing for dead corpses.

Trivial Matters: Clint Eastwood was offered the role of K, but turned it down. Both David Schwimmer and Chris O'Donnell were asked to play J, but they both turned the role down. Steven Spielberg, George Lucas, Sylvester Stallone, Dionne Warwick, Newt Ginrich, Al Roker, and Danny De Vito are all identified on the radar screen as "known aliens."

Fanboy Rating: Babes-6 Effects-6 Action-2 Brainwaves-2 Total=16

The 2002 Film Sequel: After raking in the huge box office take from "Men in Black," Columbia insisted on making a sequel. In 2002, Barry Sonnenfeld, Will Smith and Tommy Lee Jones returned for "Men in Black 2." When Serleena (Lara Flynn-Boyle), an evil Kylothian monster that disguises itself as a sexy Victoria Secret model, arrives on Earth, she just wants to have fun. Agent J (Smith) won't allow her to launch a diabolical plot against his home world, and brings Agent K (Jones) back from retirement. The two Men in Black race against time before Earth is destroyed. Not as funny as the first one, but also not without its guilty pleasures either.

Trivial Matters: Famke Janssen was initially cast as Serleena, and even filmed some of her scenes, but had to drop out of the project; that's when Lara Flynn-Boyle was hired. Tony Shalhoub, television's obsessive-compulsive detective, returns from the first film as Jack Jeebs, an alien snitch.

Fanboy Rating: Babes-1 Effects-2 Action-2 Brainwaves-2 Total=7

Men in Black

Meteor Man

Meteor Man (1993). M-G-M,100min. **Director:** Robert Townsend. **Producers:** Christopher Homes, Loretha Jones, and Robert Townsend. **Screenwriter:** Robert Townsend. **Cinematographer:** John Alonzo. **Film Editors:** Adam Bernardi, Richard Candib, Andrew London, and Pam Wise. **Production Designer:** Toby Corbett. **Cast:** Robert Townsend, Eddie Griffin, Marla Gibbs, Robert Guillaume, James Earl Jones, Roy Fegan.

First Comic Book Appearance: "Meteor Man #1" (August 1993)
Origins: Robert Townsend's "Meteor Man" was an amalgamation of every superhero cliché that had played out in comic books for the last fifty years, but still managed to transcend its stereotypical beginnings to feature a good-natured comedy. Jefferson Reed, a mild-mannered school teacher in Washington D.C., still believes in the innate goodness of all human beings even though his neighborhood is plagued by a local gang called the Golden Lords whose members sell drugs and beat up people. One night, when he stops to rescue a woman who is being terrorized by the gang, he finds himself running for his life to get away from them. Seizing an opportunity to evade them, Reed jumps into a garbage dumpster. The gang members race right on by. Upon climbing out of the dumpster, he is struck down by a green-glowing meteorite. He awakens several days later in the hospital, and discovers much to his amazement that his wounds are completely healed. More than that, he finds that he has superhuman strength and the ability to fly. Reed confides his new found powers to his parents Ted and Marla Jefferson, and they suggest that he use his superpowers to clean up his community. Reed thinks that's a good idea, and soon he is wearing the costume of Meteor Man that his mother stitched together for him. First, Meteor Man takes on the Golden Lords and their leader Simon Caine. Then he closes down a crack house and stops a robbery attempt. But with each act of bravery and heroism, Reed feels his superpowers leaving him. Eventually, he has no superpowers at all, but he does have the

convictions of a superhero. Jefferson Reed stands alone against the remaining gang members, and though he nearly dies, he proves that a man need not have superpowers to be a superhero. Marvel Comics produced a six-issue limited series that was simply titled "Meteor Man" in 1993.

First Media Appearance: Robert Townsend made his one and only media appearance as Meteor Man in 1993, and has yet to return in the role.

The 1993 Film Version: Robert Townsend wrote, directed and starred in the title role as "Meteor Man" (1993). The film has been called blaxploitation because it features black leading man and African-Americans in all of the key roles, but it is just as much of a slice of American culture as Richard Donner's "Superman." One night, Jefferson Reed (Townsend) is hit in the chest by a radiated chuck of meteor, and becomes Meteor Man, a superhero with superpowers. His friends and family (Robert Guillaume and Marla Gibbs) want him to use his powers to protect their community. He is more than able to honor their request, and decides to take on the dreaded Golden Lords who have been terrorizing his neighborhood for years.

Trivial Matters: Though "Meteor Man" is set in Washington, D.C., most of the film was shot in near-by Baltimore. Robert Townsend named his superhero's real identity after one of his childhood heroes, his favorite teacher. The original ending of the film had Reed traveling to Arizona's famed meteor crater to get his powers back. An earlier character named "The Meteor Man" appeared as a villain in the pages of DC Comics' "Doom Patrol."

Fanboy Rating: Babes-2 Effects-2 Action-5 Brainwaves-7 Total=16

Meteor Man

Misfits of Science

Misfits of Science (1985). Universal, 120min. **Director:** James D. Parriott. **Producer:** Dean Zanetos. **Screenwriter:** James D. Parriott. Based upon characters created by James D. Parriott. **Cinematographer**: Frank Thackery. **Film Editor:** Mike Hoggan. **Cast:** Dean Paul Martin, Keven Peter Hall, Mark Thomas Miller, Courteney Cox, Jennifer Holmes, Mickey Jones, Diane Cary, Eric Christmas, Larry Linville, Tawny Little.

First Comic Book Appearance: None.

Origins: In 1985, James D. Parriott attempted to introduce a diverse group of ordinary people who discover they have superhuman abilities in the episodic comedy-drama "Misfits of Science." The Misfits themselves were a motley crew of failed experiments, accidents, or genetic mutations that formed the central nexus for the show. They included: Dr. Elvin Lincoln, or "Big El," stands a whapping 7feet 4inches tall, but by using an experimental drug, he can shrink himself to seven inches. Johnny B was a rock and roll star who was electrocuted, then brought back to life with the abilities to shoot lightning bolts from his hands and to run at superspeed. Glo Dinallo is a seventeen-year-old runaway with telekinetic powers. Dr. Billy Hayes is the leader of the group, but has no special powers himself, other than a keen intellect. One other character served as the major foil. Dick Stetmeyer was the boss and central administrator at the Humanidyne Institute; he was constantly worried that the Misfits would do something wrong and cause great embarrassment to the Institute he had worked so hard to build. The Misfits often traveled around in their Fundae Sunday van, solving unexplained cases and taking the fiction out of science fiction. In one episode, they dealt with an individual who was communicating with aliens; in another, they tried to reconcile how a primitive native was able to travel 8000 miles by canoe; and then, in another, they help a part-bionic CIA agent recover a case containing a button that could trigger World War 3. Seventeen episodes in all aired for the half season that the series

ran on NBC. In many respects, the television series was the forerunner of Tim Kring's "Heroes" (2006); in fact, Kring initially wrote for "The Misfits of Science."

First Media Appearance: "The Misfits of Science" debuted on NBC television on October 4, 1985, and was cancelled in February 1986.

The 1985 Pilot Episodes: Dr. Billy Hayes (Dean Paul Martin) and Dr. Elvin Lincoln (Kevin Peter Hall) are researchers in biological oddities for the Humanidyne Institute, a top security think tank. When they find Arthur Beifneiter (Mickey Jones) still alive after being frozen for 50 years, their greedy boss Strickland (Edward Winter) sees dollar signs. Like his predecessor Dr. Momquist (Eric Christmas), he plans to sell "the Iceman" to the Military for experimentation. But then he disappears, along with his captive. Left without jobs, Hayes and Lincoln decide to pull together a group of "misfits" (including a telekinetic 17-year-old and a rock guitarist who shoots lightning from his hands) to rescue the Iceman and save their boss. Both he and Momquist are being held by a rogue military unit, under the command of General Theil (Larry Linville), that plans to use a neutron beam cannon and "the Iceman" to take over the world.

Trivial Matters: Only 16 out of the original 17 episodes aired in prime time; the 17th episode was finally aired on the Sci-Fi Channel. The two-part pilot was edited together for release overseas as an original movie. This was the first series that Courteney Cox played on before moving on to bigger and better things. Tim Kring, the creator of "Heroes" (2006), wrote several episodes of "The Misfits of Science."

Fanboy Rating: Babes-5 Effects-2 Action-2 Brainwaves-5 Total=14

Misfits

Mr. Terrific

Mister Terrific. (1967). Universal Television, 30min. **Director:** Jack Arnold. **Producer: Screenwriter:** Budd Grossman. **Cinematographer:** Richard Rawlings. **Cast:** Stephen Strimpell, John McGiver, Richard Gautier, Paul Smith, Susan Seaford Hayes, Ellen Corby, Alan Young.

First Comic Book Appearance: None

Origins: Like its NBC counterpart "Captain Nice," "Mister Terrific" was a light, airy confection that was created as a half-hour sitcom for CBS television to capitalize on the camp superhero craze of the 1960s. "Batman" had already been a huge success over at ABC, reaching the enviable status as the number one show in the nation, and both rival networks felt they needed a superhero spoof in their prime-time line-up in order to compete for the all important ratings. So, NBC created a forensics scientist who drank a special portion that made him into a superhero, and CBS sketched up similar plans for its own superhero. Both shows debuted on the same Thursday night, January 9, 1967, a half hour apart, and ran until the end of the season of the same year. Of the two, "Captain Nice" was probably the best written and produced, while "Mister Terrific" was the most bizarrely original. In the pilot, mild-mannered, scrawny Stanley Beamish (Stephen Strimpell), a gas station attendant in Washington, D.C., volunteers his free time testing drugs for a pharmaceutical company. The pharmaceutical company is really a cover for a super-secret government think-tank. Their latest creation is a drug that will presumably turn an ordinary man into a superhero, but the drug is limited in the amount of time for its duration. Most of the subjects who have taken the drug have not responded to its potential as a super pill, but when Stanley Beamish takes the pill – roughly the size of a golf ball – he becomes Mister Terrific. Like a Walter Mitty fantasy, he gains all of the superpowers that the comic book character

Superman has. B.G. Reed (John McGiver), the head of the agency, becomes his handler, and provides him with impossible missions that even the Impossible Mission Force would not dare to tackle. Dick Gautier co-starred as Stanley's pal Hal Walters. As Mister Terrific, Stanley dons a sequined costume with wings (that he must flap in order to fly). Unfortunately, trouble comes when the effects of the pill wear off and poor, timid Stanley Beamish is forced to face his evil opponents without his mighty powers. When the show ended in 1967, the episodes were never gathered into a syndication package because the main character took drugs to gain his superpowers; however, several episodes were combined into a television movie called "The Pill Caper." Unlike its counterpart "Captain Nice," "Mister Terrific" was never adapted into a comic book, because the character of Mister Terrific had already been an established superhero from the Golden Age with the secret identity of Terry Sloane; in 1997, another Mister Terrific (aka Michael Holt) served as a member of the Justice Society of America, and played a critical role in Alex Ross' "Kingdom Come" series.

The Mister Terrific Theme Song: "A scientist both wise and bold/Set out to cure the common cold/Instead he found a power pill/Which he said most certainly will/ Change a lamb into a lion/Like an eagle he'll be flyin/Solid steel will be like putty/It'll work on anybody./Then it was found this power pill/Made the strongest men quite ill/So the secret search began/To find the one and only man/Who can take this power pill specific/And turn into the most prolific, terrific, Mr. Terrific!/What they found made them squeamish/For only Stanley Beamish/A weak and droopy daffodil/Can take this potent power pill/That sent him soaring through the skies/Fighting foes and fighting spies./When he took the pill specific,/He became the most prolific, Hydrolific, MR. TERRIFIC!!!"

Trivial Matters: Most people today remember Wally Cox in the lead role of Stanley Beamish, but he was in fact played by Stephen Strimpell; part of the error comes from the fact that Cox provided the voice for Underdog, a very similar kind of superhero. The great director and producer Jack Arnold, who had been responsible for a number of Universal's great monster movies in the 1950s, directed the pilot episode.

Fanboy Rating: Babes-1 Effects-2 Action-2 Brainwaves-2 Total=7

Mr. Terrific

Mystery Men

Mystery Men (1999). Universal Pictures, in association with Dark Horse Entertainment, 121min. **Director:** Kinka Usher. **Producers:** Lawrence Gordon, Lloyd Levin, and Mike Richardson. **Screenwriter:** Neil Cuthbert. Characters created by Bob Burden. **Cinematographer:** Stephen Burum. **Film Editor:** Conrad Buff. **Production Designer:** Kirk Petruccelli. **Cast:** Hank Azaria, Ben Stiller, William H. Macy, Geoffrey Rush, Janeane Garofalo, Greg Kinnear, Tom Waits.

First Comic Book Appearance: "Flaming Carrot Comics #16" (June 1987) *Origins:* In 1984, cartoonist Bob Burden created a zany, surrealist comic book superhero named the Flaming Carrot for Aardwark-Vanaheim Comics, and unleashed him on a poor, defenseless world. The Flaming Carrot was a crime-fighter who wore a white shirt, red paints, flippers, and a giant carrot mask. He fought criminals and other deviants in Palookaville, a neighborhood of Iron City. We are told in Issue #7 that a poor man suffered brain damage after reading five thousand comics in a single sitting to win a bet and became the Flaming Carrot; several hints in other issues suggest that he is Jim Morrison of the Doors, back from the dead. His less-than-stellar character is portrayed as a womanizer who drinks hard, fights with two fists, and enjoys pissing off the Establishment with his bizarre behavior. Burden's "Flaming Carrot" stories were never meant to be taken seriously, and were more often than not satirical tales taken from the pop culture of his day. After the Flaming Carrot was rejected as a potential member for the Justice League of America and The Avengers, he formed his own group, known as the Mystery Men. The Mystery Men were actually second-tier superheroes who, for one reason or another, were not accepted by most of the established superhero teams, so their membership in the MM was seen as a last resort. The group included the Shoveller, Jackpot, Mr. Furious, Screwball, Captain Attack, Bondo-Man, Jumpin' Jehosaphat and Red Rover; their superpowers were just as screwball as their names, and included a propensity for hitting villains over the head with a shovel, jumping short distances, attacking without warning, and getting really, really mad. The Flaming Carrot fit right into the group with all of his eccentricities. The Mystery Men made their comic book debut in "Flaming Carrot Comics #16" (June 1987) as part of a flashback that the Flaming Carrot had to an earlier adventure in which his teammates faced the Vile Brotherhood and clones of Hitler's feet. Most of Burden's other MM stories were published by Renegade Press and then Dark Horse Comics between 1987 and 1993. In 1999, Universal Pictures released a live-action feature film, titled "Mystery Men." When the movie failed miserably at the box office, fans seemed to loose interest in the Flaming Carrot as his band of misfit superheroes.

First Media Appearance: Members of the Mystery Men made their first media appearance outside the confines of their comic book universe in 1999 in the Universal Pictures release "Mystery Men."

The 1999 Film Version: In Champion City, Captain Amazing (Greg Kinnear) has enjoyed a wealth of popularity and fanfare as the city's reigning superhero for a number of years, but his popularity numbers are slipping. In order to generate more revenue from endorsements, he arranges for the supervillain Casanova Frankenstein (Geoffrey Rush) to be released from prison. Captain Amazing knows that Frankenstein will return to his life of crime, and he will be there to stop him. Unfortunately, Frankenstein turns the tables on him and locks Captain Amazing away in a secure dungeon. He then unleashes a wave on terror on the city. The other would-be superheroes of the city, known as the Mystery Men, realize that it's up to them to bring Frankenstein to justice and rescue Captain Amazing. These stumblebum heroes, including the fork-flinging Blue Rajah (Hank Azaria), the shovel-wielding Shoveller (William Macy), the bowling ball-hurling Bowler (Janeane Garofalo), the flatulent Spleen (Paul Reubens), the only-when-nobody's-looking Invisible Boy, the mysterious Sphinx (Wes Studi), and the perpetually-pissed-off Mr. Furious (Ben Stiller), charge to the rescue. Universal's attempt to create a superhero franchise of its own was poorly received by fans and critics alike and tanked at the box office.

Trivial Matters: The Sphinx, also known as Ellsworth Forrester, was an established comic book character from the Golden Age, and first appeared in "Exciting Comics #2 from Better Publishing. Mr. Furious, the Spleen and the Shoveller were the only characters from the comic to make the transition to the film; the Flaming Carrot was considered far too outlandish for this bizarre little film.

Fanboy Rating: Babes-0 Effects-1 Action-2 Brainwaves-0 Total=3

Mystery Men

Nick Fury

Nick Fury, Agent of Shield (1998). 20th Century-Fox, 120min. **Director:** Ron Hardy. **Producer:** David Roessell. **Screenwriter:** David S. Goyer. Characters created by Stan Lee. **Cinematographer:** James Bartle. **Film Editor:** Drake Silliman. **Production Designer:** Douglas Higgins. **Cast:** David Hasselhoff, Lisa Rinna, Sandra Hess, Neil Roberts, Gary Chalk, Tracy Waterhouse.

First Comic Book Appearance: "Strange Tales #135" (August 1965)
Origins: Nick Fury, Agent of S.H.I.E.L.D., was Marvel Comics' answer to James Bond and the Man from U.N.C.L.E., and came into being as a creation of Stan Lee and Jack Kirby during the height of America's fascination with spies and secret agents in 1965. Fury was already an established character at Marvel. In 1963, the legendary team of Lee and Kirby launched "Sgt. Fury and His Howling Commandos" as a war comic with Fury in charge of a group of misfits that become unlikely heroes. Twenty years after Fury's distinguished service in World War 2, an older, grayer version of Sgt. Fury (now a colonel) became an agent for the Supreme Headquarters International Espionage Law-enforcement Division or S.H.I.E.L.D. He functioned like a real-world secret agent, and was sent all around the world on missions. He'd also pause, every so often during a mission, to romance beautiful women, including the Countess Valentina Allegro DeFontaine (or Val). From time to time, he would rely on Dum-Dum Dugan, his second-in-command from the war years, to complete an assignment, and he also engaged Captain America, Iron Man and the Black Widow in his fight against Hydra, the Yellow Claw and other enemies of freedom. When writer and illustrator Jim Steranko took over the creative tasks of Nick Fury with "Strange Tales #151," the comic book quickly became one of Marvel's most popular. The fact that Steranko made Fury more like James Bond than James Bond and pushed the Comics Code with his intense storylines and collection of Bond girls didn't hurt. In later

issues of the comic, Jim Starlin and Howard Chaykin pushed Fury even further, fleshing out his background. Near the end of the war, Fury left his howling commandos to become a member of the O.S.S. (a forerunner of the C.I.A.), and recovered an anti-aging formula from Berthold Sternberg. Fury took the formula and extended his life. He then segued into the C.I.A., and worked as an agent behind the Iron Curtain and in Korea gathering information.

He started wearing his trademark eye-patch due to an earlier shrapnel wound while he was still Sgt. Fury. Tony Stark (Iron Man) recruited him to S.H.I.E.L.D., and he's worked for them ever since.

First Media Appearance: David Hasselhoff, who had played a kind of superhero on the television show "Knight Rider" (1982), portrayed Nick Fury on the made-for-the-television movie "Nick Fury: Agent of S.H.I.E.L.D." (1998).

Other Media Appearances: Fury appeared as a guest-star on the animated "Iron Man" series with Philip Abbott providing his voice. Later, he also dropped in on the X-Men in "X-Men: Evolution" and the Avengers in the "Ultimate Avengers" feature. Jim Byrnes and Andre Ware provided the voice, respectively. At the time of this writing, Paramount was developing a big-screen feature-film for release in 2008.

The 1998 Film Version: Since the end of the Cold War, Nick Fury (Hasselhoff) has lived in the Yukon in a personal-kind of exile. However, when Viper (Sandra Hess), the vicious new leader of Hydra, steals a deadly virus and threatens the destruction of the United States, S.H.I.E.L.D. brings Fury out of retirement to help them fight the terrorists. Hasselhoff redeems his years of chasing beach bunnies on "Baywatch" with a fun, action-packed portrayal of Marvel's answer to James Bond. The story itself could have been so much better, but most fans were wise enough to forget the plot and just go with the flow as the action builds from one scene to the next.

Trivial Matters: The characters of Val and Dum-Dum Dugan from the "Nick Fury" comic book also appear in the film. Due to Hasselhoff's huge fan following in Europe, the film was re-edited and released theatrically overseas

Fanboy Rating: Babes-5 Effects-2 Action-5 Brainwaves-2 Total=14

Nick Fury

The Punisher

The Punisher (1989). New World Pictures, 89min. **Director:** Mark Goldblatt. **Producer:** Robert Mark Kamen. **Screenwriter:** Boaz Yakin. Characters created by Gerry Conway. **Cinematographer:** Ian Baker. **Film Editor:** Tim Wellburn. **Production Designer:** Norma Moriceau. **Cast:** Dolph Lundgren, Louis Gossett Jr., Jeroen Krabbe, Kim Miyori.

First Comic Book Appearance: "Amazing Spider-Man #129" (Feb. 1974)
Origins: Inspired by Don Pendleton's literary assassin Mack Bolan, better known as "The Executioner," Gerry Conway created one of the first of Marvel's anti-heroes with "The Punisher." He first appeared in "Amazing Spider-Man #129" wearing his distinctive, form-fitting black Kevlar bodysuit with a large, white skull emblazoned on his chest. He had been duped by the Jackal to assassinate Spider-Man, but soon learned the truth. The new character was then featured opposite Daredevil, Captain American, and just about everybody else in the Marvel Universe, With each subsequent appearance, he became increasingly more popular with fans, and they demanded to know what had driven the Punisher to become a top-notch assassin. He finally got an origin story in "Marvel Preview #2" (April 1975), even though whole parts of it seemed to be borrowed from Pendleton's Executioner. As a Marine in Vietnam, Frank Castle honed his combat skills to near perfection, and returned to the United States as an instructor at Quantico. One day, while he, his wife and their two young children were out on a family excursion in New York's Central Park, they witnessed a gangland shooting. His wife and children were subsequently killed, and he was left for dead. Devastated, Castle built himself back up, and went after those who had been responsible. His personal war didn't stop there as his crusade pitted him against the Italian Mafia, the Japanese Yakuza, the Colombian drug cartels, the Chinese Triads, bikers, street gangs, rapist, psychopaths, and other assorted hoods.
First Media Appearance: The Punisher made his first media appearance in the guise of Dolph Lundgren in the 1989 film adaptation. He then made

several appearances on "Spider-Man: The Animated Series" in the 1990s, with John Beck supplying the voice. In 2004, a second film adaptation was released with Thomas Jane in the lead role.

The 1989 Film Version: New World Pictures' 1989 adaptation turned Frank Castle (Dolph Lundgren) into an ex-cop who had witnessed the gangland executions of his wife and kids, and chosen to leave the police force in order to seek his own unique form of justice. 125 kills over the last five years, and the Punisher is no closer to settling the score than at the beginning. The executions have certainly weakened Gianni Franco (Jeroen Krabbe) and his Mafia family, weakened them so much in fact that the Japanese Yakuza under the leadership of Lady Tanaka (Kim Miyori) have decided to muscle in. A war is coming, and Frank plans smack dab in the middle of it. Louis Gossett Jr. played Frank's ex-partner Jake.

Trivial Matters: Michael Pare was the first choice to play Frank Castle. The Punisher never uses the same weapon twice; he leaves each behind for no reason. The movie's body count is 91.

Fanboy Rating: Babes-1 Effects-2 Action-2 Brainwaves-2 Total=7

The 2004 Film Version: Thomas Jane was a better choice to play Frank Castle, aka The Punisher. In the 2004 version, Castle returns home from the Gulf War, and witnesses the execution of his wife and children by Howard Saint (John Travolta), a mafia chieftain. As a former Delta Force commando, Castle suits up, and heads out to get revenge. Like the first adaptation, this one met with mixed reviews from the critics and performed weakly at the box office. A sequel with Thomas Jane as the Punisher is currently in the works, with a release date set for November 2007.

Trivial Matters: The car that nearly runs over the Punisher has the license plate "ASM 129." This is a reference to the Marvel Comic that featured the debut of the character.

Fanboy Rating: Babes-1 Effects-2 Action-3 Brainwaves-2 Total=8

The Punisher

The Punisher (2004) Lions Gate Films, 124min. **Director:** Jonathan Hensleigh. **Producers:** Ari Arad, Gale Anne Hurd, and Stan Lee. **Screenwriters:** Jonathan Hensleigh and Michael France. **Cinematographer:** Conrad Hall. **Film Editors:** Jeff Gullo and Steven Kemper. **Production Designer:** Michael Hanan. **Cast:** Thomas Jane, John Travolta, Will Patton.

Red Sonja

Red Sonja (1984). Dino De Laurentiis Productions, 89min. **Director:** Richard Fleischer. **Producer:** Christian Ferry. **Screenwriters:** Clive Exton and George MacDonald Fraser. Characters created by Robert E. Howard. **Cinematographer:** Giuseppe Rotunno, **Film Editor:** Frank Urioste. **Production Designer:** Danilo Donati. **Cast**: Arnold Schwarzenegger, Brigitte Nielsen, Sandahl Bergman, Paul Smith, Ernie Reyes, Ronald Lacy, Pat Roach.

First Appearance: "Shadow of the Vulture" *Magic Carpet* (Jan. 1934)
First Comic Book Appearance: "Conan the Barbarian #23" (Feb 1973)
Origins: Like Conan the Barbarian and Kull the Conqueror, the character of Red Sonya of Rogatino was born in the highly-gifted imagination of Robert E. Howard. She first appeared in the short story "The Shadow of the Vulture," which was published in *The Magic Carpet* (January 1934). She was a master (or should that be mistress) of martial arts and sword-wielding and had a knowledge of the supernatural. Red Sonya lived in the same Hyborian Age as Conan. When Roy Thomas and Barry Windsor-Smith were researching a story for their "Conan the Barbarian" comic series, they stumbled across her character in Robert E. Howard's writings, and decided to use her. One of the first things Thomas did was change her name to Sonja (with a "j") and make her into the "she-devil with a sword." Barry Windsor-Smith costumed her in a chain mail bikini, and invented one of comic's first bad girls with her look. Her actual origin story didn't arrive until a few years later. In "Kull and the Barbarians #3" (September 1975), we learn that Red Sonja was driven from her home when a group of mercenaries killed her father Ivor, her mother and two younger brothers. She survived as their slave, and suffered many brutal beatings and rapes. At her lowest point of shame, Sonja called out to the goddess Scathach for help, and was endowed with superior skills as a swordsman. But those skills came with a cost. She had to swear an oath of fealty "never to lie with a man" until he had first bested her in combat. Red Sonja

continued to appear in a number of Marvel Comics, and even had her own series. More recently, when Marvel failed to renew its license to print "Red Sonja," she was picked up by rival Dynamite Entertainment. It is also very likely that her character inspired that of She-Ra in the "Her-Man and the Masters of the Universe" series.

First Media Appearance: Red Sonja made her one and only media appearance in the 1985 film "Red Sonja," with Brigitte Nielsen in the title role opposite Arnold Schwarzenegger.

Other Media Appearances: Avi Lerner and Danny Dimbort's Millennium Films just acquired the rights to make and distribute a feature film based on the "Red Sonja" property, but nothing further has been set. Expect the new adaptation in 2008 or 2009.

The 1985 Film Version: Richard Fleischer's "Red Sonja" stumbles through landslides, earthquakes, sword-play, and rubbery monsters on its pathetic quest for an ancient talisman, and that is before the cameras had even started rolling. Sandahl Bergman, Arnold Schwarzenegger's love interest in "Conan the Barbarian" (1982), should have played the character of Red Sonja. But instead she is relegated to the thankless role of evil Queen Gedren, while newcomer Brigitte Nielsen – a 21-year-old model producer Dino De Laurentiis glimpsed on television – gets the titular role. She can't act, and she can't speak, but that doesn't stop her from trying. Lines of dialogue like "I have fought 177 men and the only one to survive has no legs" sound more like outtakes from "Monty Python and the Holy Grail" rather than an action-adventure film. Even Schwarzenegger looks out of place as Lord Kalidor, the only man that can best Sonja with a sword. Better to wait for the remake.

Trivial Matters: Schwarzenegger was originally signed to reprise his role as Conan, but that was changed to Kalidor so he would not upstage Nielsen as Sonja in her first film.

Fanboy Rating: Babes-1 Effects-2 Action-2 Brainwaves-0 Total=5

Red Sonja

The Rocketeer

The Rocketeer (1991). Disney, 108min. **Director:** Joe Johnston. **Producers:** Charles and Lawrence Gordon, Lloyd Levin. **Screenwriters:** Danny Bilson, Paul De Meo, and William Dear. Based upon the character created by Dave Stevens. **Cinematographer:** Hiro Narita. **Film Editors:** Peter Lonsdale and Arthur Schmidt. **Cast:** Billy Campbell, Jennifer Connelly, Alan Arkin, Timothy Dalton, Paul Sorvino, Terry O'Quinn.

First Comic Book Appearance: "Starslayer #2" (Pacific Comics, 1982)
Origins: Created by writer and illustrator Dave Stevens, the fictional character of Cliff Secord (aka the Rocketeer) blasted into the nostalgic world of 1938 Los Angeles as a back-up feature in Mike Grell's "Starslayer #2" (1982). His adventures continued in four more installments that were published in various Pacific titles, and later collected together by Eclipse Comics. In 1988 and 1989, Comico Comics published two additional stories in the *Rocketeer Adventure Magazine*. A third appeared in 1995 under the Dark Horse Comics banner. While stunt pilot Cliff Secord is testing out a new experimental plane with his friend Peevy, he gets caught in the middle of a conflict between G-men and mobsters. Subsequently, he stumbles across a powerful rocket-pack which, when strapped to his back, enables him to fly. Peevy constructs an aerodynamic helmet for him, and Cliff transforms himself into the Rocketeer. His new alter ego effectively confuses the G-men while he zooms into action and puts an end to mob rule in Los Angeles. Unfortunately, Cliff's superhuman feats do not impress his girlfriend Betty who seeks to advance her career as an actress by posing for pin-up pictures.
Influences: Dave Stevens has made no secret of the fact that his Rocketeer character was inspired by Jeff King who wore a jet-pack and fought criminals in the 1949 Republic Pictures serial "King of the Rocketmen." He also readily acknowledges that Cliff's girlfriend Betty was also based on the personality and looks of the pin-up queen Betty Page; lovely Brinke

Stevens, who was married to Dave at the time, was most likely the model that he used to create the physical appearance of Betty. The comic book series also had a retro look that was not only set in the 1930s but also reflected the superhero style more closely associated with old movie serials. The Rocketeer comic book deposits readers in a much simpler, more innocent time when one man with superior abilities could make a difference in his world.

The 1991 Film Adaptation: With the huge success of the Indiana Jones movies, most of the major studios were looking to make their own period action-adventure films set in the 1930s. Walt Disney Productions optioned "The Rocketeer" from Dave Stevens, and hired novice director and special effects wizard Joe Johnston to make the modestly-budgeted film into a big Hollywood spectacular. In the film, Cliff Secord (Billy Campbell), a young stunt pilot, stumbles across the prototype of a top secret rocket-pack, created by Howard Hughes (Terry O'Quinn). With the help of his mechanic and mentor, Peevy (Alan Arkin), he fashions himself as a high-flying masked superhero. Actor Neville Sinclair (Timothy Dalton) wants to give the rocket-pack to his Nazi confederates, and kidnaps Cliff's girlfriend Betty (Jennifer Connelly) to force a trade. High above the sky, on an exploding Zeppelin that eventually comes crashing down on the "Hollywoodland" sign, Secord rescues the girl and kills the bad guy.

Trivial Matters: The character of Neville Sinclair was loosely modeled after Errol Flynn, the swashbuckling actor who was suspected of collaborating with the Nazis; similarly, Sinclair's henchman Lothar was modeled after B-movie actor Rondo Hatton. "Beemans" was the brand of gum chewed by Howard Hughes and many other test pilots. Originally, the Hollywood sign did read "Hollywoodland," and was used to promote real estate in 1923; in 1945, when the sign was donated to the city of Los Angeles, the last four letters were removed from the sign to decrease maintenance costs. Dave Stevens cameos as the man in the test flight movie with the rocket-pack strapped to his back. "The Rocketeer" comic book celebrated its 25th anniversary at the 2007 San Diego Comic-Con.

Fanboy Rating: Babes-7 Effects-7 Action-7 Brainwaves-7 Total=28

The Rocketeer

Roger Rabbit

Who Framed Roger Rabbit? (1988). Walt Disney Productions, 103min. **Director:** Robert Zemeckis. **Producers:** Steven Spielberg, Frank Marshall, Robert Watts. **Screenwriters:** Gary K. Wolf, Jeffrey Price and Peter S. Seaman. Cinematographer: Dean Cundey. **Film Editor:** Arthur Schmidt. **Production Designers:** Roger Cain and Elliot Scott. **Cast:** Bob Hoskins, Christopher Lloyd, Joanna Cassidy, Charles Fleischer, Stubby Kaye, Alan Tilvern.

First Appearance: Who Censored Roger Rabbit? novel (1981)
First Comic Book Appearance: "The Resurrection of Doom" (June 1989)
Origins: In 1981, Gary K. Wolf wrote his clever and satirical novel, *Who Censored Roger Rabbit?*, most booksellers didn't know how to market it. The book which placed cartoon characters side-by-side with humans in the same universe seemed like it was written as a children's book. But the mystery elements of the story, which seemed borrowed from Raymond Chandler and Dashiell Hammett, were far more sophisticated than most children could handle. Though Wolf's novel featured many lovable 'toons, including the title character, his work was clearly meant for the same audience that had grown up with Chuck Jones and Walt Disney. The plot of the novel follows the efforts of hard-boiled private eye Eddie Valiant to find the murderer of Roger Rabbit, a comic strip character. At first, Roger hires Valiant to discover why the sleazy DeGreasy Brothers syndicate has gone back on an offer to feature him in a strip of his own. He is the sidekick in the "Baby Herman" strip. But when Roger is murdered as a way of "censoring" the star, Valiant takes things personally. He had grown to like the 'toon. His search for the killer takes him down a number of dark alleys, very literally, and involves more twists and turns than a Sam Spade mystery. Valiant narrows his list of suspects down to Roger's widow, Jessica Rabbit, and his former co-star, Baby Herman. But naturally there's a surprise or two waiting for him at the end. *Who Censored Roger Rabbit?* was not a success when it was first published, but when Walt Disney teamed

with Steven Spielberg to make a feature-length film, interest in the novel was re-vitalized. Wolf has since published a sequel, titled *Who P-P-Plugged Roger Rabbit?*, and several comic books have also rolled out.

First Media Appearance: Roger Rabbit made his first media appearance on June 21, 1988, when the big-screen adaptation, "Who Framed Roger Rabbit?," debuted. Roger's voice was supplied by Charles Fleischer.

Other Media Appearances: Several Roger Rabbit shorts, starting with "Tummy Trouble" in 1989, "Rollercoaster Rabbit" in 1990, and "Trail Mix-Up" in 1993, have also been released theatrically.

The 1988 Film Version: Unlike the novel, Roger Rabbit is not killed, but merely framed for a murder he did not commit in Robert Zemeckis' ground-breaking comedy. Initially, private eye Eddie Valiant (Bob Hoskins), who hates 'toons, is hired to prove that Roger's wife Jessica (Kathleen Turner) is playing pattycake with someone else. But when Marvin Acme (Stubby Kaye) is found murdered and Roger's prints are all over the crime scene, Valiant must prove his innocence. Clues lead the private eye to Maroon Cartoon studios, and then all hell breaks loose, as the world between reality and fantasy is completely shattered. The hectic pace of the film is further complicated by guest appearances by some of the most famous 'toons in cartoon history. Eventually the trail leads straight to Judge Doom (Christopher Lloyd) who wants to rub-out all 'toons.

Guest Appearances: Mickey Mouse, Minnie Mouse, Pluto, Donald Duck, Goofy, Pegleg Pete, Horace Horsecollar, Clarabell Cow, the merry darfs, Three Little Pigs, Big Bad Wolf, Peter Pig, Toby Tortoise, Max Hare, Little Red Riding Hood, Jenny Wren, Elmer the Elephant, Snow White and the seven dwarfs, Old Witch, Wynken, Blynken, Nod, Ferdinand the Bull, Pinocchio and Jiminy Cricket, the Reluctant Dragon, Dumbo, Bambi, Chicken Little, Jose Carioca, Monte the pelican, Peter, Br'er Bear, Tar Baby, Mr. Toad, Bugs Bunny, Daffy Duck, Porky Pig, Tweety, Sylvester, Yosemite Sam, Foghorn Leghorn, Marvin the Martian, Road Runner, Wile E. Coyote, Sam Sheepdog, Speedy Conzales, Koko the Clown, Betty Boop, Woody Woodpecker, Droopy, and many, many others

Trivial Matters: Producer Joel Silver cameos as the director of the Baby Herman cartoon that leads off the film; this cameo was filmed as a prank by Robert Zemeckis on Disney chief Michael Eisner. A follow-up feature, titled "Who Discovered Roger Rabbit?, was planned, but then never filmed.

Fanboy Rating: Babes-8 Effects-7 Action-5 Brainwaves-6 Total=26

Roger Rabbit

The Shadow

The Shadow (1994). Universal, 108min. **Director:** Russell Mulcahy. **Producers:** Willi Bar, Martin Bregman, and Michael Scott. **Screenwriter:** David Koepp. Based upon the character created by Walter B. Gibson. **Cinematographer:** Stephen H. Burum. **Film Editors:** Beth Besterveld and Peter Honess. **Cast:** Alec Baldwin, John Lone, Penelope Ann Miller, Peter Boyle, Ian McKellen, Tim Curry, Jonathan Winters.

First Appearance: "Detective Stories" Radio Show (July 31, 1930)
Origins: "Who knows what evil lurks in the hearts of men? The Shadow knows!" Even though most fans regard the Shadow as a fictional character created by Walter B. Gibson in the pulp magazines of the 1930s and 1940s, few remember that he was first employed by announcer James LaCurto (then later Frank Readick Jr.) as a radio persona. Beginning on July 31, 1930, the Shadow entertained radio audiences with his readings of stories drawn from the pulp magazine *Detective Stories* published by Street & Smith. The problem was that listeners found the announcer far more gripping than the stories he told, and began demanding stories featuring the Shadow. Street & Smith complied, and commissioned Gibson, a magician and former ghost-writer for Harry Houdini, to write a series of adventures. Over the next twenty years, Gibson wrote 282 novel-length stories under the pen name Maxwell Grant. In print, the Shadow was Kent Allard, a famed aviator who had crashed in the South American rain forest and, after making a considerable fortune, returned to the United States with mysterious powers. In New York City, he assumes the identity of Lamont Cranston, a wealthy socialite who was in Europe at the time; eventually, when he does meet Cranston, Cranston agrees to allow Allard to impersonate him when he is abroad. With an elaborate network of agents and other associates, the Shadow fights a never-ending battle with the forces of evil. He is armed solely with a matching pair of .45 pistols and the ability to cloud men's minds. In illustration, the Shadow is often por-

trayed wearing a wide-brimmed fedora, suit and cape with a scarf pulled up over his mouth.

First Media Appearances: Unlike most superheroes that came out of the thirties and forties, the Shadow truly was a product of radio, not print. Aside from his first appearance as a radio announcer's persona, the Shadow became a fully-fledged detective on September 26, 1937, when the then-unknown Orson Welles portrayed him on a series of half-hour radio dramas for the Mutual Broadcasting System. That same year, the Shadow made the leap to film in "The Shadow Strikes" in a low-low budget quickie featuring Rod Larocque. Columbia Studios produced a low-budget serial with Victor Jory in 1940, and then, in 1946, Kane Richmond starred in a trio of low-low budget films for Monogram, starting with "The Shadow Returns."

First Comic Book Appearance: The Shadow made his first comic book appearance in "Shadow Comic" in 1940, published by Street & Smith. 101 issues were published between 1940 and 1948. His third, and most celebrated, depiction was brought to life by Dennis O'Neil and Mike Kaluta for DC Comics (in 1970). Several other comics were published, most notably a three-issue series by Dark Horse.

The 1994 Film: Lamont Cranston (Alec Baldwin), a disaffected veteran of World War 1, trades his skills as a mercenary to brutal warlords and opium smugglers for safe passage though Asia. When he is kidnapped by Tibetan monks and brought to their monastery, Cranston is eventually re-formed, and agrees to fight evil as the Shadow. Later, returned to New York City as a wealthy socialite, he learns that Shiwan Khan (John Lone), a Chinese warlord, plans to conquer the world by holding the city hostage with an atom bomb. Relying on his extraordinary powers, the Shadow springs into action against his former friend. Universal had hoped to launch a franchise, but the movie's dismal failure at the box office caused them to rethink their plans.

Trivial Matters: The film borrows liberally from both the pulp stories by Walter Gibson and the radio show; for instance, the fact that the Shadow can become invisible is an element that was created by writers who contributed to the radio show.

Fanboy Rating: Babes-2 Effects-2 Action-5 Brainwaves-2 Total=11

The Shadow

Sheena

Sheena (1984). Columbia, 117min. **Director:** John Guillermin. **Producer:** Paul Aratow. **Screenwriters:** David Newman, Leslie Stevens, and Lorenzo Semple Jr. Characters created by Will Eisner and S.M. Eiger. **Cinematographer:** Pasqualino De Santis. **Film Editor:** Ray Lovejoy. **Production Designer:** Peter Murton. **Cast:** Tanya Roberts, Ted Wass, Donovan Scott, Elizabeth of Toro, France Zobda, Trevor Thomas, Clifton Jones.

First Appearance: "Wags #1" British tabloid (1937)
First Comic Book Appearance: "Jumbo Comics #1" (September 1938)
Origins: Created by Will Eisner and S.M. "Jerry" Iger, the sexy, white jungle goddess Sheena was conceived as a female version of Edgar Rice Burroughs' Tarzan. Unlike her male counterpart, she was not born in the jungle or raised by apes. Instead her father Cardwell Rivington brought her with him on one of his expeditions to Africa. When Rivington is killed by accident, the local witch doctor Koba raises Sheena to atone for his mistake. He imparts his wisdom and a few supernatural spells that give Sheena dominance over the animals of the jungle. Soon, she grows into a beautiful woman, and selects great white hunter Bob Reynolds as her mate. She is often clad only in an animal-skin bikini. Many of her early stories featured treacherous hunters, mysterious beasts, and cannibal tribes that, more often than not, she subdued with her native skills. Later, her origin story was revised, and she gained parents who were missionaries. Bob Reynolds became Rich Thorne, and Koba was renamed N'bid Ela. She also inherited an ape companion named Chim. Not one of her readers seemed to mind because the stories were after all about Sheena's exploits in the jungles of Africa. After a brief run as a comic strip in the British tabloid "Wags," she debuted in the United States in "Jumbo Comics #1" (September 1938). Four years later, she became the first female comic-book character with her own title in Spring 1942. "Wonder Woman #1" was still three months away. Sheena was very popular with readers, and

despite the limitations of her storylines, she kept plugging away as a Jungle Queen until 1954 when her publishing company went out of business. The last Sheena comic was presented in 3-D (in 1953). The character was revived for a short-lived television series in the 1950s and then a feature-length film in the 1980s. Marvel Comics printed a three-issue adaptation of the movie.

First Media Appearance: For her first media appearance, sexy model Irish McCalla played Sheena on a 26-episode television series that aired in syndication from 1955 to 1956. McCalla freely admitted that she was no actress, but that she had been discovered on Malibu Beach throwing a spear.

Other Media Appearances: In 1984, former "Charlie's Angels" star Tanya Roberts played "Sheena, Queen of the Jungle." Hearst Entertainment revived the character one more time in 2000, with Gena Lee Nolin in the lead role of a 35-episode television series from Columbia. In the series, Sheena also had the power to change into any warm-blooded animal.

The 1984 Film Version: John Guillermin's "Sheena, Queen of the Jungle" presented a far more fanciful adaptation of the comic book material than had ever been imagined by Will Eisner, thanks to a screen story by "Superman" scribe David Newman and Leslie Stevens. When Sheena's geologist parents Philip and Betsy Ames (Michael Shannon and Nancy Paul) are killed in an unexpected cave-in, she is raised by the mystical Shaman of the native Zambouli tribe (Princess Elizabeth of Toro). Apparently, a prophecy about a cave-in has the Zamboulis believing that Sheena is a gift from the gods. As she grows to womanhood, the Shaman teaches her the lore of the jungle and how to communicate telepathically with all of the creatures of the jungle. Outsiders disturb the natural order and take the Zambouli captive. With an America reporter (Ted Wass), Sheena (Roberts) struggles to expose the strip-mining plans of an evil Prince (Trevor Thomas) and save her beloved Shaman. The film's story was far more complicated than it needed to be, and Roberts was just out of her element as the "queen of the jungle." Eisner's first comic book heroine deserved so much better than this.

Trivial Matters: Two years prior to "Sheena," Tanya Roberts played a similar role as Kiri in M-G-M's "Beastmaster" (1982).

Fanboy Rating: Babes-9 Effects-1 Action-2 Brainwaves-2 Total=14

Sheena

Spawn

Spawn (1997). New Line Cinema, 96min. **Director:** Mark A.Z. Dippe. **Producer:** Clint Goldman. **Screenwriters:** Alan B. McElroy and Mark Dippe. Characters created by Todd McFarlane. **Cinematographer:** Guillermo Navarro. **Film Editors:** Rodd Busch and Michael Knue. **Production Designer:** Philip Harrison. **Cast:** Michael Jai White, John Leguizamo, Martin Sheen, Theresa Randle, Nicol Williamson, D.B. Sweeney.

First Comic Book Appearance: "Spawn #1" (May 1992)

Origins: Cartoonist Todd McFarlane rose to prominence in the 1980s doing "Spider-Man," which became a huge, must-read hit. But when he felt exploited by Marvel Comics, he and several others left to form Image Comics. He then created "Spawn" to capitalize on his own popularity. Like "The Punisher" and many other, latter-day comic book creations, Spawn (short for "Hellspawn") was an anti-hero. After witnessing his boss engage in several unscrupulous deals, CIA agent Al Simmons is murdered by the same man he had served loyally for many years. That left his boss' double-dealings hidden from the Agency. On the other hand, Simmons was sent straight to hell. Bitter and angry that he had never had the chance one last moment with his beloved wife Wanda to say goodbye, he made a deal with the demon Malebolgia. In exchange for his fealty for a hundred lifetimes, Simmons got a chance to see her; unfortunately, Malebolgia made it five years later, after which time, she had already re-married his best friend Terry Fitzgerald and started a family. Simmons felt betrayed by his bargain, and re-dedicated his undead life as the demon's hellspawn to get revenge on his boss and find a way out of his bargain. In the early stories, Simmons now renamed Spawn must constantly choose between good and evil as he is pulled by Clown, a short, fat demon, and Cogliostro, a homeless man who knows more than he is saying. As a member of Malebolgia's slave army of undead warriors, he struggles with every assignment he is given. He kills a pedophile who is a serial killer; he fights an angel that was sent to eliminate him; he smashes the efforts of organized crime. Eventually, he finds a way to destroy Malebolgia, and declines an offer to go to Heaven in order to keep fighting the evil that exists on Earth. Thanks (in part) to a clever marketing strategy that included the production of action figures, "Spawn" became a huge success at Image, selling more than a million copies. Alan Moore, Frank Miller, and Neil Gaiman all loved the book so much that they wrote individual issues, starting in 1993, and brought new characters to the number one comic book in the world.

First Media Appearance: In 1997, a feature-length film adaptation, starring Michael Jai White as Spawn, was released.

Other Media Appearances: Shortly after the film was released, HBO produced a critically-acclaimed animated series with Keith David as the voice of Spawn. The series won two Emmy Awards (one in 1998, and the other in 1999). Presently, a sequel to the feature film is being made for release in 2007, and a new web-comic that takes place in a "What If?" universe is being produced as "The New Adventures of Spawn."

The 1997 Film Version: New Line Cinema reimagined Al Simmons as an assassin rather than a government agent, and that subtle change adds a unique dimension to the story that never existed in the comic books. When Simmons (White) is double-crossed and murdered by his evil boss Jason Wynn (Martin Sheen as you've rarely seen him), Al makes a pact with the devil to return to Earth as Spawn in exchange for a chance to see his wife Wanda (Theresa Randle). Spawn is then ordered by the Clown (John Leguizamo) to kill Wynn, but what he doesn't know is that Wynn has made his own deal with the Clown. He plans to destroy the world with a deadly virus that will trigger the final battle of Armageddon. Knowing that will mean Hell attacks Heaven, Spawn must choose between the ultimate Good and the ultimate Evil. The film was not a huge success, but fans of the comic book like New Line's take on their favorite character.

Trivial Matters: Todd McFarlane cameos as a bum. Tim Burton was originally signed to direct the film. Martin Sheen as Wynn is asked by Clown to start "the apocalypse, now." Sheen played the lead role in "Apocalypse Now" (1979).

Fanboy Rating: Babes-2 Effects-7 Action-5 Brainwaves-4 Total=18

Spawn

Spider-Man

Spider-Man (2002). Columbia, in association with Marvel Enterprises, 121min. **Director:** Sam Raimi. **Producers:** Ian Bryce and Laura Ziskin. **Screenwriter:** David Koepp. Characters created by Stan Lee and Steve Ditko. **Cinematographer:** Don Burgess. **Film Editors:** Arthur Coburn and Bob Murawski. **Production Designer:** Neil Spisak. **Cast:** Tobey Maguire, Willem Dafoe, Kirsten Dunst, James Franco, Cliff Robertson, Rosemary Harris.

First Comic Book Appearance: "Amazing Fantasy #15" (August 1962)
Origins: Like "Superman" at DC Comics, "The Amazing Spider-Man" is the flagship comic book of Marvel Comics, featuring one of the world's most popular and enduring superheroes. Created by Stan Lee and Steve Ditko, Spiderman was the first teenage character who was not a sidekick to be featured in his own title. He first appeared in the final issue (#15) of "Amazing Fantasy," a comic book that had been designated a mature book for adults (originally titled "Amazing Adult Fantasy") and that featured the unique, often unconventional art-work of Steve Ditko. The character of Peter Parker was also an unconventional one: He was a bitter, shy young man who nobody liked and who was often the brunt of practical jokes played by members of his own peer group. He obsessed constantly over his lack of friends, his feelings of rejection and inadequacy, and his overwhelming sense of loneliness. In other words, he was the typical adolescent of his day. Lee and Ditko had become aware of the fact that more and more teenagers were reading comic books that featured superheroes, and thought that it would be a good idea to build one around the kid everybody in school picked on. Stan Lee approached Marvel publisher Martin Goodman with the idea, and after overcoming all of Goodman's objections, he was given the go-ahead to produce a one-shot for "Amazing Fantasy." At about the same time, Jack Kirby and Joe Simon had pitched a character called the Silver Spider for the Crestwood comic "Black Magic." Their idea focused on an orphaned boy who, while living with an

older couple, finds a magic ring that endows him with superhuman powers. But when that publisher went out of business, they shelved their idea. Some time later, Lee discussed his idea with long-time partner Jack Kirby, and Kirby told him about his failed project. Lee encouraged him to make his "Silver Spider" a reality, but in the end, Kirby's character was little more than Captain Marvel with the ability to make spider-webs. (Ironically, his creation with Joe Simon became the basis for "The Fly," which appeared in Archie Comics.)

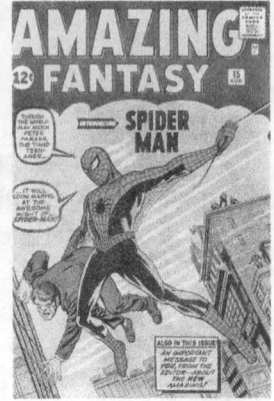

Stan Lee must have liked some aspects of his partner's idea, for when he met again with Ditko, the character of Spider-Man was much more fully fleshed out with details about his home life and alter ego in place. However, they did not anticipate the overwhelming success that Spider-Man would have in "Amazing Fantasy #15" until the fan mail started pouring in. Nearly every teenager in America wrote to say how much they could identify with Peter Parker's plight. Not long after he is bitten by a radioactive spider at a science exhibition, Parker begins to exhibit spider-like powers. He has the ability to climb walls; he has superhuman strength and agility, and he has a kind of extra-sensory perception that he calls his "spider sense." His first thought is a selfish one. Peter decides to use his powers to gain fame and fortune as a professional wrestler. But when he accidentally lets a petty thief get away, while taping a television show, that thief kills his Uncle Ben, and he realizes that he should have used his powers to prevent his uncle's death. Peter decides to dedicate himself to crime-fighting, recalling his uncle's words, "With great power comes great responsibility."

"The Amazing Spider-Man" was launched the following year, and quickly became Marvel's best-selling series. In the early issues of the comic book, Parker attends Midtown High School and works a part-time job as a stringer, selling photos to Jonah Jameson of the "Daily Bugle." Later, he attends Empire State University, where he meets Harry Osborn and Gwen Stacy. His life is quickly complicated by Harry's father Norman, who turns out to be the Green Goblin, and another supervillain known as Doctor Octopus. When the Green Goblin kills Gwen Stacy, Peter Parker turns to Mary Jane Watson for solace, and they develop a relationship. An alien symbiote attacks Spider-Man and turns his costume black while permanently trying to bond with its host. Peter is able to fight it off, but the symbiote merges with Eddie Brock instead, and creates the villain known

Spider-Man

as Venom. "The Amazing Spider-Man" and its spin-off titles have managed to remain fresh over the years because the character of Peter Parker keeps growing and changing; he continues to be a human being with all of humanity's flaws and frailties, and that is what makes him so identifiable to all of his readers. Whether he is dealing with an unauthorized clone of himself in Ben Reilly or is contemplating a break-up with Mary Jane so that he can take a job as a teacher at his old high school, Parker and Spider-Man continue to be amazing.

First Media Appearance: Spider-Man made his first media appearance on September 9, 1967, on the popular, Saturday morning cartoon series "Spider-Man" on ABC. Produced by Grantray-Lawrence Animation, the show featured the catchy opening theme, "Spider-Man, Spider-Man/ Does whatever a spider can…" and detailed many of the web-slinger's early adventures, starting with "The Power of Doctor Octopus." Paul Soles provided the voice of Spider-Man for all of its fifty-two episodes.

Other Media Appearances: In 1974, The Electric Company featured a live-action series of shorts, titled "Spidey Super Stories." The show starred Danny Seagren as Spider-Man, and was told with word balloons in place of actual dialogue. Four years later, CBS aired another live-action series, titled "The Amazing Spider-Man," with Nicholas Hammond in the familiar superhero costume. The show, which was produced by Columbia, had an impressive run of fifteen episodes, but the lack of supervillains like Doctor Octopus and the Green Goblin disappointed the show's loyal fan base. And to add insult to injury, Stan Lee voiced his objections to the series, referring to it as "too juvenile." The show ended in 1979. Spidey has also head-lined five other animated series, starting with "Spider-Man" and "Spider-Man and His Amazing Friends" (both of which first aired in 1981), "Spider-Man: The Animated Series" (1994), "Spider-Man Unlimited" (1999), and "Spider-Man: The New Animated Series" (2003).

The 2002 Film Version: Director Sam Raimi, who had previously brought "Darkman" to the big screen, delivered Columbia one of its biggest blockbusters in cinema history with the tale of an awkward high school student who is bitten by a genetically-modified spider and develops superpowers. Up until that point in time, most moviegoers had agreed that the best superhero movie was Richard Donner's 1978 "Superman." But when Tobey Maguire put on the Spider-Man costume for the first time and spun his

first web, the great debate began as audience members responded favorably to the new kid on the block. The screen story follows the familiar origin from the comic books. Once Parker is bitten, he tries to use his new-found abilities to make money for a car to take Mary Jane Watson (Kirsten Dunst) out on a date. His Uncle Ben's (Cliff Robertson) untimely death at the hands of a street thug forces him to re-evaluate his life as he develops his alter ego as Spider-Man to fight crime. He is torn by his relationship with Harry Osborn (James Franco) as he battles his father Norman (Willem Dafoe) as the Green Goblin. And he is also at odds with his employer Jonah Jameson (J.K. Simmons) who wants to exploit him for pictures of Spider-Man. His Aunt May (Rosemary Harris) tells him to relax: "You're not Superman, after all," but Peter only knows that he has to keep moving if he is to be successful in juggling all aspects of his life.

Trivial Matters: Freddie Prinze Jr. and Leonard DiCaprio were both considered for the title role before Tobey Maguire was selected. Similarly, Alicia Witt, Mena Suvari, and Elisha Cuthbert were early favorites for the role of Mary Jane Watson. Pre-production planning for the "Spider-Man" movie began in 1986 at Cannon Films. James Cameron wrote an early draft of the screenplay, and was Sony's first choice as director. Others included Jan de Bont, Ang Lee, and David Fincher.

Fanboy Rating: Babes-8 Effects-8 Action-7 Brainwaves-8 Total=31

Spider-Man 2 (2004). Columbia, in association with Marvel Enterprises, 127min. **Director:** Sam Raimi. **Producers:** Avi Arad and Laura Ziskin. **Screenwriters:** Alfred Gough, Miles Millar, and Michael Chabon. **Cinematographer:** Bill Pope. **Film Editor:** Bob Murawski. **Production Designer:** Neil Spisak. **Cast:** Tobey Maguire, Kirsten Dunst, James Franco, Alfred Molina, Rosemary Harris, J.K. Simmons.

Spider-Man

The 2004 Film Sequel: The amazing success of the first "Spider-Man" movie led to the inevitable sequel, which was in many respects better than its predecessor. Sam Raimi was once again behind the helm as director, and many of the principles from the first film, including Maguire, Dunst, Franco, Harris and Simmons, had returned to reprise their now-famous roles. As the film begins, Peter Parker (Maguire) is having a rough time balancing all the desperate elements of his life. He wants to have a meaningful relationship with Mary Jane (Dunst) who just sees him as a friend and nothing more. He's trying to comfort his best friend Harry Osborn (Franco) who blames Spider-Man for the death of his father. He feels compelled to look in on his aging aunt (Harris). He has a job as a photographer for the "Daily Bugle," and he is trying to take classes at the university in order to finish his degree. To top it all off, his double life as the superhero Spider-Man has had a devastating effect on his non-existent down-time. Peter's made up his mind to quit the superhero business for good. Unfortunately, for him, Dr. Otto Octavius (Alfred Molina) has become injured and deformed while demonstrating his new power armor before defense contractors, and been transformed into Doctor Octopus. With four huge, mechanical tentacles sticking out of his back, he strikes the city of New York, and only Spider-Man can stop him. "Spider-Man 2" was 2004's second-most successful movie in North America and third internationally, with box office grosses well in excess of $450 million. The stage seemed set for a third movie in the franchise.

Trivial Matters: With Tobey Maguire suffering severe back pains from a fall in another movie, Jake Gyllenhaal was lined up to take his place, but Maguire decided to throw caution to the wind and do the role anyway. Robert De Niro, Sam Neill, Ed Harris, and Chris Cooper were all considered for the role of Otto Octavius. Scenes featuring Spidey's battle with Doc Ock on the exterior of a subway train were actually filmed in Chicago on the famous elevated Loop. In his first film, "Raiders of the Lost Ark" (1981), Alfred

Molina had another close encounter with spiders. Raimi wanted Bruce Campbell to appear as the Lizard at the end of the film.

Fanboy Rating: Babes-7 Effects-7 Action-7 Brainwaves-7 Total=28

Spider-Man 3 (2007). Columbia, in association with Marvel Enterprises, 127min. **Director:** Sam Raimi. **Producers:** Avi Arad and Laura Ziskin. **Screenwriter:** Sam Raimi, Ivan Raimi, and Alvin Sargent. **Cinematographer:** Bill Pope. **Film Editor:** Bob Murawski. **Production Designers:** Neil Spisak and J. Michael Riva. **Cast:** Tobey Maguire, Thomas Haden Church, Kirsten Dunst, James Franco, Bryce Dallas Howard, Topher Grace, Rosemary Harris, J.K. Simmons.

The 2007 Film Sequel: "Spider-Man 3" was released on May 4, 2007, and by May 7, the film was already on its way to besting the box office take of the other two films. An alien symbiote from outer space bonds with Peter Parker and causes inner turmoil as he contends with Sandman (Thomas Haden Church), Harry Osborn's (Franco) twisted plan of revenge against Spider-Man, and temptations for Gwen Stacy (Bryce Dallas Howard) when he is still in love with Mary Jane (Dunst). If the third film follows the comic book series as closely as the two previous films, count on Gwen Stacy to meet her maker at the hands of Harry Osborn and Peter Parker's love for Mary Jane to continue as unrequited.

Trivial Matters: At the San Diego Comic-Con in 2006, Sam Raimi show attendees the first public images of Venom in the film, and fans spontaneously burst into applauds and cheers. Topher Grace left "That 70's Show" (1998) to star in "Spider-Man 3." While it is inevitable, there are presently no plans in place for a "Spider-Man 4."

Fanboy Rating: Babes-7 Effects-7 Action-7 Brainwaves-7 Total=28

Spider-Man

The Spirit

The Spirit (1987). ARRI Lighting Rental, 74min.
Director: Michael Schultz. **Producer:** Paul Aratow
and Robert Sertner. **Screenwriter:** Steven E. de
Souza. Characters created by Will Eisner. **Cinema-
tographer:** Frank Thackery. **Cast:** Sam Jones, Nana
Visitor, Garry Walberg, John Allen, Ed Cambridge,
Sarah Dammann, Philip Baker Hall, Robert Jayne.

First Appearance: "Spirit Newspaper Strip #1" (June 2, 1940).
First Comic Book Appearance: "Police Comics #22" (June 1942).
Origins: Will Eisner's "The Spirit" is one of the most recognizable of all
comic strip detectives, and one of the most classic and significant works of
the comic-art medium. He is also the character most closely associated
with his creator. From June 2, 1940, to October 5, 1952, the Spirit appeared daily, fighting the forces of evil. Presumed dead in the first three
pages of his premiere insert, young criminologist Denny Colt appears to
Central City's Police Commissioner Dolan, and explains that he has been
in a state of suspended animation as the result of one of Dr. Cobra's failed
experiments. He returned to life in Wildwood Cemetery, and decided to
use news of his death to create a crime-fighting alter ego in the Spirit. He
also uses an old tomb at the cemetery for his underground lair. (As the
Spirit, Colt wears a domino mask, a blue suit, fedora hat, and gloves for a
costume.) Dolan treats Denny Colt like a son, and agrees to go along with
his charade as long as he produces results. For the duration of the comic
strip, the Spirit fought all manner of criminals and archvillains. Sometimes
he was accompanied by Ebony White, his African-American sidekick,
and at other times, he worked alone with an invisible network of infor-
mants, assistants and collaborators. His girlfriend was Dolan's daughter
Ellen, but his relationship with her did not stop him from his share of beautiful but deadly femme fatales. In 1942, the Spirit appeared in comic book
form when Quality Comics began reprinting the daily comic strips in its

anthology series, "Police Comics." Not long after, he was given a title of his own. His comic strip came to an end in 1952, but he found a whole new generation of fans when Harvey Comics reprinted several Spirit stories in two giant-size comic books in October 1966 and March 1967. Warren Publishing and Kitchen Sink Press extended the reprints and even added a few original stories from Alan Moore, David Gibbons and Paul Chadwick. In 2006, DC Comics published a one-shot crossover featuring Batman and the Spirit as developed by Jeph Loeb and Darwyn Cooke.

First Media Appearance: Sam Jones, who had played Flash Gordon in a 1980 film adaptation, essayed the role of the Spirit in his first and only media appearance in a 1987 television movie.

Other Media Appearances: At the 2006 San Diego Comic Book Convention, Frank Miller announced that he planned to write and direct a feature film version of "The Spirit" that was targeted for release theatrically in 2008 or 2009. Odd Lot Entertainment along with executive producers Michael Uslan, Benjamin Melniker, and Steven Maier, and producers Linda McDonough and F.J. DeSanto hosted Miller's appearance at the convention, and agreed to provide financing for the film.

The 1987 Film Version: When Denny Colt (Sam Jones), a detective for the Central City Police Department, is gunned down by assassins, and miraculously survives, he takes advantage of the fact that he is legally dead. He creates the mysterious crime fighter known as the Spirit, and equips an abandoned tomb in a graveyard as his headquarters in a war against crime. The only people who know that he's still alive are Commissioner Dolan (Garry Walberg) and his daughter Ellen (Nana Visitor). His first major case pits him against P'Gell Roxton (Laura and McKinlay Robinson), a femme fatal who has criminal plans to take over the city. The television movie is played mostly for camp like the 1966 "Batman" series, and while it was produced as a pilot for an unsold series, the production values are quite low. Sam Jones is far too stiff as Colt, and Visitor is totally wrong for the role of Ellen. Thankfully, this production has been long since dead and buried in Wildwood Cemetery.

Trivial Matters: The 74-minute movie was intended as a pilot for a television series that never made it off the ground.

Fanboy Rating: Babes-4 Effects-1 Action-2 Brainwaves-2 Total=9

The Spirit

Spy Smasher

Spy Smasher (1942). Republic Pictures, 215min. **Director:** William Witney. **Producer:** William J. O'Sullivan. **Screenwriters:** Ronald Davidson, Norman Hall, William Lively, Joseph O'Donnell, and Joseph Poland. **Cinematographer:** Reggie Lanning. **Film Editors:** Tony Martinelli and Edward Todd. **Cast:** Kane Richmond, Marguerite Chapman, Sam Flint, Hans Schumm, Tristan Coffin, Franco Corsaro, Hans Von Morhart, Georges Renavent, Rudolph Anders.

First Comic Book Appearance: "Whiz Comics #2" (February 1940)
Origins: "Spy Smasher," as created by Bill Parker and C.C. Beck, was yet another flag-waving, patriotic comic book that came out in the 1940s that showed our superheroes were ready to take the fight to the fascist forces of Germany, Italy and Japan and win. Like Batman, Green Arrow, and the Crimson Avenger, Alan Armstrong masqueraded as a wealthy, carefree billionaire during the day, and fought crime as a masked avenger known as the Spy Smasher at night. He first took up the good fight when his girlfriend Eve Corby's father, an admiral in Naval Intelligence, told him that spies and saboteurs were responsible for what appeared to be a series of recent, random accidents. Armstrong made up his mind to go after these enemies himself, and built a Gyrosub (a submarine that could transform into a helicopter or a car) to give him an edge in his battle. Then, with a red cape, brown military fatigues and goggles (instead of a mask) to hide his identity, he smashed his first spies in "Whiz Comics #2" (dated February 1940). Only his girlfriend knew that he and Spy Smasher were one and the same. The character of Spy Smasher was introduced in the same Fawcett comic title that carried Captain Marvel, and together they were the most popular characters. He later got his own comic book title, and also traded his dull costume for a spiffier one, featuring a gold diamond on his chest. After World War 2 ended, Armstrong changed his name to Crime Smasher, and fought members of organized crime. The stories were not quite as entertaining or full of whimsy as the earlier ones had been. In

1953, Fawcett discontinued its line of superhero comics, and the adventures of Spy Smasher came to a temporary end. Nearly twenty years later, DC Comics obtained the rights to all of Fawcett's character, and Alan Armstrong picked up the battle right where he had left off, this time as a Cold War warrior. He was one of the heroes of Earth-S prior to the "Crisis on Infinite Earths" maxi-series. Interestingly enough, his daughter Katarina Armstrong, as created by Gail Simone, became the new Spy Smasher in the 100th issue of "Birds of Prey."

First Media Appearance: Kane Richmond played Alan Armstrong/Spy Smasher in his first and only media appearance in the 1942 serial. When the re-edited serial was shown as a feature film in 1966, Spy Smasher reached a while new generation of fans.

The 1942 Film Serial: During the early days of World War 2, Alan Armstrong (Kane Richmond) battles Nazi spies and saboteurs in Nazi-occupied

France. After his plane crashes, he lets everyone think that Alan Armstrong is dead...so that he can continue fighting the fascist forces as Spy Smasher. He manages to rescue his brother Jack (also Richmond) from a Nazi spy, and shows Jack the ring he is wearing; it matches the one that Jack is also wearing. Jack Armstrong is elated that his brother didn't die in a plane crash. Together, they return to American soil. When he learns from Admiral Corby (Sam Flint) that a German master-spy known as the Mask (Hans Schumm) plans to launch an all-out offensive with saboteurs spreading terror and destruction across the United States, Spy Smasher fights spies at home. "Spy Smasher" was Republic's finest serial. Kane Richmond is superb in his dual role as Jack and Alan Armstrong, and Marguerite Chapman makes his imperiled fiancée Eve Corby more like a real player in the drama than the typical damsel-in-distress.

Trivial Matters: The 12-part Republic serial was already in production when the United States entered World War 2, so that accounts for Alan Armstrong being identified as an "independent agent" fighting the Nazis in occupied Europe. The Mask had already been killed in the comic book series, but still made an effective villain in the serial.

Fanboy Rating: Babes-1 Effects-2 Action-2 Brainwaves-2 Total=7

Spy Smasher

Steel

Steel (1997). Warner Brothers, 97min. **Director:** Kenneth Johnson. **Producers:** Quincy Jones, David Salzman, and Joel Simon. **Screenwriter:** Kenneth Johnson. Characters created by Louise Simonson and Jon Bogdanove. **Cinematographer:** Mark Irwin. **Film Editor:** John Link. **Production Designer:** Gary Wissner. **Cast:** Shaquille O'Neal, Annabeth Gish, Judd Nelson, Richard Roundtree, Irma Hall, Ray J, Harvey Silver, Charles Napier, Gary Graham.

First Comic Book Appearance: "Advs of Superman #500" (June 1993) *Origins:* Following the much-publicized death of Superman in 1993, DC Comics green-lighted the stories of four separate superheroes who would take the place of the Man of Steel. One of them, as written by Louise Simonson and illustrated by Jon Bogdanove, was very literally a man of steel. John Henry Irons, an engineer and weapons designer, grows tired of working for the military-industrial complex, and trades his top security clearance for a simple construction worker's job. Superman had once saved his life, and Irons felt that he owed him. So, when the Man of Steel died (at the hands of Doomsday), Irons paid his debt by creating a formidable suit of armor, not unlike the one worn by Iron Man in Marvel Comics, and taking Superman's place. Irons also carried a gimmick-laden hammer, like Thor. Steel fought many of the same villains that Superman had fought, and even after Superman returned from the dead, Steel continued to fight criminals like a dedicated superhero. In 1994, Steel earned his own comic book title, and his comic sold for 55 issues and two annuals through July 1998. He then joined the Justice League of America, and distinguished himself, fighting alongside other League members. Steel was not the first superhero to use the name "Steel." In 1978, Gerry Conway and Don heck created a character named "Steel, the Indestructible Man" or "Captain Steel" for DC Comics. Hank Heywood has his body rebuilt, full of steel and mechanical devices, when he is severely injured, and goes to fight crime as one of the earliest cybernetic superheroes. Other than the

name, no other comparisons can be made.

First Media Appearance: On August 15, 1997, Shaquille O'Neal provided Steel with his first media appearance outside the world of comic books in the feature film from Warner Brothers, titled "Steel."

Other Media Appearances: Shortly after the film's release in 1997, the character of Steel became an animated one on "Superman: The Animated Series," with Michael Dorn from "Star Trek: The Next Generation" (1988) providing the voice. He also made a guest appearance in "Justice League Unlimited," voiced by Phil LaMarr.

The 1997 Film Version: Warner Brothers dropped all connections to Superman and the popular comic book series in order to create a far more urban character for the 1997 feature film. In "Steel," John Henry Irons (Shaquille O'Neal) quits his job designing weapons for the military when his latest project – a harmless neutralizer – goes up in smoke, possibly the target of sabotage. He returns to his home in the low-rent projects of Los Angeles, and finds that local gang-bangers are responsible for creating an atmosphere of fear and terror. At his Uncle Joe's (Richard Roundtree) junk yard, he tinkers together an indestructible suit of armor, and goes after the punks who have threatened his friends and family. Kenneth Johnson, who had created the series "V," does an okay job directing the film, but Shaq's poor acting skills and lack of screen charisma doomed this production even before the first frame.

Trivial Matters: The character that Annabeth Gish plays in the movie was based on the DC Comics character Oracle. Shaquille O'Neal's Superman tattoo, which is real, is the only link the film makes to Superman; all of the material about Steel's origin has had the Superman connection eliminated. Shaquille O'Neal is 7'1".

Fanboy Rating: Babes-1 Effects-2 Action-2 Brainwaves-2 Total=7

Steel

Supergirl

Supergirl (1984). Warner Brothers, 105min. **Director:** Jeannot Szwarc. **Producer:** Timothy Burrill. **Screenwriter:** David Odell. Characters created by Otto Binder for DC Comics. **Cinematographer:** Alan Hume. **Film Editor:** Malcolm Cooke. **Production Designer:** Richard MacDonald. **Cast:** Faye Dunaway, Helen Slater, Peter O'Toole, Mia Farrow, Brenda Vaccaro, Peter Cook, Simon Ward, Marc McClure, Hart Bochner.

First Comic Book Appearance: "Action Comics #252" (May 1959)
Origins: "The Supergirl from Krypton," written by Otto Binder and illustrated by Al Plastino, introduced the Man of Steel's cousin Supergirl to the DC Universe in "Action Comics #252" (dated May 1959). Kara was the daughter of Zor-El and Allura; Zor-El was the brother of Jor-El who was also Superman's father, and that family lineage made Kara, Superman's cousin. When the planet Krypton exploded, Zor-El's Argo City was flung away on a hunk of rock no larger than an asteroid. Zor-El knew that his city's resources would sustain them for only a short time, and that continued exposure to fragments of kryptonite meant his people were doomed. He prepares a rocket, in much the same way that Jor-El had prepared for Kal-El, and sent Kara in it to Earth for safekeeping with her cousin. At first, Superman does not know what to do with her, but when she acquires the same superpowers as Superman, he decides to conceal her identity for as long as he can. He gives her a brunette wig to conceal her blonde hair, and takes her as an orphan to Midvale Orphanage. Kara is coon adopted by Fred and Edna Danvers, and Supergirl adopts the secret identity of Linda Lee Danvers. Kara, the last daughter of Krypton, attends Midvale High School and then Stanhope College. After college she moves to Chicago, and tries her hand counseling, news reporting (like Clark Kent), and finally acting in a television soap opera. Her cat Streaky and her horse Comet gain superpowers and follow her on numerous adventures. In 1985, DC Comics attempted to reboot its various comic book series with the

"Crisis and Infinite Earths" miniseries. In Issue #7, Kara as Supergirl sacrifices her life for Superman and temporarily saves the multiverse from destruction. Her death was major news, and rippled throughout the entire comic book industry. Supergirl returned a few years later with a new origin and identity.

First Media Appearance: Supergirl made her first media appearance in the guise of Helen Slater in the 1984 feature film, "Supergirl."

Other Media Appearances: Supergirl also appeared on a two-part episode of "Superman: The Animated Series" in 1996; she later traded costumes and appeared in a fifth season episode of "Justice League Unlimited." More recently, on the television series "Smallville" (2001), a girl named Kara (Adrianne Palicki) has emerged, claiming to be from Krypton.

The 1984 Film Version: Following the success of the first three "Superman" movies, Alexander and Ilya Salkind produced a follow-up film featuring Superman's cousin Kara as Supergirl. The feature film should have been a success, but Warner Brothers gave the Salkinds too much freedom to tamper with the origin story, and what remains is a strange concoction that is neither a film nor a comic book. Argo City floats peacefully through the void of inner space, powered by the Omegaheadron. When the Omedheadron is lost by clumsy Zaltar (Peter O'Toole), Kara (Helen Slater) heads to Earth to find it. She soon learned that a witch named Selena (Faye Dunaway) has found it and plans to use it to conquer the world. Supergirl must stop her before Argo City dies without its power source. Christopher Reeve had been signed to reprise his role as Superman to launch his cousin in her first film, but alas, he is missing, and so is the plot!

If you like to watch beautiful women fly around, you'll love it.

Trivial Matters: John Williams' rousing Superman theme is jettisoned for a timid score from the usually reliable Jerry Goldsmith. Marc McClure cameos as Jimmy Olsen. Demi Moore was slated to play Lucy Lane, but dropped out at the last minute. Brooke Shields was the first choice for the role of Supergirl.

Fanboy Rating: Babes-9 Effects-2 Action-2 Brainwaves-2 Total=15

Supergirl

Superman

Superman, The Adventures of (1948). Columbia, 244min. **Director:** Thomas Carr. **Producer:** Sam Katzman. **Screenwriters:** Lewis Clay, Royal Cole, Arthur Hoerl, George Plympton, and Joseph Poland. Characters created by Joe Shuster and Jerry Siegel. **Cinematographer:** Ira Morgan. **Film Editor:** Earl Turner. **Cast:** Kirk Alyn, Noel Neill, Carol Forman, Tommy Bond, Pierre Watkin, Jack Ingram, Nelson Leigh, Luana Walters.

First Comic Book Appearance: "Action Comics #1" (June 1938)
Origins: In 1932, Superman was created by Jerry Siegel and Joe Shuster, two science fiction fans living in Cleveland, Ohio, and first appeared in a short story, titled "Reign of the Superman," in their self-published fanzine *Science Fiction #3* (dated 1933). He was not the Man of Steel that we've come to associate with "Truth, Justice and the American Way," but rather a megalomaniacal superior man bent on world domination. Siegel and Shuster retooled the character, one year later, as a hero, and submitted the story in comic strip form to Consolidated Book Publishing. Consolidated rejected their creation in a polite letter that claimed he was far too much like other figures of the day. They tried again, this time giving him a costume not unlike those worn by characters in the "Flash Gordon" comic strip and extraordinary abilities far beyond those of mortal men. Siegel and Shuster offered their strip to M.C. Gaines, United Features Syndicate, and finally Detective Comics. DC publisher Jack Liebowitz had been on the look-out for new talent, and needed material to fill out his new monthly anthology, titled "Action Comics." When he saw Siegel and Shuster's final work, Superman became the lead feature. Their story not only launched the superhero craze but also gave the fledgling comic book industry a real boost. Superman became the first character who originated in comic books to earn his own title, with "Superman #1" (in 1939). In terms of their story, which has had more than its fair share of minor revisions and significant alterations over the years, Superman was born Kal-

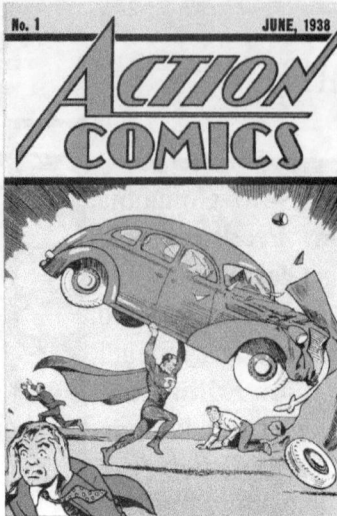

No. 1   JUNE, 1938
ACTION
COMICS

El on the distant planet Krypton to scientists Jor-El and Lara. When Jor-El discovers that Krypton is doomed, he builds a rocketship and sends his infant son rocketing to Earth mere moments before the planet's destruction. The rocket crashlands on Earth, and the child is found by passing motorists, Jonathan and Martha Kent. They adopt him and give him the name Clark Joseph Kent. Clark grows to maturity in the little town of Smallville, Kansas, and learns about his superhuman abilities. His adoptive parents teach him a strong sense of purpose and morality, and raise him to believe that his powers are gifts to be used for the betterment of mankind. (In the "Superboy" comics, which first debuted in "More Fun Comics #101" (June 1944), Clark lived at 321 Maple Street with the Kents, and wore a junior version of his costume to fight foes from the Phantom Zone. He also romanced Lana Lang, and was responsible for his friend Lex Luthor's hair loss in a laboratory fire. Superman was also given a superdog named Krypto in "Adventure Comics #210" (1955) and a female cousin named Kara in "Action Comics #252" (1959).) At age 21, Clark Kent sets out as Superman to use his powers to fight crime, and to maintain a secret identity, he takes a job as a "mild-mannered reporter" for the *Daily Star* (later changed to *Daily Planet*) in Metropolis. His editor is Perry White; his best friend is cub photographer Jimmy Olsen, and his fellow reporter and romantic interest is Lois Lane. In the early comics, Superman not only used his powers to fight crime but also to stop injustices (like the mistreatment of prison inmates) and to fight social causes (like reckless driving or the poor construction of public housing). He became a champion of the weak, and adopted a strict moral code that prevented him from killing anyone. Instead he used his arsenal of powers, which included super-strength, invulnerability, super-speed, x-ray vision, super-hearing, super-breath, and the ability to leap tall buildings in a single bound, to safeguard humanity from the forces of evil; he couldn't fly, at first, but gradually added flight to his abilities. However, Superman could do nothing to stop the ravages of the Great Depression. During the War years, Superman fought enemies of freedom in the United States; with all of his superhuman abilities, he could have probably brought an end to

Superman

World War 2 in a manner of moments, but that was not something the writers ever considered. Superman was not entirely godlike. He did have his limitations, and in time, we learned that he was most vulnerable to Kryptonite, a hunk of rock from the planet Krypton that had become radioactive. In the 1950s and 60s, Superman fought enemies from space as well as Earth-bound ones, and found himself often at a disadvantage to characters like Brainiac, Bizarro, Mr. Mxyzptlk, and General Zod. In fact, Superman was apparently killed in 1993 by Doomsday, only to return a short time later. He did team up with other superheroes, most notably Batman in "Worlds Finest" comics, and he was a member of both the Justice Society of America and the Justice League of America. The "Crisis on Infinite Earths" miniseries attempted to clean up the many inconsistencies in Superman's past by sending the Golden Age Superman off with his bride Lois Lane and killing off his cousin Kara (aka Supergirl), but that clean-up only lasted so long. Today, we look upon the Man of Steel as Earth's champion and protector.

First Media Appearance: Superman made his first media appearance in a radio series, titled "The Adventures of Superman," which premiered on New York City's WOR on February 12, 1940. Bud Collyer provided the voice of Superman. The series ran until March 1, 1951, and featured the distinctive opening that most of us probably know by heart: "Faster than a speeding bullet!/More powerful than a locomotive!/Able to leap tall buildings with a single bound!/Look ! Up in the sky!/It's a bird!/It's a plane!/It's Superman!"

Other Media Appearances: Bud Collyer also provided the voice of the animated Superman that appeared in seventeen cartoon shorts produced by the Fleischer Studios between 1941 and 1943. In 1948, Kirk Alyn became the first actor to play Superman on the silver screen in the first of two serials, simply titled "Superman," that were produced by Columbia Pictures. The second serial was titled "Atom Man vs. Superman" in 1950. Alyn was asked to return to play Superman on television, but he declined. Instead George Reeves headlined as the Man of Steel. The pilot episode, "Superman and the Mole Men," was released theatrically in 1951, and generated so much interest

that the television show, which ran from 1952 to 1958, was such an easy sell. Superman was the subject of a Broadway musical, titled "It's a Bird…It's a Plane…It's Superman," in 1966, and returned to television that same year in an animated series, "The New Adventures of Superman," with Bud Collyer again providing the voice. From 1973 to 1984, Hanna-Barbera produced the "Super Friends" series, and Superman was a regular character along with his friends from the Justice League of America. A big-budget feature film with Christopher Reeve in the title role of "Superman" opened in 1978, and broke all sorts of box office records. The film spawned three sequels, including "Superman 2" (1980), "Superman 3" (1983) and "Superman 4: The Quest for Peace" (1987), and a spin-off about Superman's cousin "Supergirl" (1984). John Haymes Newton and Gerard Christopher shared duties as Superboy in "The Adventures of Superboy" that aired in syndication between October 1988 and June 1992. In 1993, Teri Hatcher and Dean Cain played "Lois and Clark: The New Adventures of Superman," a romantic comedy that featured one of the most popular love triangles in literary history. Several other animated shows, including Ruby Spears' "Superman" (1988) and "Superman: The Animated Series" (1996), gave the Man of Steel other venues for his superpowers. The WB's "Smallville" (2001) added yet another twist to the familiar story, by showing us the early life and adventures of Clark Kent before he donned the red cape. And finally, Bryan Singer's update of Richard Donner's 1978 classic gave us Brandon Routh as Superman in "Superman Returns."

The 1948 Film Serial: Columbia Pictures had wanted to make a serial from the "Superman" comic books for a number of years, but Sam Katzman knew the cost of producing the special effects of a man in flight would be prohibitively expensive and hesitated for nearly ten years. Finally, someone on his production team saw one of the Fleischer Studios' shorts, and suggested that all of Superman's in-flight scenes be animated like a cartoon. With that major budgetary problem solved, the 15-part, black-and-white serial was given the green light, and the first of its fifteen-minute episodes premiered on January 5, 1948. "Superman" begins by recounting Jor-El's (Nelson Leigh) fateful decision to send his infant son to Earth, and then follows the early years of Clark Kent (Alan Dinehart III) as he is

Superman

raised by Eben (Ed Cassidy) and Martha Kent (Virginia Caroll). Years later, the adult Clark Kent (Kirk Alyn) lands a job with the *Daily Planet* newspaper, and goes to work for Perry White (Pierre Watkin), sharing offices with Lois Lane (Noel Neill) and Jimmy Olsen (Tommy Bond). Several chapters into the serial, Carol Forman as the Spider Lady emerges as a formidable foe who wants to enslave the world with her deadly raygun. Superman comes to the rescue, many times in the appropriate cliff-hanger form, and ultimately defeats the evil woman. The serial was a popular success for Columbia, and spawned a 1950 sequel. It also launched the careers of Kirk Alyn and Noel Neill. In retrospect, "Superman" may well have been the most successful serial of its time.

Trivial Matters: Every shot of Superman in flight was animated, and then simply superimposed onto live action shots; thus, after Kirk Alyn as Superman takes a few steps and then jumps, he stops being a real person and turns into a cartoon figure. Kirk Alyn was not credited as Superman, only Clark Kent. In fact, the publicists at Columbia even suggested to the press that the real Superman was portraying himself. Kirk Alyn's double broke his leg jumping off a building.

Fanboy Rating: Babes-4 Effects-3 Action-3 Brainwaves-4 Total=14

The 1950 Film Sequel: Spencer Gordon Bennet directed Columbia's 43rd serial, "Atom Man Versus Superman," in 1950, and proved the old adage that bigger was better in this follow-up to the highly successful "Superman." Masquerading as Atom Man, Lex Luthor (Lyle Talbot) has threatened to destroy the city of Metropolis if the politi-

Atom Man Vs. Superman (1950). Columbia Pictures, 252min. **Director:** Spencer Bennet. **Producer:** Sam Katzman. **Screenwriters:** David Mathews, George Plympton, and Joseph Poland. Characters created by Joe Shuster and Jerry Siegel. **Cinematographer:** Ira Morgan. **Film Editor:** Earl Turner. **Cast:** Kirk Alyn, Noel Neill, Lyle Talbot, Tommy Bond, Pierre Watkin, Jack Ingram.

cal officials don't agree to his blackmail terms. He has apparently invented a number of deadly gadgets to accomplish his threat, including a disintegrating machine which reduces people to their basic atoms. Perry White (Pierre Watkin), editor of the *Daily Planet*, assigns Lois Lane (Noel Neill), Jimmy Olson (Tommy Bond) and Clark Kent (Kirk Alyn) to get the exclusive story. But Superman manages to thwart each and every one of his schemes. Since Kryptonite can rob Superman of his powers, Luthor decides to create a synthetic form of Kryptonite and spends part of the serial assembling the necessary ingredients. He then springs it on the Man of the Steel who subsequently collapses. His goons grab the incapacitated hero, and make him vanish into "The Empty Doom." But we all have confidence that Superman will escape the empty doom and save the city of Metropolis. This is one of the few sequels that is just as good, if not better, than the original. The flying sequences are much improved, and without needing to retell the origin story at the beginning, the story leaps right into action. Certainly well worth the effort!

Trivial Matters: Lyle Talbot was the first actor to play Lex Luthor on screen. Footage from Superman's origin story is placed strategically in the sequel to heighten tension and suspense for the audience. Atom Man's disintegrator/integrator was a forerunner of the transporter on "Star Trek."

Fanboy Rating: Babes-4 Effects-4 Action-3 Brainwaves-4 Total=15

Superman and the Mole Men (1951). Lippert Pictures, 58min. **Director:** Robert Maxwell. **Producers:** Robert Maxwell and Barney Sarecky. **Screenwriter:** Richard Fielding. Characters created by Joe Shuster and Jerry Siegel. **Cinematographer:** Clark Ramsey. **Film Editor:** Al Joseph. **Cast:** George Reeves, Phyllis Coates, Jeff Corey, Walter Reed, J. Farrell MacDonald, Stanley Andrews.

The 1950 Film Version and Television Show: "Superman and the Mole Men" (1951) was produced by Barney Sarecky and directed by Lee Sholem as the pilot for the syndicated television series, "The Adventures of Superman." But when the studio saw how very good the fifty-eight minute was, they decided to release it theatrically first. The film, which premiered on November 23, 1951, finds mild-mannered reporter Clark Kent (George Reeves) and Lois Lane (Phyllis Coates) in the small town of

Silsby reporting on the world's deepest oil well. What no one realizes is that the well has penetrated the underground home of the "Mole Men," and these furry beings have come up to the surface to investigate. But everything they touch turns phosphorescent. The townspeople are whipped up into a frenzy by Luke Benson (Jeff Corey) to destroy the "monsters," but naturally, Superman intervenes and saves the townspeople from themselves. The Mole Men return to their underground home, and the well is sealed forever. The pilot and many of the early episodes of the television series were very well done, and showed a great deal of intellect and adult themes. Tinkering by syndicated sponsors later made it a kiddie show. When Kirk Alyn passed on the television show (and pilot), George Reeves stepped into the part and made it truly his own. In fact, before Christopher Reeve left such an indelible performance, Reeves was always the actor most associated with Superman and Clark Kent. Phyllis Coates makes an acceptable Lois Lane, but it wasn't until the second season that Noel Neill returned to the part that she was born to play. Jack Larson played Jimmy Olsen and John Hamilton was Perry White. The opening narration of the television show expanded on the narration used in the 1940s cartoons: "Faster than a speeding bullet! More powerful than a locomotive! Able to leap tall buildings at a single bound! ("Look! Up in the sky!" "It's a bird!" "It's a plane!" "It's Superman!")... Yes, it's Superman ... strange visitor from another planet who came to Earth with powers and abilities far beyond those of mortal men! Superman ... who can change the course of mighty rivers, bend steel in his bare hands, and who, disguised as Clark Kent, mild-mannered reporter for a great metropolitan newspaper, fights a never-ending battle for truth, justice, and the American way!" The show first aired on September 19, 1952, and the series ran until April 28, 1958. Many of the 104 episodes were made in black-and-white; some were shot in color. After all of the fan mail, producers planned to make two more year's worth of episodes, starting in 1959, but Reeves untimely and unresolved death ended all of those plans. A proposed series, featuring Jack Larson as "Superman's Pal, Jimmy Olsen," never got very far beyond the planning stages.

Trivial Matters: At first, Kirk Alyn was not interested in doing television; then, he wanted too much money per episode; eventually, they settled on George Reeves who was on his way to becoming a big star. "Superman and the Mole Men" was cut in half, and aired as a two-parter on the television series.

Fanboy Rating: Babes-4 Effects-3 Action-4 Brainwaves-5 Total=17

Superman (1978). Warner Brothers, 143min. **Director:** Richard Donner. **Producers:** Alexander Salkind and Pierre Spengler. **Screenwriters:** Mario Puzo, David and Leslie Newman, Robert Benton, and Tom Mankiewicz. Characters created by Joe Shuster and Jerry Siegel. **Cinematographer:** Geoffrey Unsworth. **Film Editors:** Stuart Baird and Michael Ellis. **Production Designer:** John Barry. **Cast:** Christopher Reeve, Marlon Brando, Gene Hackman, Margo Kidder, Ned Beatty, Glenn Ford, Trevor Howard, Valerie Perrine.

The 1978 Film Version: Thirty years after the first "Superman" movie, producers Pierre Spengler, Alexander and Ilya Salkind teamed with director Richard Donner to create a classic – what many consider to be the greatest of all superhero films. The Warner Brothers production was huge, even by today's standards, and featured some of the industry's greatest actors and actresses in key roles. In the lead role was Christopher Reeve, an unknown actor who would define Superman for a whole generation. When he is unable to convince the ruling council of Krypton that their world will be destroyed, Jor-El (Marlon Brando) sends his infant son Kal-El to Earth. There, under the Earth's yellow sun, he will gain great strength and powers. Raised by the Kents (Glenn Ford and Phyllis Thaxter), young Clark Kent (Jeff East) learns that his super-

Superman

human abilities must be used to benefit all of mankind. The adult Clark Kent (Christopher Reeve) travels to Metropolis, takes a job with Perry White (Jackie Coogan) at *the Daily Planet* and tries to romance fellow reporter Lois Lane (Margo Kidder). He also emerges as a caped wonder known as Superman, performing amazing feats that stun the city. Meanwhile, Lex Luthor (Gene Hackman), the world's greatest criminal mind, plots to destroy the West Coast in the greatest real estate swindle of all time. Naturally, Superman is there to stop him, and rescue Lois from an alternate time-line in which she died. The great John Williams provides a magnificent score that captures Superman's greatest feats in musical form, and the special effects masters capture lightning in a bottle with their green-screen effects. Donner gives us action, drama, romance, comedy, and good-old-fashioned American values in a heart-warming film that we are likely never to see again in any other film.

Trivial Matters: At one time or another, many different actors were considered for the role of Superman, including Burt Reynolds, Arnold Schwarzenegger, Robert Redford, Warren Beatty, James Caan, Kris Kristofferson, Nick Nolte, Jon Voigt, Bruce Jenner, and Patrick Wayne. Similarly, Anne Archer, Lesley Ann Warren, Deborah Raffin, Susan Blakely, Stockard Channing, and Holly Palance were considered as likely Lois Lanes. Kirk Alyn and Noel Neill are featured in cameos. Both "Superman" and "Superman 2" were shot at the same time, using many of the same sets; when it appeared Richard Donner was not going to make his deadline, shooting on "Superman 2" ceased.

Fanboy Rating: Babes-9 Effects-7 Action-8 Brainwaves-10 Total=34

Superman 2 (1981). Warner Brothers, 127min. **Director:** Richard Lester. **Producers:** Alexander Salkind and Pierre Spengler. **Screenwriters:** Mario Puzo, David and Leslie Newman, and Tom Mankiewicz. Characters created by Joe Shuster and Jerry Siegel. **Cinematographers:** Robert Paynter and Geoffrey Unsworth. **Film Editor:** John Victor-Smith. **Production Designer:** John Barry. **Cast:** Christopher Reeve, Gene Hackman, Margo Kidder, Ned Beatty, Terence Stamp, Valerie Perrine.

The 1980 Film Sequel: Though much of "Superman 2" had already been filmed by Richard Donner, the Salkinds dismissed him, and hired Richard Lester to take over the reigns of the production. What remains is a very good, commercial film that shows moments of brilliance and moments of mediocrity. Ironically, the Richard Donner version, which was finally released in 2006 on DVD, has its own moments of brilliance and mediocrity. Very likely, the screen story by four different writers is at the heart of the film's dichotomy. When Superman (Christopher Reeve) rescues Lois Lane (Margo Kidder) from nuclear terrorists in Paris, he unwittingly frees three Kryptonian supervillains (Terence Stamp, Sara Douglas, and Jack O'Halloran) from the Phantom Zone with the nuclear explosion. Apparently, these are the same supervillains his father Jor-El imprisoned at the start of the previous film. They travel to Earth and start wreaking havoc, while Superman is busy romancing Lois at his Fortress of Solitude at the North Pole. Superman agrees to sacrifice his powers to marry Lois, but soon comes to regret his decision when they return to Metropolis as a couple. Now, Superman has to find a way to restore his superpowers or watch the world crumble at the hands of these supervillains. The Last Son of Krypton comes to realize that he must sacrifice his love to keep the Earth safe. The motion picture sequel was a huge success when it was released in 1980, and made stars out of most of the principles. Most fans enjoyed the battle of the superpowers in Metropolis between Superman and his three adversaries. But there was still something lacking from the production. Perhaps it was Donner's old-fashioned take on the material? Or Lester's lack of understanding? Or the loss of cinematographer Geoffrey Unsworth?

Trivial Matters: Another version of the film, known as the Richard Donner version, was released in 2006; that version significantly alters the overall feel of the picture, while maintaining the original storyline. Richard Lester scrapped the epic look of Donner's footage, which was shot by the late Geoffrey Unsworth, in favor of a more gritty appearance. The whole sequence in Paris with the nuclear terrorists was created for the Lester film; in Donner's version, Zod and his companions from the Phantom Zone were released when Superman threw one of Luthor's missiles from the first movie into space. Gene Hackman did not return for "Superman 2"; all

Superman

of the footage of Hackman as supervillain Lex Luthor had been previously filmed by Richard Donner.

Fanboy Rating: Babes-8 Effects-7 Action-8 Brainwaves-7 Total=31

Superman 3 (1983). Warner Brothers, 125min. **Director:** Richard Lester. **Producer:** Ilya Salkind and Pierre Spengler. **Screenwriters:** David and Leslie Newman. Characters created by Joe Schuster and Jerry Siegel. **Cinematographer:** Robert Paynter. **Film Editor:** John Victor-Smith. **Production Designer:** Peter Murton. **Cast:** Christopher Reeve, Richard Pryor, Jackie Cooper, Marc McClure, Annette O'Toole, Annie Ross, Robert Vaughn, Pamela Stephenson, Margot Kidder.

The 1983 Film Sequel: The second sequel found Christopher Reeve's Superman playing second banana to Richard Pryor's comic villain Gus Gorman. When wealthy businessman Ross Webster (Robert Vaughn) discovers that one of his employees (Pryor) is a computer genius, he decides to use his talents to gain economic control of the world. But first, he must get rid of Superman (Reeve). He has Gorman create a synthetic form of Kryptonite, which acts like Red Kryptonite on Superman, splitting the Man of Steel into a good half and a bad half. The two do battle, and eventually, the good Superman emerges victorious. Then Webster instructs Gorman to create a Kryptonite laser which he also uses on Superman. Ultimately, Superman beats the corporate magnate, and saves Gorman from a life of crime. "Superman 3," which was also directed by Richard Lester, is a total mess, with very few redeeming qualities. The best part of the picture is when Clark Kent returns to Smallville for a high school reunion and meets his old flame Lana Lang (Annette O'Toole), but those scenes are very short-lived. Instead Lester focuses too much on comedian Richard Pryor, and forgets this is supposed to be a Superman movie. *Trivial Matters:* On the television series "Smallville" (2001), Annette O'Toole plays Martha Kent. The original title of the film was "Superman Versus Superman." Brainiac was supposed to have been the villain, but was changed to accommodate Richard Lester's desire to use Pryor as the comic villain.

Fanboy Rating: Babes-6 Effects-6 Action-5 Brainwaves-4 Total=21

Superman 4: The Quest for Peace (1987). Cannon Films, 90min. **Director:** Sidney Furie. **Producers:** Yoram Globus and Menahem Golan. **Screenwriters:** Christopher Reeve, Lawrence Konner, and Mark Rosenthal. Characters created by Joe Shuster and Jerry Siegel. **Cinematographer:** Ernest Day. **Film Editor:** John Shirley. **Production Designer:** John Graysmark. **Cast:** Christopher Reeve, Gene Hackman, Margot Kidder, Marc McClure, Jon Cryer, Sam Wanamaker.

The 1987 Film Sequel: With the Salkinds gone and Warner Brothers temporarily out of the superhero business, Yoram Globus and Menahem Golan of Cannon Films hired Sidney J. Furie to direct a very traditional Superman movie. Regrettably, "Superman 4: The Quest for Peace" is only marginally better than "Superman 3." Most the blame rests with Furie; in an effort to turn out a film like Donner's original, he lifts whole sequences from the first two movies. He then races through the material without providing enough context or characterization. So, what remains is a 90-minute trailer for "Superman" and "Superman 2," with a few cool extras thrown into the mix. At the urging of a young boy (Damien McLawhorn), Superman (Christopher Reeve) crusades for nuclear disarmament, and manages to hurl most of the world's nuclear weapons into the sun. However, Archvillain Lex Luthor (Gene Hackman) has other plans. With his nephew Lenny (Jon Cryer), he uses the DNA from a strand of Superman's hair to create a radiation-charged Nuclear Man (Mark Pillow). Meanwhile, Perry White (Jackie Cooper) fights David Warfield (Sam Wanamaker) for control of the *Daily Planet*, and Clark Kent (Reeve) romances Warfield's daughter Lacy (Mariel Hemingway). In the explosive finale, Superman and Nuclear Man duke it out on the Moon, New York, Italy, China, and other locales around the planet, while the Man of Steel saves the Statue of Liberty, Mount Etna, and the Great Wall of China from destruction. Christopher Reeve provided the story for the film, and while on paper, the story is a good one…Furie is

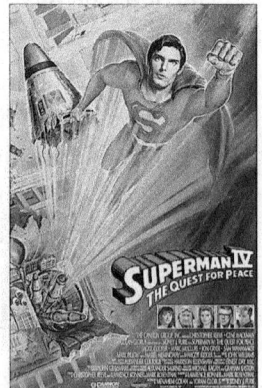

Superman

unable to ignite the fire of creativity on screen. Golan and Globus should have spent another couple of million, hired Richard Donner, and made a truly epic film; instead what remains is a flawed film that could and should have been so much better.

Trivial Matters: Superman and Lois' romantic flight around Manhattan from the first film was recreated here. Though Christopher Reeve receives credit for the story, a current trend in the comic book found Superman experiencing nightmares about nuclear war and the end of the world. At the end of the film, Superman tells Lex Luthor that he will see him in twenty (meaning twenty years); "Superman Returns" was released 19 and a half years later.

Fanboy Rating: Babes-8 Effects-3 Action-5 Brainwaves-7 Total=23

Superman Returns (2006). Warner Brothers, 154min. **Director:** Bryan Singer. **Producers:** Gilbert Adler, Jon Peters, and Bryan Singer. **Screenwriters:** Michael Dougherty, Dan Harris, and Bryan Singer. Characters created by Joe Shuster and Jerry Siegel. **Cinematographer:** Newton Thomas Sigel. **Film Editor:** Elliot Graham and John Ottman. **Production Designer:** Guy Dyas. **Cast:** Brandon Routh, Kate Bosworth, Kevin Spacey, James Marsden, Parker Posey, Frank Langella, Marlon Brando, Eva Marie Saint.

The 2006 Film Version: After dozens of scripts and nearly a dozen years in development hell, Bryan Singer's magnificent "Superman Returns" (2006) demonstrates that some of the best things in life are worth waiting for. Singer achieves, what most fans and critics alike believed was, the impossible...resurrecting the Superman franchise without Christopher Reeve. For most of us, Reeve was the Man of Steel, and the untimely accident that put him in a wheelchair on live support (and eventually led to his death) was a crushing blow to all those that wanted to see Reeve put on the red cape and take to the skies one more time. Actors like Josh Hartnett, Brendan Fraser, Jerry O'Connell, Ian Somerhalder, Nicolas Cage, and Ashton Kutcher would never have been able to fill Reeve's red boots, let alone project his congenial, nice-guy image. But Brandon Routh who sort of looks like Reeve and reflects Reeve's inno-

cent character makes an acceptable substitute as both Clark
Kent and Superman. In fact,
when he quotes statistics about
air travel safety to Lois Lane
(Kate Bosworth), he seems to be
channeling the late Christopher
Reeve as if his ghost was inhab-
iting Routh's body. Singer delivers a Superman movie that has
the epic sense of grandeur that Richard Donner's original film had, and
makes his feature fun and relevant to today's audience. Kevin Spacey is
terrific as Lex Luthor, as are most of the other actors. The one weak note
is Bosworth as Lois Lane; most fans and critics had a hard time believing
this young actress was a mother with a five-year-old son, a career and a
Pulitzer. Another, more mature actress would have been better suited for
the role. The story is simple, and yet somehow complicated: After a five-
year long visit to the lost remains of the planet Krypton, the Man of Steel
(Routh) returns to Earth to discover that things have gotten worse. People
need him even more now than they once did, everyone that is except Lois
Lane (Bosworth) who has a son named Jason (Tristan Lake Leabu) and
fiancé Richard White (James Marsden). Lex Luthor (Spacey) compli-
cates matters even more with his obsession for beach-front property and
a new scheme to control the world. Yes, the world needs Superman more
than ever! At the 2006 San Diego Comic-Con, Singer announced that a
sequel, titled "Superman: Man of Steel," was being prepped for a 2009
release; Warner Brothers chairman Alan Horn confirmed that a few weeks
later in a *Los Angeles Times* article.

Trivial Matters: Tim Burton, McG, Brett Ratner, J.J. Abrams and many
others were considered to direct the new film; the closest any one of them
came to a green light was Tim Burton in 1993 for "Superman Lives"; the
script by Kevin Smith was based on the comic book story arc featuring
Superman's death at the hands of Doomsday. Elisha Cuthbert, Claire
Danes, and Keri Russell were all considered for the role of Lois Lane.
Anthony Hopkins was set to play Jor-el when Brett Ratner was attached
as director. Bryan Singer used archival footage of Marlon Brando as Jor-
El from the Richard Donner Film.

Fanboy Rating: Babes-8 Effects-7 Action-7 Brainwaves-8 Total=30

Swamp Thing

Swamp Thing (1982). Embassy Pictures, 91min. **Director:** Wes Craven. **Producers:** Benjamin Melniker and Michael Uslan. **Screenwriter:** Wes Craven. Characters created by Len Wein and Bernie Wrightson. **Cinematographer:** Robert Goodwin. **Film Editor:** Richard Bracken. **Production Designer:** Robb Wilson King and David Nichols. **Cast:** Louis Jourdan, Adrienne Barbeau, Ray Wise, David Hess, Nicholas Worth, Dick Durock.

First Comic Book Appearance: "House of Secrets #92" (June-July 1971) *Origins:* Like its Marvel counterpart in "Man-Thing," Lein Wein and Berni Wrightson's "Swamp Thing" was a muck monster that had gained sentience after a man was murdered and dumped in a swamp. The account from their first story in "House of Secrets #92" (dated June-July 1971) had scientist Alex Olsen caught in a lab explosion purposely triggered by his rival Damian Ridge for his wife Linda's attention. Olsen's body is resurrected as a swamp creature that seeks vengeance for Damian's betrayal. After he murders Ridge, he finds that Linda knew all about his plans. The swamp "thing" tries to kill her, but cannot bring himself to kill the woman he loved. Story resonated with a lot of fans, and called out to be adapted into a running series. So, in October 1972, the comic book "Swamp Thing" was born. The revised plotline had Alec Holland tinkering on a secret formula that would change deserts into forests. But when Holland is killed by a bomb planted at his Louisiana laboratory by a mysterious Mr. E, he mutates into a "muck-encrusted mockery of a man" called Swamp Thing. The comic book series ran 24 issues until 1976, and detailed Swamp Thing's efforts to find the men that killed his wife and turned him into a creature. He also sought a way to transform himself back into a man. When sales plummeted in 1976, every effort was made to revive the series by introducing aliens and other monsters, but that simply wasn't enough. After the series was canceled, Swamp Thing made a number of guest appearances. Then, following the moderate success of the Wes Craven film, the Swamp Thing came back in a book titled "Saga of the Swamp Thing," and followed him on a series of adventures around the globe as he tried to stop a woman from destroying the world. Later, Alan Moore's "Swamp Thing" brought the book back to its horror roots and even resembled a book that EC Comics' may have published in the 1950s. Moore's stories gathered together forgotten and minor characters from the DC universe, and created a whole mythology that was continued by Neil Gaiman. Thanks to John Constantine, Holland learns that he is truly dead and that his swamp creature is actually a "plant elemental" capable of superpowers. More recently, the Swamp Thing stories have focused on Holland's daughter and her connections to a supernatural realm.

First Media Appearance: Actor and stuntman Dick Durock played the creature in his first media appearance in "Swamp Thing" (1982).

Other Appearances: A sequel, titled "Return of the Swamp Thing," was filmed in 1989, again with Dick Durock in the title role. A short-lived television series, shot at Universal Studios Florida, also featured Durock as the Swamp Thing. In 1990, a "Swamp Thing" cartoon series was produced by DiC Entertainment.

The 1982 Film Version: Released on July 30, 1982, Wes Craven's "Swamp Thing" told the familiar story of a scientist (Ray Wise) who is transformed into a muck monster when his laboratory explodes in the depths of a murky swamp. Dr. Alec Holland had been trying to create a new species, which was a combination of plant and animal life, but he becomes the victim of his own experiment. Rival scientist, Dr. Anton Arcane (Louis Jourdan), wants Holland's secret formula, and will stop at nothing to get it. Adrienne Barbeau

plays Alice Cable, the Swamp Thing's love interest. Craven filmed most of the picture on location in Charleston, South Carolina, and nearby Johns Island, because of the picturesque swampy scenery. The film inspired a direct-to-video sequel and a short-lived television series, which ran on the USA Network. Re-runs of the series' seventy-two episodes are still seen on the Sci-Fi Channel.

Trivial Matters: In the early comic book series, Dr. Anton Arcane is the Swamp Thing's most notable adversary; though he only appeared in two issues, his obsession with gaining immortality drove him to madness.

Fanboy Rating: Babes-8 Effects-3 Action-1 Brainwaves-3 Total=15

Swamp Thing

TMNT

Teenage Mutant Ninja Turtles (1990). New Line Cinema, 93min. **Director:** Steve Barron. **Producers:** David Chan, Kim Dawson, and Simon Fields. **Screenwriter:** Bobby Herbeck and Todd W. Langen. Characters created by Kevin Eastman and Peter Laird. **Cinematographer:** John Fenner. **Film Editors:** William D. Gordean, Sally Menke, and James R. Symons. **Production Designer:** Ray Forge Smith. **Cast:** Josh Pais, David Forman, Michelan Sisti, Leif Tilden, Jay Patterson.

First Comic Book Appearance: "Teenage Mutant Ninja Turtles #1" (1984)
Origins: In 1984, after an evening of creative brainstorming, Kevin Eastman and Peter Laird came up with the idea for their first issue of "Teenage Mutant Ninja Turtles," and turned the comic's world on its back with a book that became an overnight success and box office champion. Their comic was intended as a parody of Marvel Comics' "The New Mutants," a comic which featured teenaged mutants, and Frank Miller's "Daredevil," which dealt with ninja clans vying for supremacy of New York City's underworld. The origin story introduces us to four turtles – Michaelangelo, Leonardo, Raphael and Donatello – that have managed to escape from a pet store into the sewers beneath the city. When the same radioactive canister that falls off a truck and endows Daredevil with his super senses continues to spread its deadly radiation into the sewers, it turns the turtles into mutants. The four turtles gain sentience and superpowers. They train with a rat named Splinter, who is supposed to remind readers of Stick from "Daredevil," and learn to become ninjas. Eastman and Laird tried to sell their very novel concept to Marvel and DC, but neither company was interested in a comic book about turtles. So, they scraped together enough money (with much of it coming from a tax refund) and published the work themselves, using "Mirage Studios" as they imprint. The first three thousand copies sold very quickly; then the second printing of double the number of copies sold in half the time of the first, and the third printing was even more. Within a couple of months, they had sold 50,000 copies, and

parlayed their original creations into a huge licensing deal with Mark Freedman. The deal included t-shirts, action figures, Halloween costumes, and coffee mugs. Overnight, Eastman and Laird became millionaires. An animated series was produced in 1987. In 1988, Archie Comics licensed the kid-friendly version that had run on television, and published a series of comic books aimed at children. In 1996, Image Comics took over their publishing efforts, and have been producing the TMNT comics ever since. Recently, the Turtles have been featured in a 15-issue manga from Japan.

First Media Appearance: Michaelangelo, Leonardo, Raphael and Donatello – better known as the Teenage Mutant Ninja Turtles – made their first media appearance on December 10, 1987, in an animated cartoon series by Murakami-Wolf-Swenson Film Productions. The Saturday morning syndicated series began with a five-part miniseries that established the Ninja Turtles as four wise-cracking superheroes who were obsessed with pizza and fighting criminals. The show went through several changes between 1987 and 1994, but remained essentially the same.

The Four Film Versions: In 1990, the first of three live-action movies featuring the Ninja Turtles reached the big screen. "Teenage Mutant Ninja Turtles" (1990), as directed by Steve Barron and scripted by Todd Langen and Bobby Herbeck, returned the story to its humble origins as told in the very first comic book, and dealt with Michaelangelo, Leonardo, Raphael and Donatello's first confrontation with Shredder and his Foot Clan. The Ninja Turtles came to life thanks to the outstanding puppetry work of Jim Henson studios. A follow-up film, titled "Teenage Mutant Ninja Turtles 2: The Secret of the Ooze," premiered one year later, and dealt with a canister of dangerous chemicals that make them revert back to infant turtles. The third of these movies, "Teenage Mutant Ninja Turtles 3," concerns a magical scepter the boys Michaelangelo, Leonardo, Raphael and Donatello take back in time to feudal Japan. They end up fighting Lord Norinaga and an English trader Walker to prevent a war; Norinaga and Walker were parodies of the characters that Toshiro Mifume and Richard Chamberlain had played in "Shogun" (1980). All three films were made with kids in mind, and features little content that adults would find interesting. A fourth feature film, simply titled "TMNT," was released on March 23, 2007, and showcased the groundbreaking computer-generated imagery of Imagi Animation Studios. Instead of puppets and actors in rubber suits, the Ninja Turtles and their various friends and allies were digitally-rendered. With a grittier look that reflects the earlier comic books, this film promised to be the best of the bunch, and was designed to appeal to both adults and kids.

TMNT

Unbreakable

Unbreakable (2000). Touchtone Pictures, 106min. **Director:** M. Night Shyamalan. **Producers:** M. Night Shyamalan, Barry Mendel, and Sam Mercer. **Screenwriter:** M. Night Shyamalan. **Cinematographer:** Eduardo Serra. **Film Editor:** Dana Tichenor. **Production Designer:** Larry Fulton. **Cast:** Bruce Willis, Samuel L. Jackson, Robin Wright Penn, Spencer Treat Clark, Charlayne Woodard, Eamonn Walker, M. Night Shyamalan.

First Comic Book Appearance: None

Origins: David Dunn, the Unbreakable Man, was the creation of M. Night Shyamalan for his motion picture about the world of comic books and how their mythic dimensions intersect with the real world. In "Unbreakable" (2000), the writer-director also tells a parallel story about the birth of a supervillain. Elijah Price is born with osteogenesis imperfecta, a rare genetic disease that renders all of the bones in his body weak (and easy to break). In fact, he was even born with broken limbs. His fellow school mates make fun of his abnormality, called him "Mr. Glass," due to his fragility. Dejected and outcast, he finds the world of comic books his only safe retreat. He grows to manhood, looking for answers that are not easy to find. His comic books suggest to him that, if he exists on one end of the spectrum as a weak, easily broken man, then there must be someone on the other end with greater strength and invulnerability. Meanwhile, David Dunn has grown up never having had a cold or major childhood disease or injury. He represents the other side of the spectrum from Price, but he does not know it. To marry Audrey, he gave up a promising career as a football player, and took an undemanding job as a security guard. They have a son named Joseph, but David still feels an emptiness in his life that something is missing. After surviving a fatal train crash that kills 131 people, David is visited by Price. Price believes that David Dunn is a superhero, and he wants to train him for his future ahead. Initially, Dunn resists, but in time, he comes to accept the truth. He has finally found a purpose for his life, and begins to feel whole again. For his first "heroic" act, David dons a security poncho (that looks like a cape) and stops a psychotic murderer from killing a Philadelphia family. Later, Price holds a comic book convention at his store, and David discovers that Price was responsible for the train bombing. "Mr. Glass" tells him that, for every superhero, there must be a supervillain, and he is that character. Hero and villain are opposites that sometimes start out as friends, but then become mortal enemies.

First Media Appearance: Bruce Willis played David Dunn in "Unbreakable," the character's one and only media appearance.

The 2000 Film Version: M. Night Shyamalan's tribute to comic book superheroes was unfairly criticized when it was released in 2000 for being far too slow, but upon multiple viewings, "Unbreakable" holds together rather well as a suspense thriller. Security Guard David Dunn (Bruce Willis) walks away as the sole survivor of a horrific train crash outside Philadelphia that killed 131 people, and left him without a scratch. His marriage to Audrey (Robin Wright Penn) starts to fall apart as Dunn tries to deal with his survivor's guilt, and he just cannot connect with his son Joseph (Spencer Treat Clark) any more. Into his life walks Elijah Price (Samuel L. Jackson), a comic book collector and fan who has been sickly his entire life; he was nicknamed "Mr. Glass" due to a genetic condition that has rendered all of the bones in his body weak and easy to break. Price has a theory that comic book superheroes are based on real-life people, and he thinks Dunn is one of them. David Dunn is "unbreakable," has incredible strength, and possesses the uncanny ability to tell what someone is about to do. At first, Dunn doesn't believe him, but gradually, as Price coaches him, he comes to see that he does have superpowers that ordinary men don't have. His first action saves a Philadelphia family from a psychotic murderer. But that is far from the end of the story. Shyamalan has made better films ("The Sixth Sense") and worse films ("The Lady in Water"), but one of his most remarkable films was "Unbreakable" and defied classification. Yes, the film is terribly slow, but it also details the origin story of David Dunn, the Unbreakable Man.

Trivial Matters: Elijah's clothes are purple, similar in fact to the Joker and Lex Luthor. David Dunn has an alliterative name like Bruce Banner or Matt Murdock. David is afraid of water, similar to Superman's fear of Kryptonite.

Fanboy Rating: Babes-3 Effects-3 Action-3 Brainwaves-8 Total=17

Unbreakable

Vampirella

Vampirella (1996). Concorde-New Horizons, 86min. **Director:** Jim Wynorski. **Producers:** Roger Corman, Jim Wynorski, and Paul Herzberg. **Screenwriter:** Gary Gerani. Characters created by Forrest J. Ackerman. **Cinematographer: Film Editor: Production Designer: Cast:** Talisa Soto, Roger Daltrey, Richard Joseph Paul, Brian Bloom, Corinna Harney.

First Comic Book Appearance: "Vampirella #1" (September 1969)
Origins: Forrest J. Ackerman, the editor of *Famous Monsters of Filmland*, created the character of Vampirella for a horror-comics magazine that Warren Publishing had decided to publish in 1969. Jim Warren had a long history of publishing magazines that were somewhat exploitative, including "Creepy" which featured grisly horror stories. Vampirella was intended to be his first continuing character, and under the direction of writer Archie Goodwin, she performed well for fourteen years. The character was later acquired by Harris Comics in 1991, and lasted until 2007. The premise was a rather familiar one, one that readers of the Superman comic would clearly know. Vampirella lives on the planet Drakulon, a world where the rivers flow red with blood and its vampire inhabitants find their thirst for blood easily quenched. When her home-world is devastated by solar radiation from one of the planet's twin suns, she knows that she must escape and find a new world to live. She climbs aboard a rocketship from Earth, and using the astronauts for her nourishment, she travels back home with them. Once there, her adventures begin in earnest. She is able to transform herself into a bat, sprout wings and fly. Vampirella comes to see the difference between good and evil, and decides to become a "good" vampire, fighting the evil vampires who live on Earth. She continued to fight the good fight until 1983 when Warren Publishing folded. The company's assets were purchased by Harris Publications. Vampi's character laid dormant for several years, while Harris tried to figure out what to do with her. In the Warren magazines, she was the least-dressed woman in comics. Finally, in 1991, Harris gave Vampirella a full-scale re-launch.

The re-launch meant tinkering with her origin story, which was subsequently rewritten by Kurt Busiek; in the new origin, Vampi was the daughter of Lilith, the first wife to Adam, and not an alien from another planet. When Lilith sought redemption from God for her sins, she offered Vampirella as a vampire-hunter to kill all evil vampires on the Earth. In later issues, she fell in love with Adam Van Helsing, and teamed with Catwoman, Lady Death, and the Witchblade.

Similarities: When Forry Ackerman first created Vampirella, he had just played a very minor role in the sci-fi horror movie, "Queen of Blood" (1966); in the movie, astronauts find a lone survivor on Mars, and take her aboard their spaceship. On their journey back to Earth, she attacks them, one-by-one, draining them of blood. Florence Marley played the titular role. Ackerman was also close friends with Maila Nurmi, the actress who created the character of Vampira as a horror host for late night horror movies. She also played a vampire character in "Plan 9 from Outer Space."

First Media Appearance: Many actresses and models vied for the opportunity to wear the Vampirella costume, but it was Barbara Leigh in 1978 that gave Vampi her first media appearance. Since then, Brinke Stevens, Julie Stain, Cathy Christian, Sascha Knoft, Maria DiAngelis, Kitana Baker, and Angelique Trouvere have all appeared as Vampirella.

The 1996 Film Version: In 1996, Showtime and Roger Corman's New Horizons made "Vampirella" into a made-for-cable movie. The titular character (Talisa Soto), a sexy vampiress in a skimpy costume, travels to Earth from Drakulon to destroy the vampire who murdered her father. His name is Dracula (Roger Daltrey), and Vampirella must rely on the help of an earthman, Adam Van Helsing (Richard Joseph Paul), to destroy him. Fans of the comic book hated the movie adaptation, in particular the casting of Soto as the busty and nearly-always-naked Vampirella. As this book goes to press, there was renewed interest in making a big-screen version, but no casting or production information had been released.

Trivial Matters: Forry Ackerman makes a cameo appearance as the old man who is briefly shown dancing while the band plays. The space scenes, featuring Vlad Dracula and his cohorts leaving Drakulon, was borrowed from "Not of This Earth" (1988), and run backwards so no one but director Jim Wynorski would know the difference.

Fanboy Rating: Babes-7 Effects-2 Action-2 Brainwaves-3 Total=14

Vampirella

Witchblade

Witchblade (2000). Warner Brothers, 91min. **Director:** Ralph Hemecker. **Producers:** Brad Foxhoven, Perry Husman, and David Wohl. **Screenwriter:** J.D. Zeik. Characters created by Marc Silvestri. **Cinematographer:** Anghel Decca. **Film Editors:** Norman Buckley and Gordon McClellan. **Production Designer:** Jasna Stefanovic. **Cast:** Yancy Butler, Anthony Cistaro, Conrad Dunn, David Chokachi, Will Yun Lee, Kenneth Welsh, Eric Etebari.

First Comic Book Appearance: "Witchblade #1" (November 1995).
Origins: Created by cartoonist Michael Turner, "Witchblade" was an original comic book series that was published by Top Cow Productions, an imprint of Image Comics, from 1995 to 2006. In the series, the "witchblade" is actually an ancient, sentient weapon that has been wielded by heroic women like Cleopatra, Joan of Arc, and Queen Isabella. The weapon has an armored gauntlet that bonds with the wearer and a powerful blade that cannot be beaten in combat; the weapon may have extraterrestrial origins, and is believed to be one of thirteen similar weapons; the weapon also has its evil side that must be forever subdued by good. Tough-as-nails homicide detective Sara "Pez" Pezzini takes possession of the weapon, seemingly by chance, when her partner Michael Yee is killed and she must defend herself from his killer. But we later learn the spirit dwelling within the weapon called out to her subconscious mind and induced her to put it on. The weapon can have only one owner at a time, and can only belong to a woman. Throughout the early issues of the comic book, Sara struggles to hone the awesome powers of the Witchblade while fighting low-life criminals and mob bosses. She also struggles to maintain a personal life. Sara soon learns that the "witchblade" was discovered in Greece by Kenneth Irons and displayed in his antique shop for many years. Irons tells her that she has formed a symbiotic bond with the weapon that will only end when she is dead, but that she has a higher purpose in life wielding the weapon. Many of the later stories have found her fighting demons, ghosts,

magical forces, and religious maniacs who believe the "witchblade" signals the coming Apocalypse. Sara has teamed with many prominent comic book characters from other universes, including the Justice League of America and Lady Death.

First Media Appearance: In 2000, Yancy Butler played Pez and gave the "witchblade" its first media appearance in the made-for-television movie "Witchblade." Though a new "Witchblade" movie is planned for release in 2008, no other actresses have wielded the supernatural sword.

The 2000 Film Version: Turner Network Television co-financed the project with Warner Brothers in an effort to bring the popular comic book series to life with Yancy Butler in the central role as the guardian of the "Witchblade." NYPD detective Sara "Pez" Pezzini has put her career and life on the line to bringing down Tommy Gallo (Conrad Dunn), the Mafia assassin who killed her father. When she finds herself trapped in the Museum of History with one of Gallo's thugs – and out of bullets – she seizes the Witchblade from one of the museum's displays to defend herself. The enchanted gauntlet covers her right arm, and allows her to defect his bullets. She then takes the thug down with the weapon's extended blade. Later, Sara finds herself unable to shake off the bracelet that has attached itself to her wrist. Both Kenneth Irons (Anthony Cistaro) and his enigmatic and lethal compatriot Ian Nottingham (Eric Etebari) have been waiting for the Witchblade to find its owner, and now that it has, both seem eager to control Sara's use of the supernatural weapon. The film was critically acclaimed and popular with audiences, and led to a short-lived television series, also with Butler. "Witchblade" ran for two seasons on TNT, each featuring 12 episodes with a cliffhanger, season-ending finale. The first episode aired on June 12, 2001, and the last episode aired on August 26, 2002. Production on a third season was discussed, but due to Yancy Butler's alcoholism, the producers didn't want to take a chance. A new movie version has been projected for a 2008 release, even though no production details are available at this time.

Trivial Matters: Sara Pezzini's costume in the comic book series is considerably more revealing than the outfits Yancy Butler wore on the television series.

Fanboy Rating: Babes-8 Effects-3 Action-3 Brainwaves-6 Total=20

Witchblade

Wonder Woman

Wonder Woman (1975). Warner Brothers, 120min. **Director:** Jack Arnold. **Producer:** Wilfred Lloyd Baumes. **Screenwriters:** Margaret Armen and John D.F. Black. Characters created by William M. Marston. **Cinematographer:** Joe Jackman. **Film Editor:** Carroll Sax. **Cast:** Lynda Carter, Lyle Waggoner, Tom Kratochvil, Norman Burton, Carolyn Jones, Richard Eastham, Beatrice Colen, Saundra Sharp.

First Comic Book Appearance: "All Star Comics #8" (December 1941)
Origins: In 1940, after serving on an advisory board for DC Comics, psychiatrist William Moulton Marston created the character of Wonder Woman in an effort to establish some balance in the male-dominated world of superheroes. Writing as "Charles Moulton," he crafted a female character that was equally heroic so young women would have a hero with whom to identify. Wonder Woman's story begins with United States Army pilot Steve Trevor's crash-landing on Paradise Island, home to a warrior race of Amazonian women. Diana, their princess, nurses him back to health with a purple ray, and falls in love with him. When their goddess Aphrodite determined that Trevor should be returned to his own world by one of their own kind, Diana participates in a tournament to be the one chosen. Even though her mother Queen Hippolyte forbids her, Diana does it anyway, hiding her identity behind a mask. She eventually emerges as the winner, and her mother relents in her decision, giving her daughter a magic lasso of truth and bulletproof bracelets. Diana Prince travels to "Man's World" as Trevor's nurse, and fights crime and the evils of fascism as Wonder Woman. She was assisted by the Holliday Girls, a sorority run by Etta Candy. Between 1940 and 1945, Wonder Woman fought Nazis, spies and saboteurs at the side of Steve Trevor, who was promoted to Army Intelligence. Later, she joined the Justice Society of America as its first female member. At one point, Diana surrendered her powers, gave up her signature costume, and studied martial arts to become a secret agent. Thankfully, Wonder Woman's powers and traditional costume were

restored, in large part due to the popularity of the 1975 television series. DC's "Crisis on Infinite Earths" (1985) also helped to explain how Wonder Woman could have served in World War 2 and was also active as a superhero in the modern era. When sales of her own book declined in 1986, she married Steve Trevor, and lived happily ever after. Well, at least for one year, until DC decided to reboot her book, and start over, with George Perez directing the new Wonder Woman. In 2006, Diana had returned to being a secret agent in a skin-tight jumpsuit.

First Media Appearance: Wonder Woman made her first media appearance in 1967 in a four-and-a-half-minute test film, titled "Who's Afraid of Diana Prince?" Ellie Wood Walker played Diana, while Linda Harrison (Nova from "Planet of the Apes," 1968) played her alter ego. The test reel was shot by Greenway Productions, the company behind the "Batman" television series. They had hoped to launch a half-hour series, but the test was not very well received, and plans for the show were then abandoned.

Other Appearances: In 1974, Cathy Lee Crosby starred as Wonder Woman in a 90-minute television movie that bore little resemblance to the comic books. Some critics have suggested the movie's plotline was influenced by Diana's short stint as a secret agent. Television producers got it right, one year later, by remaining faithful to the character's origins with "The New, Original Wonder Woman," featuring Lynda Carter in the lead.

The 1975 Pilot Movie and Television Series: After the false start with Cathy Lee Crosby, producers went back to Diana's origin story when she first met Steve Trevor (Lyle Waggoner). Set during World War 2, Wonder Woman (Carter) nurses Trevor back to health, then helps him battle Nazis and spies and saboteurs. The pilot aired on November 7, 1975, and was such a huge ratings success that ABC ordered two more, two-hour movies, including one featuring Debra Winger as Wonder Girl. Despite strong ratings, ABC lost the show to rival CBS, which consequently switched the time period to the present day. Waggoner returned as Steve Trevor Jr., a spy who worked for the CIA, and Wonder Woman helped him battle Communist spies and saboteurs in Seasons 2 and 3. Joss Whedon is now writing a big-screen version of "Wonder Woman" for release in 2008/09.

Fanboy Rating: Babes-9 Effects-5 Action-6 Brainwaves-4 Total=24

Wonder Woman

The X-Men

X-Men (2000). 20th Century-Fox, in association with Marvel Enterprises, 104min. **Director:** Bryan Singer. **Producers:** Lauren Shuler Donner and Ralph Winter. **Screenwriters:** Tom DeSanto, Bryan Singer, David Hayter. **Cinematographer:** Newton Thomas Sigel. **Film Editors:** Steven Rosenblum, Kenin Stitt, John Wright. **Cast**: Hugh Jackman, Patrick Stewart, Ian McKellen, Famke Janssen, James Marsden, Halle Berry, Anna Paquin.

First Comic Book Appearance: "The X-Men #1" (September 1963)
Origins: The group of mutant superheroes known as The X-Men was created by Stan Lee and Jack Kirby, and debuted in "The X-Men #1" (published in September 1963). What distinguished them from Spiderman or The Fantastic Four, two other comic book series about superheroes set in the Marvel Universe, was that they were born with latent superhuman abilities as the direct result of some unknown leap in human evolution. Lee had originally intended to title his new series "The Mutants," but publisher Martin Goodman objected. Eventually, they agreed upon "The X-Men," partially as a tribute to Professor Charles Francis Xavier, or Professor X, the wealthy mutant who founded the comic book's fictional academy to train and protect mutants. Professor Xavier's School for Gifted Youngsters was located on a large country estate at 1407 Graymalkin Lane in Salem Center, a small town in Westchester County, New York. The original group of X-Men consisted of five teenagers, including Scott Summers (Cyclops), Hank McCoy (Beast), Bobby Drake (Iceman), Warren Worthington (Angel), and Jean Grey (Marvel Girl). The team's arch nemesis was Magneto and his Brotherhood of Evil Mutants. The comic book series ran for six years, but declining sales saw Marvel cap the series with issue #66. (Issues 67-93 were reprints of older stories from the past.) In 1975, Len Wein and Dave Cockrun revived the series by introducing a whole new team in Giant-Size X-Men #1, and continued with their new group in all-new issues, beginning with issue #94. Instead of focusing on

teenagers, they unleashed a group of adults who represented different nations and cultures. The new team was made up of John Proudstar (Thunderbird), Piotr Rasputin (Colossus), Kurt Wagner (Nightcrawler), and Ororo Munroe (Storm). As Cyclops, a member of the original team, Scott Summers assumed the role of leader. Other characters, like Shiro Yoshida (Sunfire), Sean Cassidy (Banshee), and Logan (Wolverine), appeared. But it wasn't until Jean Grey rejoined the team as Phoenix (particularly Dark Phoenix) that the series gained international super stardom with artwork by John Byrne and stories by Chris Claremont.Over the years, other members have joined the X-Men, including Rogue, Dazzler, Psylocke, Gambit, Northstar et al; Professor Xavier briefly returned to command, and divided the X-Men into two strike teams, one gold and one blue; Magneto took charge of the X-Men for a short time, and a group of younger mutants were introduced as "The New Mutants," and then later, "Generation X." The conflict between mutants and normal humans remained the same, but resonated with some of the comic book's mainstream readers as allegories about racial and ethnic cleansing, metaphors about diversity and sexual intolerance, and fears about AIDS and other diseases that had created divides between people. Fears and anxieties about the Red Scare, anti-Semitism, racism, bigotry, prejudice, homosexuality and other social issues were explored in the pages of the comic book as Middle America faced each of those issues for the first time. The Sentinels and other anti-mutant hate groups are often though to represent those oppressive forces in our society, like the Ku Klux Klan, that seek to deny civil rights to certain groups. In 2000, Marvel Comics attempted to consolidate a number of its comic titles, and killed off some of its characters as part of an event called "Revolution." Grant Morrison took over as

The X-Men

the new writer, and started reforming much of the X-Men team. One of his first important changes, in "E is for Extinction," gave Cassandra Nova license to destroy Genosha, Magneto's island refuge to sixteen million mutants. He did away with the bright spandex costumes that had been long associated with the X-Men, and replaced them with black leather street clothes. He added new characters, like Xorn; revised older ones, like Juggernaut and Mystique, and instigated an extramarital affair between Emma Frost and Cyclops, who was at the time mar-

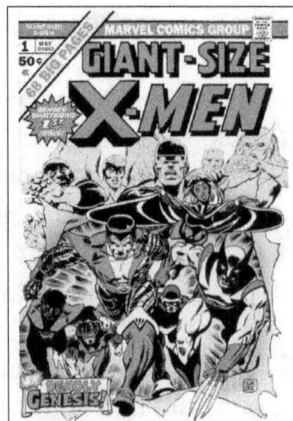

218

ried to Jean Grey. Joss Whedon, the creator of "Buffy the Vampire Slayer," replaced Morrison, and authored a new X-title called "Astonishing X-Men." Several short-lived spin-offs and mini-series have also followed the exploits of familiar team members.

First Media Appearance: Thirty-four years before 20th Century-Fox released Bryan Singer's big-screen adaptation, the X-Men made their first ever media appearance on "The Marvel Super Heroes" (1966). The animated, Saturday morning cartoon by Grantray-Lawrence Animation featured the original X-Men line-up of Angel, Beast, Cyclops, Iceman, and Marvel Girl. They were not called the X-Men, but rather referred to as Allies for Peace, and they did battle with the Sub-Mariner in part one of a two-part story titled "Doctor Doom's Day." Ironically, Grantray-Lawrence had originally wanted to showcase the Fantastic Four, not the X-Men; but when they were contractually prohibited from using Reed Richards and his team, they had to settle for the X-Men. The characters were allowed to keep their yellow spandex costumes and maintained the same identities from the comics even though they lost the name X-Men.

Other Media Appearances: The X-Men made regular appearances on "Spiderman and His Amazing Friends," a Saturday morning cartoon produced for NBC (1981). Bobby Drake (Iceman) and Angelica Jones (Firestar) were college students with Peter Parker (Spiderman) at Empire State University, and the trio would often team-up with other mutants to fight supervillains. In 1989, Marvel Productions made a pilot for a proposed X-Men television series for NBC, titled "Pryde of the X-Men," but the series was never picked up by the network. Several years later, Fox produced an animated series, featuring the most popular roster of X-Men, that ran from 1992 to 1997. Rival Warner Brothers ran a similar animated show, titled "X-Men: Evolution," on its network from 2000 to 2003. In 1996, Fox also tried to launch a live action show, based on the comic book series "Generation X," but the low-budget show which featured two less prominent X-Men (Banshee and Emma Frost) as the headmasters of Xavier's School was not very well received. Plans to develop a series for syndication were later scrapped by Fox. In 2001, Marvel Studios succeeded in producing a low-budget, live-action series titled "Mutant X" which chronicled the adventures of four genetically-altered mutants. The series ran for three seasons in syndication, and while it's connection to the X-Men universe is a tenuous one (at best), the television series was hugely popular with Generation X-ers.

Film Development: Marvel Comics had been eager to have its prized

property developed in the early eighties along with "Spiderman" and "The Hulk," but each time "The X-Men" movie was optioned, something prevented the property from being made. At first, James Cameron, the director of "The Terminator" (1984) and "Aliens" (1986) was attached to the project as a producer and director. After Cameron wrapped production on "Terminator 2: Judgment Day" (1991), he lost interest, and moved on to pursue "Spiderman." (Eventually, Cameron gave up on "Spiderman" and instead made "Titanic," 1997.) The film was then in development at Carolco Pictures, when the studio went bankrupt in early-'90s thanks to box office bombs like "Showgirls" (1995) and "Cutthroat Island" (1995). And finally, when Fox produced the low-budget spin-off "Generation X" and it tanked, "The X-Men" movie seemed to be doomed. The openly gay director Bryan Singer, who had made "The Usual Suspects" (1995) and "Apt Pupil" (1998), brought his own experiences with prejudice and bigotry to the project, and demonstrated a rare understanding of the material. He saw the mutant condition as analogous to his own homosexuality. Gay men and lesbian women often keep the secret of their sexuality from the world for fear that their difference will not be understood and accepted. Singer saw "X-Men" as a metaphor for acceptance of all people for their special and unique gifts. His sensitivity to the material encouraged 20th Century-Fox to green-light the project with a budget of $75 million. The 2000 film was an instant hit and took in over $296 million worldwide.

Plot Summary: When his family is exterminated by the Nazis in one of the death camps at the end of World War 2, Magnus, a mutant with extraordinary magnetic powers, vows vengeance on all humanity. Following the war, Professor Charles Xavier, a mutant with superior mind control, begins to take note of children being born with a X-factor in their genetic make-up that gives them superhuman abilities: Cyclops can fire a beam of force from his eyes; Angel can sprout wings and fly; Storm can control the weather, and Jean Grey can read men's minds. These "children of the atom" are very unique, and need to be trained to harness their extraordi-

The X-Men

nary powers. Xavier gathers many of them together at a special school with the hope of protecting and teaching them to use their powers for the benefit of mankind. Unfortunately, most people fear these mutants as freaks and monsters that need to be destroyed. The seeds of a new Holocaust are sewn in Congress by Senator Robert Kelly (Bruce Davidson) who sets in motion a series of events that will have catastrophic consequences. Kelly's eagerness to destroy the mutants is all that Magnus, now renamed Magneto, needs to assemble an army of mutants (including Sabertooth and Mystique) to fight the humans. He has also created a machine that will speed up the mutation process and turn everyone into mutants. Xavier and his X-men seek a solution where humans and mutants can peacefully co-exist. The battle-lines are drawn, and it's the good mutants against the bad mutants. Newcomer Wolverine helps Xavier and tips the balance of power. Magneto's dastardly evil plan to destroy the world is stopped. He and a number of his followers are rounded up and placed in maximum security cells, while Xavier promises peaceful co-existence with the humans.

Trivial Matters: Originally, Dougray Scott was cast to play Wolverine; Aaron Eckhart and Viggo Mortensen were both considered to replace him, but in the end, Hugh Jackman got the nod. During casting, Bryan Singer also considered Mel Gibson, Russell Crowe, Edward Norton, and Keanu Reeves. Sarah Michelle Gellar and Jada Pinkett Smith were front-runners for the roles of Rogue and Storm, respectively, but lost out to other actors. Jeri Ryan and Maria Bello were similarly considered for Mystique and Jean Grey. Rebecca Romijn as Mystique is totally naked in the film, covered only by body paint and a few, well-placed pieces of latex prostheses. Neither Patrick Stewart nor Ian McKellen knows how to play chess. Stan Lee makes a cameo as the man near the hot dog stand. Cyclops' remarks about "yellow spandex" were added by Bryan Singer as a dig at those fans who complained online about the X-Men's leather costumes. And finally, Singer played a practical joke by hiring an actor to dress up as Spiderman and comfront the X-Men on the set.

Fanboy Rating: Babes-7 Effects-7   Action-7 Brainwaves-7 Total=28

X2: X-Men United (2003). 20th Century-Fox, in association with Marvel Enterprises, 133min. **Director:** Bryan Singer. **Producers:** Lauren Shuler Donner and Ralph Winter. **Screenwriters:** Zak Penn, David Hater, Bryan Singer, Michael Doughterty. **Cinematographer:** Newton Thomas Sigel. **Film Editors:** John Ottman and Elliot Graham. **Cast:** Hugh Jackman, Patrick Stewart, Ian McKellen, Famke Janssen, James Marsden, Halle Berry, Brian Cox.

The 2003 Film Sequel: Loosely based on the 1982 graphic novel "God Loves, Man Kills," Bryan Singer's 2003 follow-up to "X-Men" proved to be a bigger blockbuster than the original. "X2: X-Men United" grossed $407.5 million for 20th Century-Fox, and established the Uncanny X-Men as the leading superhero box office champs. When an unknown mutant assassin attempts to kill the President (Cotter Smith), General William Stryker (Brian Cox) expresses renewed support for the Mutant Registration Act, which would identify all mutants. Most of those in the United States government agree. Stryker takes steps a bit further, and leads an offensive strike against the X-Men mansion and school. He wants to eradicate all mutants, even though he may have been behind the experiments that created Wolverine (Hugh Jackman). While Jean Grey (Famke Janssen) and Storm (Halle Berry) search for the assassin believed to be Nightcrawler (Alan Cumming), Professor Xavier (Patrick Stewart) confers with Magneto (Ian McKellen) in his prison cell. They must find a way to stop the madness. News of the strike against the school reaches each of the team members. Magneto escapes from his plastic prison, and forms a temporary alliance with the X-Men. Together they fight against Stryker and his plans for a mutant-free world. During the battle, Jean Grey is killed, but we are meant to think she lived on as the Phoenix as she gives the final voiceover. The second X-Men movie was not only a huge financial success but also a critical one as well. Most critics likened the film to problems around

The X-Men

The X-Men

the globe related to ethnic cleansing. In the graphic novel, Stryker kills his wife and infant son when he learns that she gave birth to a mutant. He believes that he has been chosen by God to destroy mutants, and sees his military exploits as a holy war against the mutant forces. Those themes also resonate with fans and critics alike who view the X-Men's storyline as a reflection of the direction our country has moved toward fascism.

Trivial Matters: The mansion used for Xavier's school is the same one that appears as Lex Luthor's home on "Smallville" (2001). Ian McKellen worked alongside Bryan Singer and the screenwriters to make the scene in which Bobby Drake (Iceman) reveals that he is a mutant to his family members to look like a scene in which a gay man might "come out" to his parents. Neil Patrick Harris auditioned for the role of Nightcrawler, but lost out to Alan Cumming who was Singer's first choice. Both Professor Xavier and Magneto share T.H. White's *The Once and Future King* in common as shown in two different scenes.

Fanboy Rating: Babes-7 Effects-7 Action-7 Brainwaves-7 Total=28

X-Men: The Last Stand (2006). 20th Century-Fox, in association with Marvel Enterprises, 104min. **Director:** Brett Ratner. **Producers:** Lauren Shuler Donner and Ralph Winter. **Screenwriters:** Simon Kinberg and Zak Penn. **Cinematographer:** Dante Spinotti. **Film Editors:** Mark Goldblatt, Mark Helfrich and Julia Wong. **Cast:** Hugh Jackman, Patrick Stewart, Ian McKellen, Famke Janssen, James Marsden, Halle Berry, Anna Paquin.

The 2006 Film Sequel: With Bryan Singer off directing "Superman Returns," Brett Ratner took over the directorial reigns, and delivered what most fans and critics agree is the best film in the trilogy, "X-Men: The Last Stand." When a cure is found to treat the mutant threat, the government forces all mutants to take the cure or register their whereabouts with the Mutant Registration Act. Some of them reluctantly submit to the cure, while others remain protected by Professor Charles Xavier (Patrick

Stewart) at his school for mutants. Still others band together as the Brotherhood, under Xavier's former ally, Magneto (Ian McKellen). The battle lines are drawn between the might of the U.S. military and Magneto's band of mutant forces, with the X-Men right in the middle. The appearance of Jean Grey (Famke Janssen) as the Dark Phoenix tips the balance, and launches an all-out war. With the help of new recruits Beast (Kelsey Grammer) and Angel (Ben Foster), the X-Men emerge victorious, but not without suffering some significant losses, including Xavier, Cyclops (James Marsden), and Jean Grey.

Trivial Matters: Halle Berry had chosen not to return as Storm, but when Singer left and her film "Catwoman" (2004) was trounced at the box office, she agreed to take the role as long as her part was significantly expanded. Summer Glau auditioned for the role of Kitty Pryde. Initially, Singer had planned to make the Dark Phoenix saga as it had appeared in the comic books with Signourney Weaver as Emma Frost, but his departure meant a change in direction for the script. As this book goes to press, there was no discussion about making another X-Men film; however, Fox had announced plans to spin-off Magneto and Wolverine into their own films, with possible release dates set in 2008 and 2009.

Fanboy Rating: Babes-7 Effects-6 Action-7 Brainwaves-6 Total=26

The X-Men Updates:

Wolverine (2008): Slated for a 2008 release, David Benioff's "Wolverine" features Hugh Jackman in the role that made him famous. This prequel to "The X-Men" finds Wolverine, who has been living the mutant life, seeking revenge against Victor Creed (who will later become Sabertooth) for the death of his girlfriend, and ultimately ends up going through the mutant Weapon X program. Brian Cox and Ken Watanabe are rumored to be Jackman's co-stars.

Magneto (2009): David S. Goyer, who had produced and written two of the three "Blade" films, was hired to develop "Magneto" with an eye on directing and writing the screenplay with Sheldon Turner. The storyline looks at the early life of Eric Lensherr, an escapee from a Nazi concentration camp, and his friendship with Charles Xavier, and how the one-time allies became mortal enemies. At the time of this writing, no casting had been announced, but Ian McKellen was being sought for a cameo.

The X-Men

Youngsters

The Adventures of Sharkboy and Lavagirl (2005). Troublemaker Studios, 93 min. **Director:** Robert Rodriguez. **Producer:** Elizabeth Avellan. **Screenwriters:** Robert, Racer and Marcel Rodriguez. **Cinematographer:** Robert Rodriguez. **Film Editor:** Robert Rodriguez. **Cast:** Taylor Lautner, Taylor Dooley, Cayden Boyd, George Lopez, David Arquette, Kristin Davis, Jacob Davich.

The popularity of superhero films in the last few years has given rise to a whole new generation of superheroes who have by-passed the traditional comic book route and debuted directly on film. Many of these films feature youngsters in the role of would-be superheroes, and they are presented here for the sake of completeness. The first of these is "The Adventures of Sharkboy and Lavagirl" (2005).

First Comic Book Appearance: None

Film Version: The success of Robert Rodriguez's "Spy Kids" movies encouraged him to make a superhero film, featuring Taylor Lautner as Sharkboy and Taylor Dooley as Lavagirl. In the film, a lonely, eleven-year-old boy named Max (Cayden Boyd) dreams the "Planet Drool" into existence, and populates the imaginary world with all sorts of interesting and exotic creatures. One day, Sharkboy (Lautner) and Lavagirl (Dooley) arrive on Earth in their spaceship, and demand that Max help them. An alien intelligence threatens his beloved Planet Drool with darkness. At first, Max doesn't believe them, but later, he takes off on a wild and dangerous journey with Sharkboy and Lavagirl to save the helpless denizens of the Planet Drool. Will they be able to stop the alien intelligence in time? Is the whole situation real, or just a figment of his imagination? This superhero movie for the pint-sized crowd won't score many points with adults, but it remains a favorite of those pre-pubescents who don't demand a whole lot from their entertainment. Released on June 10, 2005, the feature film was savaged by critics and ignored by ticket buyers.

Primary Superheroes: Sharkboy (Taylor Lautner) was the son of a great oceanographer who studied and befriended great white sharks. When he is separated from his father during a great storm at sea, his rescued by a talking shark named Kraken. Kraken teaches him how to survive like a shark, and soon he learns how to use great strength and speed in every task he is given. Lavagirl (Taylor Dooley) does not know much about her origins; she is partially composed of living lava, and can radiate great heat, destroying most of what she touches. Max (Cayden Boyd) has the power to generate powerful dreams that affect other worlds.

Trivial Matters: The story was dreamed up by Robert Rodriguez's seven-year-old son Racer. Professional wrestler Dean Roll, whose stage name is Sharkboy, filed a lawsuit against Miramax, claiming his trademark had been infringed upon.

Fanboy Rating: Babes-1 Effects-1 Action-2 Brainwaves-2 Total=6

Sky High (2005). Walt Disney Pictures, 100 min. **Director:** Mike Mitchell. **Producer:** Andrew Gunn. **Screenwriters:** Paul Hernandez, Robert Schooley, and Mark McCorkle. **Cinematographer:** Shelly Johnson. **Film Editor:** Peter Amundson. **Cast:** Michael Angarano, Kurt Russell, Kelly Preston, Danielle Panabaker, Christopher Wynne, Kevin Heffernan.

First Comic Book Appearance: None

Film Version: Sky High, as imagined by Paul Hernandez, Robert Schooley, and Mark McCorkle, is a high school for training superheroes and their sidekicks. The school itself hovers about the cloud layer, using anti-gravity technology, and its location is known only to a handful of people, including the school bus driver, Ron Wilson (Kevin Heffernan). The student body is comprised of the children of superheroes who have superhuman powers and a handful of others whose powers have yet to (and may never) emerge. Not unlike a real high school, the heroes and sidekicks find themselves divided into jocks and geeks. When Will Stronghold (Michael Angarano), the son of the world's most legendary superheroes, shows up for the first day of classes, he does not possess any superpowers. His desire to join

Youngssters

the Hero class is foiled, and he is relegated to being just a Sidekick and the brunt of practical jokes by the upperclassmen. But since this is a Disney movie, Will eventually discovers his powers, and must use them against an evil villain who threatens his family, friends, and the sanctity of his new school. "Sky High" was modestly successful when it premiered on July 29, 2005, and showed that a family film from the Mouse didn't have to be saccharine sweet to be fun.

Primary Superheroes: The Commander (Kurt Russell) is one of the world's most powerful superheroes, with superstrength and invulnerability; he wears a red, white and blue costume, but hides his identity as Steve Stronghold behind glasses, like Clark Kent. His wife Josie is Jetstream (Kelly Preston); she has the ability to fly and engage in hand-to-hand combat. She also wears a red, white and blue costume. Nurse Spex (Cloris Leachman) has the superhuman ability of x-ray vision.

Trivial Matters: Actress Lynda Carter plays the principal of the school, and at one point in the film delivers the line "I'm not Wonder Woman you know." Kurt Russell's superhero suit had a cooling system built right in.

Fanboy Rating: Babes-6 Effects-1 Action-2 Brainwaves-1 Total=10

Zoom (2006). Sony Pictures Entertainment, 83 min. **Director:** Peter Hewitt. **Producers:** Todd Garner, Jennifer Todd, Suzanne Todd. **Screenwriters:** Adam Rifkin and David Berenbaum. Based upon *Zoom's Academy* by Jason Lethcoe. **Cinematographer:** David Tattersall. **Film Editor:** Lawrence Jordan. **Cast:** Tim Allen, Courteney Cox, Chevy Chase, Spencer Breslin, Kevin Zegers, Kate Mara, Michael Cassidy, Rip Torn.

First Book Appearance: Zoom's Academy by Jason Lethcoe
Film Version: Former superhero Jack Shepherd (Tim Allen), also known as Captain Zoom for his super-speed, is called back into service to work as an instructor at a private facility known as Area 52. There, he is tasked with transforming a group of kids with superpowers into superheroes to defend the world against a presence, possibly alien, heading towards the

Earth. With the help of clumsy scientist Marsha Holloway (Cox) who has read all of his comic book exploits, Shepherd auditions all of the hopeful candidates. Out of all of the kids who are interviewed; only four are chosen: Dylan (Michael Cassidy) has the power to become invisible; Summer (Kate Mara) has telekinetic powers; Tucker (Spencer Breslin) can enlarge his body, and Cindy (Ryan Newman) has superstrength. They become Houdini, Wonder, Mega Boy and Princess. They board a flying saucer that has been leftover from the Cold War days, and battle the evil force that threatens our planet. Peter Hewitt's film is cute and has all of the right elements, but after the similarly-themed "Sky High" (2005), "Zoom" lacked superpowers at the box office.

Primary Superheroes: Captain Zoom (Allen), who possessed super-speed, was the leader of a superhero team called "Team Zenith." When the military tried to increase the group's superpowers with Gamma radiation, Zoom apparently lost his powers, and the other members, including his brother, died in an explosion. Concussion, Zoom's brother (Kevin Zegers), had the ability to project shockwaves. Marsha Holloway (Courteney Cox) discovers, in the course of the film, that she has the power to blow rainbow-colored wind.

Trivial Matters: Tim Allen is best known for playing a different kind of hero, Captain Peter Quincy Taggart on "Galaxy Quest" (1999). Courteney Cox played superhero Gloria Dinallo on "Misfits of Science" (1985).

Fanboy Rating: Babes-3 Effects-1 Action-1 Brainwaves-2 Total=7

Youngssters

Selected Bibliography

Ackerman, Forrest J., editor. *Famous Monsters of Filmland* Magazine. Philadelphia: Warren Publishing, 1958.

_____. *Monsterland* Magazine, nos. 1-6. Los Angeles: New Media Publishing, 1986.

Barney-Hawke, Syd. *Marvel Encyclopedia, Volume Two*. N.Y.: Marvel Comics, 2003.

Bogart, David. *Marvel Encyclopedia, Volume One*. N.Y.: Marvel Comics, 2002.

Brooker, Will. *Batman Unmasked: Analyzing a Cultural Icon*. N.Y.: Continuum International Publishing Group, 2001.

Brosnan, John. *Science Fiction in the Cinema*. N.Y.: Paperback Library, 1970.

Brozik, Matthew David and Jacob Sager Weinstein. *The Government Manual for New Superheroes*. N.Y.: Andrews McMeel Publishing, 2005.

Conroy, Mike. *500 Great Comic Book Action Heroes*. N.Y.: Barron's Educational Series, 2003.

_____. 500 Comic Book Villains. N.Y.: Visible Ink Press, 2004.

Fingeroth, Danny. *Superman on the Couch: What Superheroes Really Tell Us About Ourselves and Our Society*. N.Y.: Continuum International Publishing Group, 2004.

Flynn, John L. *The Films of Arnold Schwarzenegger.* N.Y.: Carol Publishing, 1993.

_____. *Phantoms of the Opera: The Face Behind the Mask*. N.Y.: Image Press, 1993. Maryland: Galactic Books, 2006.

Franklin, Joe. *Classics of the Silent Screen*. NY: Citadel Press, 1959.

Garrett, Greg. *Holy Superheroes: Exploring Faith and Spirituality in Comic Books*. N.Y.: Navpress Publishing Group, 2005.

Goulart, Ron. *Comic Book Encyclopedia: The Ultimate Guide to Characters, Graphic Novels, Writers, and Artists in the Comic Book Universe*. N.Y.: Harper Entertainment, 2004.

Gresh, Lois H. and Robert Weinberg. *The Science of Superheroes*. N.Y.: Wiley, 2002.

Halliwell, Leslie. *Halliwell's Film Guide*. New York: Scribner's, 1984.

Jimenez, Phil et al. *The DC Comics Encyclopedia*. N.Y.: DK Publishing, 2004.

Kiefer, Kit and Jonathan Couper-Smartt. *Marvel Encyclopedia, Volume Two*. N.Y.: Marvel Comics, 2003.

Kraucauer, Sigfried. *From Caligari to Hitler*. New Jersey: Princeton University Press, 1964.

Kyrou, Ado. *Le Surrealisme Au Cinema*. Paris: 1964.

Laclos, Michael. *Le Fantasique Au Cinema*. Paris: 1958.

Lee, Walt. *Reference Guide to Fantastic Films*. Los Angeles: Chelsea-Lee Books, 1978.

Markstein, Donald D. *Don Markstein's Toonopedia* <http://www.toonopedia.com/> 1999-2006.

Morris, Thomas V. *Superheroes and Philosophy: Truth, Justice and the Socratic Way*. N.Y.: Open Court Publishing Company, 2005.

O'Neill, Cynthia. *Spider-Man: The Ultimate Guide*. N.Y.: DK Publishing, 2006.

Powell, Michael. *The Superhero Handbook*. N.Y.: Sterling, 2005.

Rovin, Jeff. *Encyclopedia of Superheroes*. N.Y.: Facts on File, 1987.

Sanderson, Peter. *Marvel Universe*. N.Y.: Harry N. Abrams, 1998.

_____. *X-Men: The Ultimate Guide*. N.Y.: DK Publishing, 2006.

Settel, Irving. *A Pictorial History of Television*. New York: Frederick Ungar Publishing, 1983.

Simpson, Paul et al. *The Rough Guide to Superheroes*. N.Y.: Rough Guides, 2004.

Terrace, Vincent. *Complete Encyclopedia of Television Programs*. N.Y.: A.S. Barnes, 1979

Wallace, Daniel et al. *The Marvel Encyclopedia*. N.Y.: DK Publishing, 2006.

Wright, Bradford. *Comic Book Nation: The Transformation of Youth Culture in America*. Baltimore, MD: Johns Hopkins University Press, 2003.

Bibliography

Index of Superheroes

About the Author

Dr. John L. Flynn is a three-time Hugo-nominated author and long-time science fiction fan and critic who has written twelve books, countless short stories, articles, reviews, and two screenplays. He is a college teacher and administrator at Towson University in Maryland. Born in Chicago, Illinois, on September 6, 1954, he has a Bachelor's and Master's Degree from the University of South Florida and a Ph.D. from Southern California University. He is a member of the Science Fiction Writers of America, and has been a regular contributor and columnist to dozens of science fiction magazines. In 1977, he received the M. Carolyn Parker award for outstanding journalism for his freelance work on several Florida daily newspapers, and in 1987, he was listed in *Who's Who Men of Achievement*. He sold his first book, *Future Threads*, in 1985. His other books include *Cinematic Vampires, The Films of Arnold Schwarzenegger, Dissecting Aliens, Phantoms of the Opera, Visions in Light and Shadow, War of the Worlds: From Wells to Spielberg, The Jovian Dilemma, 75 Years of Universal Monsters,* and *50 Years of Hammer Horror*. With Dr. Bob Blackwood, he wrote *Future Prime: The Top Ten Science Fiction Films*.

Index

www.ingramcontent.com/pod-product-compliance
Lightning Source LLC
LaVergne TN
LVHW051625080426
835511LV00016B/2185